York St John
Library and Information Services

Eating Disorders, Food and Occupational Therapy

D

Dedication
To my husband Paul and son Timothy

Eating Disorders, Food and Occupational Therapy

JOAN E MARTIN

University of Ulster

Whurr Publishers Ltd

© 1998 Whurr Publishers Ltd
First published 1998 by Whurr Publishers Ltd
19b Compton Terrace, London N1 2UN, England

British Library Cataloguing in Publication Data
A catalogue record for this book is available from the British Library.

ISBN 1 86156 105 9

Printed and bound in Great Britian by Athenæum Press Ltd, Gateshead, Tyne & Wear.

Contents

PART 1
Anorexia nervosa:
an overview

Chapter 1
Anorexia nervosa

History

Anorexia nervosa must be viewed as a serious clinical syndrome in that it is one of the few psychiatric conditions that can result in death. It has been argued that voluntary self-starvation is not a recently developed syndrome but that it has been seen throughout history. Bemporad (1996) reports that forms of eating disorders have existed since ancient times although varying in frequency, manifestation and possible motivation and being influenced by certain sociocultural factors that might inhibit the form or frequency of the condition. Moses fasted for 40 days before receiving the Ten Commandments. Fasting was seen as a means of penance or purification as individuals denied themselves the pleasure of eating.

Bell (1985) published a book called *Holy Anorexia*, which drew attention to the existence of self-starvation in a large number of European women from the thirteenth to seventeenth centuries. However, the author does not vigorously contend that the cases that he described are in fact illustrative of anorexia nervosa as we know it today, although he does highlight some similarities in the 261 documented cases of holy fasting which he uncovered.

At the time of the Reformation starving women were seen as being possessed by the devil, or to be physically or mentally ill. Brumberg (1988) describes a fairly typical pattern whereby they existed only on delicate objects such as rose petals or, in the case of one woman, only by the smell of a rose.

Bliss and Bruch (1960) cite a case described in a letter by the philosopher Hobbs in 1669. The girl is said to have lost her appetite completely and is thought to have existed by wetting her lips from a feather dipped in water. Hobbs portrays her as so emaciated that her stomach touched her backbone. The girl was frequently visited out of curiosity by onlookers who were charged a small payment to view her pathetic state.

However Richard Morton (1689) is generally credited with the first medical description of the condition. He was a Fellow of the College of

Physicians in London and the appointed physician to the King of England. Morton described anorexia nervosa as a nervous disorder with an emotional or psychiatric basis. He labelled the disease a 'nervous consumption' and described his first case involving a 20-year-old woman when he wrote 'I do not remember that I did ever in all my practice see one that was conversant with the living so much wasted with the greatest degree of a consumption – like a skeleton only clad with skin.' Morton's publication in London of his *Treatise of Consumption* was the first reported effort towards differentiating anorexia nervosa from tuberculosis.

The disorder then re-emerged as a distinct clinical entity with the descriptions by two physicians, Gull (1868) in England and Laseque (1873) in France. These physicians are in fact responsible for initiating the concept of anorexia nervosa as we know it today. Gull, who was physician to the Court, offered a positive treatment response in his description of his case. He recommended the administration of regular nutrition and psychological treatment. Such sound advice still holds today! Laseque, on the other hand, highlighted the ineffective efforts of families who used persuasion or threatening methods but he also drew attention to the amenorrhea suffered by the patients.

The representation of women in art and media forms in Western cultures has changed through the ages. Rubens in the seventeenth century painted his favourite women as plump, sensual and with a certain roundness of form. However women's shapes changed in the nineteenth century with the use of corsets producing the hourglass figure. Women wanted to mirror Marilyn Monroe in the 1950s, with her very shapely figure and large breasts. However, in the late 1960s the ideal shape changed yet again with the arrival of Twiggy, the supermodel who had almost no breasts at all. The ideal shape for women changed again in the 1980s to broad shoulders and nipped-in waists. So throughout history, feminine beauty has had different models, some associated with ample body size rather than thinness. Nowadays, however, only slender models with whom the majority of women can scarcely identify are presented as ideal. These often emaciated bodies are used to sell everything from clothes, shampoos, foods, cars and other consumer goods.

The term 'anorexia nervosa' literally means 'nervous loss of appetite'. Early accounts of the illness by Laseque (1873) and Gull (1868) considered the lack of appetite to be the primary disturbance, but it is now accepted that there is no appetite loss. Anorectics report that they are constantly hungry and obsessed with food. They will spend hours reading recipe books, preparing gourmet meals to feed to others and gazing at food in supermarkets.

While anorexia nervosa was once thought to be rare, it has now become an important public health concern in Western society (Garner, 1993). It affects mostly young females and the central feature of the illness is the abnormally low weight achieved through extreme caloric restriction. Eating disorders result from a combination of emotional, physical and sociological factors and are encouraged by a society that places great emphasis on appearance as a measure of worth. Once believed to be a problem largely of young female adolescents, the condition can now be seen among children, men and elderly women. It also manifests itself in particular populations and in a wide variety of cultural groups. Whereas anorexia nervosa now occurs across the full social class spectrum, most studies indicate a higher preponderance among social classes I and II. However, this social class bias could be seen as a result of the structures, norms and thresholds of the healthcare system.

Anorexia nervosa – the condition

The anorectic's behaviour has been described as a 'relentless pursuit of thinness' (Bruch, 1962), 'a morbid fear of fatness' (Russell, 1970) or 'an adolescent weight phobia' (Crisp, 1967). Anorexia nervosa develops as a response to the inevitable body changes that occur in puberty with the concomitant increases in body fat. The onset of puberty brings with it increased sexual attention. The fears of managing sexual relationships with men or experiencing sexual drives can be reduced by the anorectic through losing body weight to below the menstrual threshold. As the anorectic diets and loses weight, friends and family congratulate her on her appearance. This reinforces her behaviour and encourages her to lose more. She feels, possibly for the first time in her life, to be in control and perhaps winning over others who had begun to diet with her. Fearing that her weight may return, she diets even more stringently and may increase her exercise activity. Her body image then becomes distorted. She sees nothing wrong in what she is doing and is reluctant to give up this new-found feeling of control and self-worth. Friends and relatives often admire the anorectic's slimness and she is congratulated on her sense of self-control. Even though the anorectic loses weight, she is unhappy at her new-found weight level and wants to lose more. This may progress until the individual is emaciated to such a dangerous level that it can result in death. The reported mortality rates range from 5–10%.

It is now the case that for an overwhelming number of females in Western society, chronic dieting has become a way of life. Eating disorders are predominantly female disorders and in our society slenderness in females is not only regarded as a normal requisite of beauty, but also symbolizes a sign of health and evidence of success. However, no single cause has been established for anorexia. The condition is thought to result from an amalgamation of physical, emotional, sociological and family factors. There is also some support for the hypothesis that it may be genetically based.

Classification of anorexia nervosa

One of the greatest advances in psychiatry over the past four decades has been the development of a criterion-based classification of mental illnesses. Clinical entities are classified for several reasons. One is that of communication in that clinicians need to know what they are talking about if meaningful communication is to take place. Research is also based on clinical entities and is essential if studies are to be replicated. The classification of clinical entities is required to elucidate the phenomena that one is investigating. After a clinical entity has been established, research can proceed in a particular direction. Clinical entities are essential for the purpose of treatment. This process of classification began in, 1952 with the introduction of the Diagnostic and Statistical Manual of Mental Disorders (DSM-1) by the American Psychiatric Association and was followed in 1968 by the DSM-II. The subsequent publication of three editions DSM-III (1980) DSM-IIIR (1987) and DSM-IV (1994) are representative of significant rapid strides in the advancement of psychiatry.

'Binge-eating disorder' appears in DSM-IV as a new diagnostic category requiring further investigation, but many express the view that patients with binge-eating disorder show strong similarities to those with the non-purging form of bulimia nervosa. This is a view that this author subscribes to, so this book will only consider anorexia nervosa and bulimia nervosa.

DSM-IV (1994) diagnostic criteria for anorexia nervosa

- Refusal to maintain body weight at or above a minimally normal weight for age and height (e.g. 85% of that expected).
- Intense fear of gaining weight or becoming fat, even though underweight.
- Disturbance in the way in which one's body weight or shape is experienced, undue influence of body weight or shape on self-evaluation, or denial of the seriousness of the current low body weight.
- In post-menarcheal females, amenorrhea, ie, the absence of at least three consecutive menstrual cycles.

(Diagnostic and Statistical Manual of Mental Disorders IV, 1994 by the American Psychiatric Association.)

In DSM-IV anorexia nervosa is divided into two subtypes a restricting type (AN-R) and a binge-eating/purging type (AN-B/P). The latter group includes those anorectics who vomit and take laxatives or diuretics. However, the presence of exercise as a method of weight control without purging or laxative abuse does not warrant a diagnosis of AN-B/P.

The developed and most thoroughly researched assessment inventory for anorexia nervosa is the Eating Attitudes Test (EAT) devised by Garner and Garfinkel (1979). The EAT is a 40-item, self-report rating scale, covering a broad range of target behaviours and attitudes. It has also been used as a screening device for assessing anorexia nervosa in high-risk populations. The EAT is seen as a useful tool as an objective measure of the symptoms of anorexia nervosa and can prove useful in following behavioural and attitudinal change during treatment.

Differential diagnosis

The differential diagnosis encompasses both psychiatric and medical disorders that produce weight loss. Anorexia nervosa should be considered in the differential diagnosis of any unexplained weight loss and may for example be confused with insulin-dependent diabetes mellitus, thyrotoxicosis, malignancy, malabsorption syndromes or infective conditions such as HIV. Medical conditions such as Crohn's disease and psychiatric illnesses such as major depression may sometimes lead to diagnostic confusion. However the central feature of fear of fatness is not seen in these other conditions.

Anorexia nervosa may also be confused with a depressive disorder, but in depression there is a disinterest in food rather than avoidance. The other psychiatric differential diagnosis includes affective disorders, obsessive-compulsive disorder, somatization disorder and schizophrenia. Schizophrenia with delusions about food is relatively easy to discount since the delusions are not concerned with the food's caloric content and the impaired contact with reality will usually be observed in other spheres. The diagnosis of anorexia nervosa is finally achieved by confirming a morbid fear of fatness and a relentless pursuit of thinness.

Chapter 2
Epidemiology

Epidemological studies of eating disorders assess the incidence of prevalence rates of the disorders within populations and compare these results against different population groups. Incident rates represent longitudinal events whereas prevalence rates represent cross-sectional events. Incidence rates are defined as the number of new cases in the population in a certain period of time. In eating disorders the rates cited do not represent the onset of the illness but rather the moment when it was first detected. Incidence rates are expressed as the rate per 100 000 of a population per year. The prevalence rate is the actual number of cases in a defined community at a certain time. Prevalence rates have been estimated for specified populations where the risk for the disorder might be expected to be high and also in more broadly based populations. For eating disorders the incidence rates are those cases presenting for health intervention as it is impossible to screen a large population of 100 000 for a year or longer. The studies have used psychiatric case registers, medical records or morbidity registration by general practitioners. It is felt that all studies of eating disorders will grossly underestimate the true incidence of the conditions, as not all cases will be referred for healthcare.

Anorexia nervosa appears to have become more common, especially among young women. It is common in adolescence but the age of onset can range from children through to older women. Most cases are women with men constituting 5–10% of those presenting for treatment. It is no longer seen as a disorder just of the upper social classes but now it seems to cross the full class spectrum as well as being found in both rural and urban settings. It could also be argued that increased public awareness of eating disorders has led to presentation by anorectic patients at an earlier, milder stage and perhaps such patients might not have come to medical attention in previous decades. So doubts can exist as to whether increased incidence is due to a better detection and earlier referral.

In 1970, Theander published the results of what was the first epidemiological study on anorexia nervosa. His study marks a very significant development in the history of the study of eating disorders. Theander (1970)

8

examined the number of hospitalized cases over a 30-year period from 1930 to 1960 in southern Sweden. He reported an increase in incidence from 0.08 female patients per 100 000 inhabitants in the first decade, to 0.45 per 100 000 in the last decade, supporting his view that there had indeed been an increase. He argued that better medical records and accurate diagnosis along with a greater tendency to hospitalize cases could all provide alternative explanations for the rise in the admission rates. Theander also found that the fertility of women with anorexia nervosa is low and in his long-term follow-up study he found only 36% had borne children. This, the author argues, would in itself lead to a decline rather than an increase in the disorder. Nylander (1971) also carried out a study in Sweden of 1241 schoolgirls aged 14 and over. He found that half thought they were fat and one-third had been dieting.

The prevalence of distorted eating among young United States' women has increased markedly over the past few decades. Rosen et al. (1990) argue that at any one time between half and two-thirds of all high-school females are on a diet, many of them unnecessarily. In England, the often-cited study of Crisp et al. (1976) looked at nine populations of schoolgirls in seven private and two state-run schools. They found that in private schools the prevalence was one severe case in approximately every 200 schoolgirls, but in those aged 16 and over, it amounted to one severe case in every 100 girls at private school. This was in contrast to the state schools where the prevalence was less – about one case per 550 investigated.

In Sweden, Rastram et al. (1989) also carried out a survey of an entire school population of 15 year olds and found a prevalence rate of 0.84% for girls and 0.09% for boys. Nielsen's (1990) study in Denmark, for the period 1973 to 1987, investigated the increased incidence of anorexia nervosa in the population and/or among psychiatric inpatients. The survey was of psychiatric admissions in Denmark for 1973 to 1987 and showed that the prevalence of anorexia nervosa is not increasing in the population. The female-to-male ratio was 12:1. Males were younger than females at first admission for anorexia nervosa and readmission rates for females were more than 10 times greater than for the males. This finding is also supported by Willi et al. (1990) who found there to be no significant increase in the disorder. Their study investigates all Swiss women in the canton of Zurich who developed anorexia nervosa between the ages of 12 and 25 years and who were hospitalized between 1983 and 1985. Data were compared with the earlier studies. The authors found that the incidence of anorexia nervosa did not significantly increase but that there was a more frequent use of vomiting and abuse of laxatives, which could signify an increase in cases with mixed features of anorexia nervosa and bulimia.

Lucas et al. (1991) who investigated the incidence of anorexia nervosa in Rochester, Minneapolis, do not support such findings. The study aimed to determine prevalence and incidence rates and long-term trends in incidence of anorexia nervosa by identifying all those persons residing in the community during a 50-year period from 1935 until 1985. The authors concluded that anorexia nervosa is more common than previously thought. Among 15 to 19 year olds it is a very common chronic illness. Its incidence had increased among females between 15 and 24 years old but not among older women or among males.

Minority groups

Eating disorders have been considered culture specific in that they tend to be found in young females who live in societies in which food is plentiful and where thinness is valued. Anorexia nervosa appears to be associated with developed Western societies. Studies from underdeveloped countries are lacking, although this could be due to limited psychiatric resources. However, different cultural attitudes to weight and shape would also have a bearing on this. There is a strong impression that, whereas eating disorders are rarer in developing countries, they become more common as a country develops economically (Hsu, 1990).

Most research on eating disorders has been conducted on Caucasian women. There has been much uncertainty concerning its presence in ethnic minorities. It is not clear as to whether eating disorders are more or less prevalent among minorities. Some studies report the incidence to be low among minorities (Abrams et al., 1993) but others have found no difference between groups of Caucasian and non-Caucasians in the diagnosis of bulimia nervosa (Gross and Rosen, 1988). Some have even reported a higher incidence of eating disorders in minority populations (Story et al., 1994).

Fisher et al. (1994) administered the Eating Attitudes Test (EAT) to two populations of high school students in an effort to measure abnormal eating. One was a group of 268 suburban females (mean age 16.2 years) and the second was a group of 389 females and 281 males (mean age 16.0 years) in a city school, with 92% black or Hispanic students. The subjects were also weighed and measured for health screening. Significantly more suburban females (63%) considered themselves overweight compared with both urban females (35%) and males (19%), yet only 14% of suburban females were calculated as being more than 10% over ideal body weight, compared with 45% of urban females and 39% of urban males. Contrary to the authors' expectations, self-esteem was higher and anxiety lower in the urban students than the suburban students. The authors concluded that abnormal eating attitudes were present among both urban and suburban students, although there were important differences in their manifestation and implications.

Anorexia nervosa is often considered culture-bound to Western Europe and North America, this assumption can no longer be valid since the condition is now being reported in Hong Kong, Taiwan, Malaysia, China,

India, Japan and Singapore (Khandelwal et al., 1995; Goh et al., 1993; Suematsu et al., 1985). Although the incidence of eating disorders is thought to be rare in non-Western countries, non-Western immigrants are more likely to develop anorexia nervosa than their counterparts in the homeland, like Arab college students in London (Nasser, 1986) and Greek and Turkish females in Germany (Fichter et al., 1988). There is also clinical evidence that reports anorexia nervosa in immigrant families, suggesting that immigration and acculturation stress are key factors in triggering the illness.

Silber (1986) suggests that as minority groups become more upwardly mobile and progress up the socio-economic scale, the number of cases of eating disorders among them will also increase. Silber found that an overwhelming number of minority groups came from families who had already achieved a higher socio-economic level. Such findings are supported by Suematsu et al. (1985) who found that the healthcare system in Japan was also seeing an increasing number of anorexia nervosa patients.

Children

Children are now being influenced by the cultural shift towards over-valuing appearance as a measure of personal worth. The prevalence rates are highest in girls from upper socio-economic groups but it has been reported in pre-pubertal children as young as eight years of age (Jacobs and Issacs, 1986). It is clear that for significant proportions of children there is a definite desire to be thinner and the practice of weight control begins before adolescence, particularly in girls. In order to investigate children's attitudes and behaviours associated with eating and weight control, Maloney et al. (1988) developed a children's version of the Eating Attitudes Test (Garner and Garfinkel, 1979). Maloney et al. claim that the EAT is incomprehensible to young children and they produced a slightly modified version – the Children EAT (Ch EAT). It was designed to be used with children aged eight to 13 years. The Ch EAT is a 26-item, self-report inventory that assesses dieting behaviours, food pre-occupations, bulimia and concerns about being overweight. A score of 20 or above can suggest, but not necessarily diagnose, an eating disorder. Almost 7% of the 318 children surveyed scored within the anorectic range on the Ch EAT, which is consistent with reports on the use of the EAT in older individuals.

Rolland et al. (1997) looked at the desire for thinness among pre-adolescent Australian children to assess any gender differences. Their study included 244 children from grades three to six who completed the children's version of the Eating Attitudes Test (Ch EAT). The children reported whether they had ever wanted to be thinner or if they had ever tried to lose weight. They were also shown selected pictures ranging from thin to fat to depict their current and ideal body image. The results showed that 50% of girls and 33% of boys wanted to be thinner and 40% and 24% respectively had attempted to lose weight. Percentages of girls and boys scoring above the Ch EAT screening threshold for anorexia risk were 14% and 9% respectively. High Ch EAT scores among such young (grade three) children raise the question as to whether very young children can fully understand such a questionnaire.

Studies are also now indicating the presence of anorexia in children from various ethnic groups, a situation once thought of as rare.

Older women

It is important to ask why women experience eating disorders in later life. It can develop soon after childbirth, as the literature on the association between pregnancy, motherhood and eating disorders has been reported (Fahy and O'Donoghue, 1991). Seeing anorexia nervosa solely as a disorder of adolescence could prevent older women from seeking treatment and only when this group is investigated further can we obtain a true indication of its prevalence. It is common to see women in their middle to late years with eating disorders. Some have harboured a distorted body image since youth. They also realize the full long-term side effects of the condition and the negative influence it has had on their personal, social and work lives. Often their eating disorder has been kept a secret from their spouses or other family members. Of course, in the elderly, anorexia nervosa needs to be separated from patients with depression and those whose delusional belief is that food is poisonous.

Hall and Driscoll (1993) report on two cases of older patients. One patient was a 64 year old with a nine-year history of symptoms while the other patient was a 61-year-old woman with a 12-year history. The authors argue that they had less insight into their illness than younger patients and, despite intensive therapy, they died from their illness two and five years later. It could be argued that increased pressure on older women to maintain their sexuality may have been related to development of their eating disorder. Zerbe (1996) describes the skeletal grandmother who equates thinness with youthful looks. The problem with elderly patients can be their reluctance to discuss psychological issues, eating habits or sexual issues with anyone. However, of those who do, they will recount memories of traumatic experiences of being criticized and teased relentlessly for their excessive weight in childhood.

Males

One in every 10 patients with an eating disorder is male. Young men who participate in seasonal sports that require a particular weight (such as wrestling and boxing) or that stress appearance and body build (running, skating, jockeying) are at particular risk of developing an eating disorder.

There is also an increased incidence of eating disorders in the male homosexual population. Andersen (1990) found that 20% of males with an eating disorder were homosexual, which is significantly greater than the general population. It could be argued that the 'gay' male culture places greater value on men being slender than does 'straight' culture. The eating disorder may be first noted by excessive exercise and relentless attempts to maintain a slender figure. This is then followed by a drastically calorie-reduced diet. There is also the suggestion (Andersen, 1990) that male patients with eating disorders have a high incidence of substance abuse. It seems that the eating problem is part of an impulse control problem in which alcohol, drugs and food are misused to calm emotional distress.

Szyrynski (1973) found that anorexia nervosa occurs mostly in pre-adolescent or conspicuously immature adolescent boys. The author suggests that, in these cases, it appears alongside inadequate sexual identity in boys who have not yet accepted themselves as males. Wiener (1976) however suggests that apart from a younger age of onset there seems little that distinguishes the male cases from comparable cases in females.

Few authors nowadays would dispute the existence of anorexia in male patients but its occurrence is rare and only 5 to 10% of the clinical population of anorexia nervosa is male. For this reason most studies have been limited by the low number of patients included (Burns and Crisp, 1984; Oyebode et al., 1988; Beumont et al., 1972).

Sport, exercise and dance groups

Serious athletes walk a fine line between healthy eating and an eating disorder. College athletes engaging in intense competition may have highly abnormal dietary patterns. Rosen et al. (1986) in their survey found that up to 14% had engaged in self-induced vomiting, 6% had abused laxatives, 25% routinely used diet pills and as many as one-third had at least one unhealthy eating habit. Among female college gymnasts, 62% reported having unhealthy eating behaviours and two-thirds said their coaches told them they were too heavy. This would support the viewpoint that those who participate in dance, gymnastics, running, rowing or other sport for which thinness is essential are at risk of developing eating disorders. It may be first recognized by teammates or coaches who remark on the progressive weight loss in an athlete or comment on the smell of vomit in the changing room.

Many anorectics can also misuse exercise by expending huge amounts of energy keeping constantly on the move. This can involve fidgeting, running on the spot as well as other forms of exercise. This cycle needs to be broken and often the only way to do this is by hospital admission. Often the anorectic will exercise excessively despite exhaustion, injuries and warnings to stop from both doctors and coaches. There are, however, some that have developed anorexia after they became serious runners and had lost weight consequent to their increased activity level and not because of an initial conscious decision to embark on a diet. Others have developed the disorder following an illness that resulted in a weight loss. It is therefore possible that weight loss, by itself, can serve as a precipitating factor for anorexia in a vulnerable individual.

Garner and Garfinkel (1980) also suggest that the pressure to be slim, experienced by those for whom it is professionally essential to be so, combined with their own expectations of achievement, are definite risk factors. The authors surveyed a group of 183 professional dance students and 56 modelling students. In both groups the prevalence of dieting and anorexia nervosa was greater than in other students. The authors noted that music students exposed to similar competitive pressures did not score as highly on attitudes to eating as did the dancers. Garner and Garfinkel concluded that a pressure for thinness, when combined with a competitive environment, may constitute a strong risk for anorexia nervosa.

Anorexia nervosa in twins

Twin and family studies indicate a considerable likelihood of a significant genetic contribution in developing anorexia nervosa. This has been supported by Holland et al. (1988) and their findings, which indicate that in a sample of 45 twin pairs, the rate for anorexia nervosa in non-identical (dizygotic) twins was 5%, whereas concordance for identical (monozygotic) twins was 56%. It has always been accepted that physical illnesses can have a genetic basis, but psychiatric disorders are not so clearly defined. However, the presence and extent of any genetic vulnerability can be verified using family, twin and adoption groups.

Bruch (1969) reported two pairs of identical female twins, each pair discordant for anorexia nervosa, finding in both cases that the affected twin was the smaller, weaker, more dependent and non-dominant of the two. Both order and birth weight were inconsistent factors because in one set the affected twin was born first and weighted 'slightly less' whereas in the second set the affected twin was born six minutes later and weighed much less. Debow (1975) has also described the condition occurring in identical twins. The author discussed the problems of twinship, especially the failure to establish separate identities as complicating what were already major psychological issues in a disturbed family with anorexia nervosa. In the hospital setting, much difficulty occurred around the issue of separating the twins and, consequently, they were allowed to be in the same room.

The incidence of anorexia nervosa in a male twin was reported by Wiener (1976), he describes a case of anorexia nervosa in one of prepubertal identical male twins. The author reported that the patient twin was more perfectionistic, achieved in athletics and had a greater fear of failure than his brother who was more phobic, experienced nightmares and paradoxically was perceived as the less competent and dependent twin.

More recently Wade et al. (1996) looked at eating problems in an Australian twin population. Questionnaires were administered to a group of 3869 female twins. The results indicated that for those women experiencing problems with eating, five groups could be identified. These were overweight women who were dissatisfied with their weight and shape, underweight women struggling with anorectic behaviour, those with bingeing problems, those using vomiting, laxatives and starvation as a means of weight control and overweight women using slimming and fluid tablets for weight controls.

Prevalence rates for anorexia nervosa are equivocal as many anorectics do not see themselves as ill and in need of seeking out health care advice. The anorectic also has a great fear that treatment will mean weight gain and in her eyes becoming 'fat' is to be avoided at all costs. Methodological disparity in prevalence studies, with regard to how data are collected and analysed, has also influenced reported prevalence rates. Differences in target populations, sampling methods, co-operation rates, assessment instruments and case definition used, may in part explain some of the discrepancies found between prevalence rates. Anorexia nervosa does not affect all cross sections of the population at the same rate. Gender, race and age are the three most influential demographic factors in the development of an eating disorder.

Fombonne (1995) suggests that the apparent increase in the incidence of anorexia nervosa could be explained by demographic changes in the general population and by higher readmission rates. The figures on the incidence of anorexia nervosa do not, of course, include the additional numbers of adolescent girls who will engage in less extreme, but still unhealthy, dieting behaviours. Some would argue that dieting frequencies remain at epidemic levels and it is unusual to find a girl by the age of 18 who has not dieted at some time in her life. It could also be that there is a sizeable population with eating disorders who have not yet sought attention. This is because we have, inherent in our population, established etiological factors for eating disorders, such as the cultural emphasis on the thin ideal body shape, the high degree of competitiveness and the over-indulgence of eating as a favourable past time.

It is, however, unlikely that the trend in the increased number of anorexia nervosa cases could continue at previously reported rates. It would appear that the condition reached a peak in the early 1980s, when bulimia nervosa first became recognized as a separate clinical entity. This condition, allowed some women to binge-purge and maintain their weight around the normal range.

Chapter 3
Etiology

It is unlikely that anorexia nervosa has a single discrete cause, but more likely that it is an illness that is precipitated by a complex change of events. The etiology of anorexia nervosa has primarily been seen in terms of psychological and cultural factors but there is also the possibility that there may be a genetic basis. This has not yet been extensively researched, although it has been recognized.

Crisp (1967) sees anorexia nervosa as rooted in the biological aspects of normal adult weight. Starvation in the anorectic represents a phobic avoidance of adult weight. Anorexia nervosa can therefore be seen as a disorder of weight pivoting around specific maturational changes of puberty, both biological and psychological. Bruch (1962), on the other hand, describes anorexia nervosa in three fundamental aspects. These are the anorectic's inability to appreciate the necessity for adequate nourishment, a disturbance of body image perception preventing the patient from seeing how thin she really is and, finally, the intense feeling of ineffectiveness. This feeling stems from the parents' attitude to their daughter and their wish to provide everything for her and in return control her in such a way that she no longer sees herself as an individual. Most anorectics acknowledge that the decision not to eat is the first time in their lives that they have asserted their own will. In contrast to Bruch (1962), others argue that anorexia nervosa can be used to avoid independence and all that it entails and that, by reducing her body weight, the anorectic remains a child.

During puberty, girls' bodies undergo numerous physiological changes, predominant among them is a significant increase in body fat. This, in turn, causes many adolescent girls to become concerned about their body image, as they seem to be moving away from what they view as ideal. So they attempt to diet in order to return to their thinner, prepubertal physique. So girls who mature early are at a greater risk of developing eating problems and females who experience a conflict between developmental needs and cultural expectations will be at risk for eating disorders as opposed to those who, while recognizing society's values regarding women, can reject them.

Cauffman and Steinberg (1996) carried out a study based on the premise that eating problems develop in young girls as a result of interactions between two distinct aspects of adolescent development – that is the specific challenges of puberty, alongside the psychological and social challenges of early adolescence. They argue that a developmental change that usually accompanies puberty is the onset of hetrosocial activity including participation in mixed sex social activities, the beginning of formal dating and initial experimentation with sex. The authors argue, however, that there are indications that show that menarchal status may indeed affect dieting and disordered eating. Dating is also strongly correlated with dieting and disordered eating tendencies among girls who have recently experienced menarche. Their findings indicate that physical involvement with a boyfriend increases the likelihood of dieting and disordered eating among adolescent girls. However, as the eating disorder progresses, a shift of emphasis takes place so that their interest in sexual activity is exchanged for a feeling of sexual inadequacy.

Familial predisposition

The role of the family in the etiology of anorexia nervosa has been researched widely with most writers agreeing the families to be dysfunctional. However, it is not useful to imply that the families are to blame. Clinical and family therapists have emphasized the importance of the dynamics and interactions within families in which eating disorders develop and are maintained. Family influence in the etiology of eating disorders may have both environmental and genetic components. For some adolescents this can be related to a problematic family structure and communication within that family. The presence of psychiatric disorders in a parent with its resulting effects on family relationships can also be important for the onset of an eating disorder. It could also follow that if the parental problems have an underlying genetic basis then this could be transferred to the offspring in biological make-up, thus creating an additional influence on the eventual development of an eating disorder.

Kalucy et al. (1977) found that there were a number of families of anorectics who shared certain common features. These included an unusual interest in food, weight and shape, an unusual incidence of phobic avoidance and obsessive compulsive character traits and unusual vulnerability to seemingly ordinary life events and a tendency to be unusually close, loyal and mutually interdependent. The common denominator was that families were ill equipped for – and prepared their children inadequately for – the adolescent phase of development.

Sibling rivalry is often cited as a factor in the development of the illness, although no particular grouping appears important. The condition may arise in the youngest, middle, eldest, or only child and brothers or sisters or both may be affected (Dally and Gomez, 1980). Sibling rivalry was also recorded by Morgan et al. (1975) as 32% in their study.

A father's death can also be a precipitating factor in the development of anorexia nervosa. In studies reported by Dally and Gomez (1980) a mother and her daughter both began dieting competitively after the husband committed suicide. Two sisters also developed the condition after their father's death and a 15-year-old girl stopped eating all solids when her father died. In all these cases Dally has interpreted the girl's behaviour as a bid for the mother's affection and attention, a reminder of her maternal role. Similar cases have been reported by Kalucy et al. (1977) and others.

Parent's divorce and separation can also precipitate the condition. Halmi (1974) found 18% came from broken homes, this being a slightly higher incidence than Theander's (1970) reported 13%.

Minuchin et al. (1978) described the anorectic family as being charac-terized by enmeshment, over-protectiveness, rigidity and the lack of conflict resolution. The authors argue that, in an enmeshed family, autonomy and independence are sacrificed for the sake of loyalty and collective protection. They see over-protectiveness as the social facade of enmeshment.

Santonastaso et al. (1997) looked at the family psychiatric histories of 115 subjects with a diagnosis of anorexia nervosa or bulimia nervosa. The authors argue that the association between a positive family psychiatric history (found in 40% of their sample) and a more serious eating psychopathology is suggestive that family psychiatric morbidity may have an impact on the development of eating disorders. In their study, the most reported diagnoses among relatives were affective disorders (50%), anxiety disorders (19%), alcoholism (10%) and eating disorders (13%). In 63% of the cases the psychiatric problems involved the mothers of the eating disordered patients.

Another study that examined families of anorectics was that of Wallin et al. (1996), who looked at 49 families with a child suffering from anorexia nervosa. The aim was to assess these families to see whether they are different with regard to perceived psychopathology in the family members, differences in perceived family function and in the degree of the eating disorder in the anorexia nervosa patient. However, they found no clear differences between the families regarding the severity of the patients' eating disorders. There was also no clear evidence that different family functions gave rise to different degrees of eating disorders.

Attempts to identify a typical anorectic mother or father have resulted in no consistent findings. Parents are often preoccupied with outward appearance and success. They are frequently over-protective and control-ling. However, it can often be the case that, as the anorectic's condition improves, the parents' psychoneurotic morbidity increases and this is particularly so of the father.

Women with anorexia nervosa will frequently report that their parents are highly disapproving of their behaviour and their achievements and are seen as setting impossibly high standards for success. Mothers of anorectics have been described as dominant, intrusive and ambivalent, whereas fathers have been seen as passive and ineffectual. Some report that the father and not the mother is the overprotective parent. Childhood eating problems display an association with food preferences and fussiness. Anorectics report being part of a family that is characterized by low levels of cohesion, over-protectiveness, high levels of criticism and low levels of emotional warmth. Parents have been found to discourage psychological growth in the areas of self-expression and autonomy was not encouraged. Garfinkel and Garner (1982) suggest that families with anorectic children often show a preoccupation with weight and eating, emphasizing physical appearance and relying on external standards of measuring self-worth and success. The families also report a history of affective disorder (depression or alcoholism) and experience difficult parent–child interactions.

Striegel-Moore and Kearney-Cooke undertook a large study in 1994, which also looked at the parents' attitudes and behaviours about their children's physical appearance. This included the child's physical appearance, eating habits and exercise behaviours and the parents' efforts to influence their child's physical appearance. The sample included 1276 adult men and women who had a child aged between two and 16 years. A majority of parents were generally satisfied with their child's appearance, eating habits and exercise behaviour. However, as the child's age progressed, the parents' attitudes were less positive. The authors found few gender-related differences between male and female respondents but women did appear to have more influence and were also held responsible for their children's physical appearance. Some of the questions asked by the authors related to gender difference and the greater importance of beauty for women compared with men. Striegel-Moore and Kearney-Cooke, however, suggest that men are increasingly becoming included in our culture's mandate to value and pursue physical attractiveness. Fathers were as likely as mothers to help their child lose weight.

For girls, the development of body image concerns and disordered eating are closely linked to the physical changes associated with puberty. It could also be the case that parents show a similar pattern of increasingly negative perceptions and attitudes regarding their child's physical appearance at this stage in development as well. Parents who place great emphasis on their own physical appearance may in turn place greater importance on, or be more critical of their child's appearance than those parents who consider their own physical appearance to be relatively unimportant. Families with an anorectic child are more than normally concerned with appearances. To them social acceptability is paramount. In the Striegel-Moore and Kearney-Cooke study (1994), they found that, although boys were heavier (as measured by Body Mass Index) than girls, parents felt that girls were fatter than boys, a difference that increased as the children reached adolescence. This would support the view that there are different beauty ideals for men and women in our culture. Parents will often compare their daughter's body to an unrealistically thin ideal and arrive at a distorted view of her body size. Girls would tend to receive more praise for their physical appearance, as opposed to boys, who tend to get more praise for athletic and sporting skills.

Anorectic mothers

In childhood anorexia, a common, though important cause, is being confronted by disturbed attitudes about food by mothers who themselves have an eating disorder or are preoccupied with weight and appearance. The occurrence of anorexia nervosa in biological relatives of anorectics has been found by Strober and Humphrey (1987). First-degree relatives of anorectics are more likely to have an eating disorder than are relatives of normal controls. Some cases of eating disorders do appear to stem from family vulnerability, although how genetics and the environment interact to produce anorexia nervosa is unclear.

Timimi and Robinson (1996) examined case records of 11 women with eating disorders who had children to determine the prevalence of recorded disturbance in the children. Disturbances were found in nine children of six mothers. Some mothers had disturbed perceptions of their children, believing the child to be fat or greedy. Some children displayed unusual behaviour such as simulated vomiting and periodic overeating. The children's attitudes on the other hand recorded their concern regarding their mother's thinness. The authors stated that there is evidence to show that children of eating disordered parents appear to be at risk from a variety of disturbances afflicting their emotional and physical development. Scourfield (1995) discussed the presentation of three different cases of abnormal eating behaviour in children of anorectic women. The author describes this as anorexia by proxy. The Canadian study of Woodside and Shekter-Wolfson (1990) examined parenting of patients with eating disorders and found that few were happy with the role of parent and most experienced serious difficulties, with two out of 12 parents abandoning their children.

Hodes et al. (1997) study examined the extent of psychiatric disorders and abnormalities of weight and growth in children whose mothers had eating disorders and were attending a specialist eating disorder service. It included 13 mothers and their 26 children who participated in the study. Their findings indicate that the mothers suffered from chronic eating disorders, high rates of mental difficulties and separation. Of the children, 50% had psychiatric disorders and 32% had abnormalities of weight or growth. The female offspring, were, on the whole, of low body weight as the mothers tended to underestimate their children's dietary needs. Half of the children had psychiatric disorders including severe conditions such as anorexia nervosa and obsessive compulsive disorder. One-third had abnormal weight or growth. Professionals working with mothers who have anorexia nervosa should automatically inquire about the children as it may be necessary to provide help with parenting skills in order to meet the child's physical and emotional needs.

Brinch et al. (1988) found, in their retrospective study of women who had anorexia nervosa, that 29% of their children had eating problems beyond the first year of life and that prenatal mortality was six times the expected rate. Mothers with eating disorders often report fears that their babies are overweight and do admit to resorting to slimming their babies. The quality of these mothers' parenting skills can place their children at great risk. Not only is there an increased risk of low birthweight babies, but Lacey and Smith (1987) reported that 15% of mothers were trying to slim their babies within their first year of life. The anorexia nervosa itself can preoccupy the mother to such an extent that she does not have time to look after her child properly.

Personality

Most researchers have found that the premorbid personality of the anorectic is characterized by substantial emotional instability. Lifetime prevalence rates of depression have also been reported ranging from 25% to 80% (Herzog et al., 1992b; Halmi, 1996) across different samples. The most common anxiety symptoms found are obsessive-compulsive. Anorectic women have poorer coping skills, less confidence in their ability to solve problems and a tendency to avoid confronting problems.

In the face of inadequate coping skills, anorexia nervosa may occur in response to new experiences such as puberty, leaving home and entering university. Adverse life events can also trigger the condition. Meyer (1997) looked at stressful events in the development of eating disorders and a striking finding in their study showed an association with an alcoholic family member (33%) or experience with a chronic stressful event (34%) such as abuse, parental illness or death and mental illness.

There is also a strong association between perfectionism and anorexia nervosa. Perfectionism can be seen as a dimension of the rigid, obsessive behaviours that may contribute to resistance to treatment and relapse in anorexia nervosa. Bastiani (1995) looked at this issue of perfectionism and concluded that the characteristics of perfectionism persist after weight restoration, as well as a drive for thinness. Thus, perfectionism may be an innate personality characteristic existing both in a malnourished state and still persisting after weight restoration. Their study showed that perfectionism in anorexia nervosa is a behaviour that cannot be easily changed, even by improved eating.

Self-esteem is one particularly important psychological variable in determining whether a young woman moves beyond the common concern with avoiding fatness to the more severe concerns and behaviours that lead towards a recognized eating disorder. Button et al. (1996) carried out the first prospective study to investigate the role of self-esteem in etiology prior to the onset of an eating disorder. In their study they measured self-esteem in 594 schoolgirls aged 11–12. Almost 400 were successfully followed up at age 15–16 when they completed a questionnaire examining eating and other psychological problems. The results indicated that 12% of girls with low self-esteem at age 11–12 were at significantly greater risk of developing the more severe signs of an eating disorder alongside other psychological problems by the age of 15–16 years. Of course their results might also indicate that problems at school around the age of 11–12 years might also be a predictor of more severe problems.

Sociocultural influences

There is a suggestion that females are becoming more dissatisfied with their body shape and are developing weight concerns from the age of eight years. A review of children's attitudes towards thinness carried out by Feldman et al. (1988) found that children acquire cultural values of beauty before adolescence and their longing for thinness is desirable before their longing for beauty.

Throughout history, people have demonstrated a tendency to change their bodies to conform with the physical ideal of their particular era. Especially for women, the current Western standard for beauty and attractiveness is thinness. It appears that women believe men find them more attractive if they are slim. However, there is no evidence to support this claim (Smith et al., 1990). Women's striving for thinness involves much more than imitation of cultural role models. Psychodynamic and feminist approaches emphasize the symbolic power of food by seeing eating and food as a means through which women attempt to establish an adult female identity and sense of personal control. Others argue that the creation of eating disorders reflects the subordinate position of women in society. Eating disorders represent an indirect method of gaining power and control because it is very difficult to force an anorectic to eat. Women's roles as nurturers and care-givers have also been highlighted as contributing to the development of anorexia nervosa as they reflect the social mandate to be self-sacrificing and focused.

Boskind-White and White (1986) argue that, whereas women are expected to actively participate in previously male domains, they are still seen as the traditional female stereotype with characteristics of 'passive, fragile and frightened of competitiveness'. Women, they argue, go on to develop an excessive concern regarding weight and appearance as they cannot live up to the ideal expected of them. Stereotypical standards of beauty and social success transmitted through advertising and other mass media are often blamed for the incidence of dieting and disordered eating among young women. This, of course, does not explain why some young women develop eating disorders whereas others, still exposed to the same mass media, do not. The moderators here may include biological, cognitive and personality factors.

The media have often been implicated as playing an important causal role in the development of anorexia nervosa. It is argued that, by constantly presenting a barrage of idealized images of extremely thin women, the media are promoting a standard of thinness for women that is impossible to achieve without resorting to unhealthy means. In recent years, however, this thinness has had added to it an image of fitness. Regular exercise is presented as necessary to improve body tone and as a weight loss strategy. Media images of thin attractive women can therefore contribute to body dissatisfaction and body size distortion. Ogden and Mundray (1996) carried out a study that examined the effects of acute exposure to images of thin pictures compared to images of overweight individuals in both men and women. Twenty men and 20 women completed measures of body satisfaction before and after viewing images of either thin or overweight individuals matched for the subject's gender. Their results indicate that subjects of both genders reported feeling less satisfied with their bodies as measured by rating scales (measuring the extent to which they felt fat, attractive and so forth), body silhouettes and body size estimation after viewing the thin pictures, while indicating improved body satisfaction after viewing the overweight pictures. This response was greater in the female than in the male subjects for some of the measures (such as feeling fat, feeling toned) and was unrelated to levels of restrained eating.

There is evidence that the ideal body for females has changed over the course of this century. Garner et al. (1980) compared weights of *Playboy* centrefolds and Miss American pageant contestants from, 1959–1978 to actuarial statistics on the average women of the same age and height. They found a significant trend towards slimness. All measurements of *Playboy* centrefold girls, except for height and waist, decreased significantly, so, for instance, in 1959 the average 'Playmate' weighed 91% of average for her age and height, but by 1978 she weighted only 83.5% of the average for her age and height. The Miss American pageant winners since 1970 had a mean weight of only 82.5% of the average for their age and height and they also weighed significantly less than the average contestant. Wiseman et al. (1992) provided an interesting update to these pageant contestants and showed that they continued to get thinner during the period 1979–1988, although centrefolds appeared to have levelled off. Female magazine models also became increasingly thin from the 1970s through the early 1980s, as did female film actresses from 1940 until the 1970s (Silverstein et al., 1986; Snow and Harris, 1986). However, no such data are available for men. At the same time, the number of diet articles in six women's magazines had increased substantially during the previous 20 years (Garner et al., 1980). All this is at a time when the general population is actually becoming heavier.

Mondini et al. (1996) analysed 347 articles on eating disorders, nutrition, fitness, beauty and body care, cosmetic surgery and fashion models in Italian newspapers and magazines. The results showed that, while there was an agreement between the information given by the media and scientific reporting on clinical symptoms and sociocultural causes of the eating disorder, the media did not tend to portray eating disorders as a mental illness but would blame the parents for causing the eating disorder.

Another study by Nemeroff et al. (1994) also assessed magazine article content while examining gender differences, time trends and magazine audience type. They looked at four types of article content – health, fitness, beauty and weight loss in order to capture the major aspects of body focus. The number of articles containing such content were counted over a 12-year period in a sample of magazines aimed at three separate audiences – traditional, high fashion and modern. Large gender differences were seen with female-targeted magazines, as expected, outstripping male targeted ones for all content categories assessed. However, time-trend analysis indicated a decrease in emphasis on weight loss in women's magazines and a slight increase in health consciousness over the period studied, and a statistical move towards an increase in weight loss focus in men's magazines.

Dittmar and Blayney (1996) however found that advertisements featuring food aroused more negative emotions than non-food adverts, but this was only found in women who already suffered from an eating disorder with disturbed attitudes towards body and weight. The authors found that the greatest difference in negative emotions appeared with the chocolate advert. This advert, of course, gives out a most contradictory message about beauty and eating behaviour as it promotes the view that women can be slim and beautiful while at the same time eating such a high-calorific and non-essential food.

Some now argue that there is an obvious trailing off in articles in magazines for women to lose weight (Wiseman et al., 1992). However, the authors found that exercise articles, which they see are weight loss articles in disguise, had in fact surpassed diet articles over an eight-year period. The authors continue to argue that, as both are putting on pressure to lose weight, then this pressure was still increasing.

Fashion magazines, it can be argued, provide a psychosocial stimulus, triggering body dissatisfaction and encouraging weight-control behaviours. These images encourage girls to present a body image that gains social approval and acceptance. Body dissatisfaction encourages the instigation and maintenance of weight control behaviours that, in turn, lead to the downward spiral, ending with anorexia nervosa. Whereas a distorted body image has been seen as a crucial aspect of eating disorders for many years, a similar distorted body image has been reported in some individuals without an eating disorder (Martin, 1985).

Stice et al. (1994) carried out an investigation that assessed the relationship of media exposure to eating disorder symptoms and tested whether gender-role endorsement, ideal body stereotype internalization and body satisfaction mediated this effect. They used 238 female undergraduates. The results supported the assertion that internalization of sociocultural pressures mediates the adverse effects of the thin ideal. Gender-role endorsement was related to ideal body stereotype internalization, which, in turn, predicted body dissatisfaction. There was also a significant relation between body dissatisfaction and eating pathology.

Several studies have examined the association among populations that must maintain a thin body shape. Wrestlers and jockeys frequently lose weight to meet the weight requirement for their prospective sports (King, 1991). Studies of their eating patterns, behaviour and attitudes found abnormal eating behaviours to be common including fasting and purging. Female ballet students are another such group. Garner et al. (1987) investigated 55 female ballet students aged between 11 and 14 years in Canada and found 25.7% to be anorectic, 2.9% to be bulimic and that 11.4% had partial symptoms of anorexia nervosa and bulimia nervosa. The authors concluded that eating disorders were common in an environment that emphasized thin body shape.

Sexual abuse

The role of childhood sexual abuse and the development of eating disorders has received considerable attention in recent years. Oppenheimer (1985) drew attention to features shared by patients with eating disorders and those who had been the victims of childhood sexual abuse. Such features included low self-esteem, shame, and a negative attitude towards one's body and sexuality. Palmer et al. (1990) investigated 158 women seen in an eating disorder clinic and reported one-third as having had an unpleasant and uninvited sexual experience with an adult before the age of 16 years. In addition, over half reported various later adverse sexual experiences. In the cited cases of sexual abuse in anorectics, it was traditionally their fathers, grandfathers and uncles who were suspected as the perpetrators of such acts. However, there is now evidence coming forth to suggest that maternal incest may also be a factor.

If an adolescent is being sexually abused, weight loss with accompanying reduction of secondary sexual characteristics can be an effective deterrent to the abuse.

Zinc deficiency

There is often a zinc deficiency in the anorectic due to her intake of meat being strictly limited. The demand for zinc is increased during growth so that some teenagers harbour a latent zinc deficiency. Bakan et al. (1993) were the first to speculate that zinc deficiency may play a role in the etiology of anorexia nervosa, while examining the similarity of the symptoms of anorexia nervosa and those of zinc deficiency such as weight loss, appetite loss, skin lesions, nausea and disorders of sexual development. Bakan cites three factors as contributing to a zinc deficiency. These are stress, oestrogen and dietary habits. If the patient persistently refuses to eat, then zinc administration can, of course, be effective.

Chapter 4
Clinical features

The features of anorexia nervosa that usually attract attention at first are the patient's complete resistance to eating 'fattening foods', progressive and/or major weight loss, irritability with the rest of the family and amenorrhea. The anorectic may also produce bizarre eating patterns, which may include bingeing, vomiting and purging. If this is the case then profound metabolic disturbances may occur, with their accompanying clinical complications. The common physical findings include amenorrhea, emaciation, bradycardia, hypertension, pallor, ankle oedema, breast atrophy and scanty pubic hair. Halmi (1974) reported on the high number of females who begin dieting following humiliating comments on their physiques. As opposed to the 'normal' dieter who is happy when she has reached her weight goal, the anorectic will set herself lower and lower weight goals.

Woodside (1995) highlights the signs of a developing disorder. They are:

- Dieting that is associated with decreasing weight goals.
- Dieting that is associated with increasing criticism of the body.
- Dieting that is associated with increasing social isolation.
- Dieting that is associated with amenorrhea.
- Evidence of purging.

Of course it is possible that such individuals may be prevented from developing anorexia nervosa if the warning signs are recognized by family, friends, health services or school medical officer. The patient will often deny the problem if confronted and an interrogational approach is not fruitful. A sympathetic approach is more helpful in getting the anorectic to talk about her problem.

The anorectic may be secretive in her eating, refusing to eat with the family, even hiding food in the house. She may leave the table immediately after having eaten in order to vomit in the toilet. Anorectics can exist on less than 400 calories a day. If their starvation continues they appear as walking skeletons with the typical appearance of the protruding pubic bone. When they do eat they will often cut their food into very small pieces and show deliberate slowness over chewing, swallowing and finishing their meal.

A typical feature frequently observed in anorectic patients is their lack of interest in, and at times open refusal of, treatment. Halmi et al. (1977) found that 52% of patients were actively in favour of hospitalization but 23% were strongly opposed. In 71% of patients another person was influential in causing the hospitalization. Bruch (1974) also witnessed the anorectics' denial of their condition and their vigorous defence of their emaciated bodies as not too thin but as just right or as normal. Bruch feels that such a complete denial of such an emaciated appearance is pathognomic, for true anorexia nervosa patients, and patients with severe weight loss due to other reasons, will openly admit or complain about their shape.

Often patients will state on a self-report form that 'there is nothing wrong with me that a few days rest couldn't cure'. Crisp (1974) reported that such delusions as the patient's insistence that she feels and appears normal despite the 'starved' appearance could be explained by the fact that she is now as she needs to be. The atrophying gastrointestinal tract and reduced basal metabolic demands result in her hunger perception becoming distorted.

The issue of determining the age of onset is controversial as some authors view the onset of dieting or dieting behaviour while others use the date of the last menstrual period as signifying the beginning of the illness. This can also be compounded by the anorectic's wall of secrecy regarding her condition, which is so typically seen in the disorder. Hindler et al. (1994) studied 827 patients diagnosed with anorexia nervosa who attended the eating disorder unit at the Middlesex and St George's hospital from 1960 to 1990. The results indicated a stable age of onset but a lengthening in the duration of the illness with an associated increase of age at presentation. The authors concluded that there had been no change in the age of onset of anorexia nervosa during the previous 30 years. The authors argue that the delay in presentation may be attributed more to the processes of referral, which have in fact altered.

The Beck et al. (1996) study looked at 11 cases of truly late onset whose average age at presentation was 60 years. The authors found that 1% of all cases of eating disorders occurred at ages in the range of 40 to 77 years, their average onset being 56 years. Age itself is no barrier to the onset of anorexia nervosa, which can occur whenever self-starvation and/or binge-purge behaviour becomes entrenched.

In contrast, Lask and Bryant-Waugh (1992) looked at anorexia nervosa with an early onset. Their study deals with the eight to 14 years age group. Case definition in childhood, however, can be difficult as the strict criteria for defining anorexia nervosa to include amenorrhea cannot be used. In an attempt to overcome this problem Fosson et al. (1987) adapted existing diagnostic criteria to formulate their own criteria for younger children. These included:

- Determined food avoidance.
- Weight loss or failure to gain weight during the period of pre-adolescent accelerated growth (10-14 years) and the absence of any physical or mental illness.
- Any two or more of the following:
  (a) preoccupation with body weight
  (b) preoccupation with energy intake
  (c) distorted body image
  (d) fear of fatness
  (e) self-induced vomiting
  (f) extensive exercising
  (g) laxative abuse. (Fosson et al., 1987)

However, stunted growth is a common, if not a constant, sign of anorexia nervosa if the condition is of more than six months' duration in the pre-pubertal period. This is usually much more undesirable for male anorectics than females. Fohlin (1978) found that for pre-pubertal girls with long-standing anorexia, growth ceased. Even following restoration of normal weight, none of the girls showed any increase in height.

Psychopathology

Anorexia nervosa is a serious psychological disturbance causing mental, emotional and physical deterioration. Anorectics are not able to think clearly or to perceive reality logically. The illness causes emotional fluctuations between states of euphoria and periods of despair, self-loathing, loneliness and utter desperation. Anorectics are often reported as being compliant, approval seeking, self-doubting, conflict avoidant, excessively dependent, perfectionistic and socially anxious. Cognitive disturbances may play a predisposing part and may also maintain the disorder once it has been initiated. The conviction that weight, shape or thinness is central to the individuals feeling of self-worth is central to anorexia nervosa.

Obsessive-compulsive behaviours are also common among patients with anorexia nervosa. Rituals encompass almost every aspect of their lives, from food to body shape to daily tasks and activities. They often hoard food, or cut it up into tiny pieces, arranging and rearranging it on their plates to delay having to eat it. Anorectics tend to eat what they see as 'low calorie' food. Often these foods will be eaten in specific quantities – for example, six slices of cucumber, two tablespoons of yoghurt and half an orange. They will count the calories in everything including chewing gum, toothpaste and medicines. They will indulge in daily weighing and measuring body parts. They become obsessed with burning up calories, which leads to incessant exercising. Anorectic patients then tend to socially isolate themselves as a result of their low self-esteem and a fear of breaking out of their highly ritualistic lifestyle. Garner (1993) has described restricting patients as more obsessive-compulsive, stoical, perfectionistic, introverted and emotionally inhibited, while binge-eating, purging patients are described as impulsive, depressive, socially dysfunctional, sexually adventurous and substance misusers, with high levels of general emotional distress.

Fosson et al. (1987) found a high incidence of depression in children with early-onset anorexia nervosa. The authors found that 56% of children in their study (aged seven to 13 years at onset) were clinically depressed. However, Lask and Bryant-Waugh (1992) concluded that the characteristic psychopathology of anorexia nervosa in children is similar to that for older subjects. They describe the key features as a preoccupation with body weight and shape, a distorted body image, low self-esteem and a tendency towards depression and perfectionism. Rollins and Piazza (1978) also found accompanying depression apparent in 77% of the anorexia nervosa patients in their study. They also found neurotic symptoms and secondary diagnoses were also made to include personality disorder, neurosis and psychosis.

Bruch (1977) has recognized that these girls skip the classic period of resistance early in life and they continue to function with the morality of a young child, remaining convinced of the absolute rightness of 'grown-ups' and of their obligation to be obedient. It is common for them to have become socially isolated during the year preceding the illness and some will explain that they have withdrawn from their former friends whereas others feel they have been excluded.

Stealing

Dally and Gomez (1980) remark on compulsive stealing as an unexpected manifestation of anorexia nervosa. Occasionally this can happen in the initial stage when the patient is imposing controls on her urge to eat, or later when she has begun to give way to surges of appetite and to eat compulsively. The authors found that stealing is usually restricted to food and drink associated with fatness or trinkets and jewellery representing femininity. Such behaviour is totally contrary to the patients' previous high moral standards and such action is always associated with shame and regret.

A number of studies have found a relatively high incidence of compulsive stealing (shoplifting) among eating-disordered patients. The Crisp et al. (1980) study of 102 anorectic/bulimic patients found that 14% admitted compulsive stealing, four of whom were prosecuted. Almost all were in a bulimic phase at the time. Vandereycken and Van Houdenhove (1996) also investigated the characteristics of stealing behaviour and eventual associated psychopathology in a large group of 155 females with eating disorders. The study revealed that 47.1% admitted to stealing. The authors state that stealing certainly appears to be more frequent than expected and is associated with loss of control. The stealing mostly concerned food/and or money. At least 40% of the 'stealers' had been caught at least once – usually in a supermarket – and one-third had been fined.

Fasting provides a steady build-up of a 'craving for food' and this leads to an urgent need for food and compulsive action to obtain and consume food as quickly as possible – especially high carbohydrate foods. Stealing by anorectics is usually of money or food on the one hand, or clothes, make-up and toiletries on the other (Bridgeman and Slade, 1996). Crisp et al. (1980) concluded that the stealing of food probably reflected a basic effect of starvation, whereas the stealing of other items is seen as a combination of impulse and what the anorectic views as 'bad' objects. The authors see the anorectic who steals as being characterized by high levels of anxiety and depression and it is their view that the anorectic is not responsible for her action.

Body-image disturbances

A classic symptom in the condition of anorexia nervosa is the nearly delusional disturbance in the patient's body image as they are unable to 'see' themselves and the severe emaciation realistically. This distortion must be viewed as part of their misperceptions on a much wider scale. The distorted body image is marked by indifference to their emaciation, which is always defended as normal and right (Bruch, 1974). Many clinicians agree that patients with anorexia nervosa see themselves as abnormally fat. However Garner et al. (1976) found that the anorectics' body size estimations were unrelated to the degree of emaciation in their anorectic patients and neither were they related to the duration of illness.

It is now accepted that dissatisfaction with body shape remains common. As age increases, increasing numbers of girls see themselves as overweight, so that by late adolescence 50% see themselves as too fat and 80% want to lose weight. Nearly half of the underweight girls in the Whittaker et al. (1989) study still wanted to lose weight. As the anorectic loses weight she becomes more and more critical of her body shape and size, which then develops into a distorted body image. This preoccupation with body shape can be found in children as young as six years. Maloney et al. (1989) found that 60% of six-to-12-year-old girls in their study saw themselves as too fat, with 35% reporting having been on at least one diet in an effort to improve their appearance.

The anorectic can see particular body parts or her entire body as fat. She sees her body as larger than it actually is and states she feels 'fat'. Her feeling of fat is what convinces her that what she sees is what she feels and what she is. There is a question over whether body image distortion is perceptual or emotional in nature but this debate is purely academic to the anorectic. As far as she is concerned, she looks fat to herself and feels fat, so she must be fat!

Exercise

Many anorectics indulge in excessive exercise in order to control weight and even at a very low weight they may become hyperactive with endless energy. They can walk at a brisk pace for one to two hours daily, even at a very low weight. This endless energy can give parents the wrong message that there is nothing seriously wrong with their daughter, thus putting off seeking help.

Sleep patterns

As a result of food being restricted for any length of time, people will generally become increasingly restless and this is the case with those suffering from anorexia nervosa. Dally and Gomez (1980) found that in anorectic patients, sleep at the beginning and end of the night is restless and the total sleep time is reduced. In particular, the periods of deep sleep and dream sleep are reduced. Other studies report a similar finding – especially the pattern of early morning wakening (Lacey et al., 1976; Crisp et al., 1971).

Academic work

Many parents comment on their anorectic daughters' time spent on homework, which will amount to many hours depriving themselves of time out to eat a single bite of food. Everything is completed to perfection. Crisp (1974) referred to the patient's increased interest in academic work as providing the patient with a welcome and safe diversion from her other more disturbing preoccupations.

Bruch (1977) describes the anorectic as perfectionistic and academic performers who also excel in athletics. Halmi et al. (1977) also reported above average performance in schoolwork. Such excellent school records are often attributed to the anorectic's perfectionistic traits. Over two-thirds of the cases in their study were above average intellectually.

At school, the anorectic may be seen as very thin when dressed for sport, but at other times this will be disguised by the use of bulky sweaters, even in warm weather. These sweaters have a dual purpose of disguising her shape while also providing heat for her thin, cold body. The teachers and pupils will describe her as a 'model pupil' who excels academically. However, faints or collapses may begin to occur at school as her weight plummets to a very low level.

The anorectic male

Although the earliest writers on anorexia nervosa included male patients (Morton, 1694; Gull, 1868) its existence in males was contested during the middle of this century. Some argued that since amenorrhea is widely regarded as essential for the diagnosis of anorexia nervosa then men had to be excluded. However, few clinicians today would doubt the existence of anorexia in the male and new current diagnostic criteria now allow males to be included.

Anorexia nervosa in males is, despite its growing recognition, still seen as somewhat unusual. This has resulted in some cross-sectional research in this area with its associated limitations and constraints (Steiger, 1989; Beaumont et al., 1972). The prevalence of the condition in males is difficult to assess. Following extensive literature searches it has only been possible to trace approximately 20 studies of males with anorexia nervosa. The largest study was that of Crisp and Burns (1983) which reported on a series of 36 male patients. However, a national survey (Gallup, 1985) found that 4% of teenage boys had serious symptoms of anorexia nervosa.

Olivardia et al. (1995) compared a group of 25 college men suffering from an eating disorder with a group of 25 control men found through a college newspaper. They also had a second comparison group comprising 33 women with an eating disorder. The results indicated that the men with eating disorders closely resembled the women with eating disorders but they differed greatly from the comparison control group of men in phenomenology of illness, rates of co-morbid psychiatric disorders and dissatisfaction with body image. The authors did not find homosexuality to be a common feature of men with eating disorders. Childhood physical and sexual abuse appeared slightly more common in the eating disordered men than in the comparison men.

Although it is possible to find a vast literature examining the features of women with eating disorders, the data for men are very limited. However, it does appear that men and women with eating disorders generally display similar phenomenology. The main differences frequently reported are the apparent higher incidence of homosexuality or gender identity disturbance in men with eating disorders (Wiener, 1976; Steigner, 1989 and Buckley and Walsh, 1991). Sharp et al. (1994) examined the clinical features at presentation of 24 males with anorexia nervosa. The study confirmed the view that males display the classical syndrome of anorexia nervosa. The mean age at onset was 18.6 years and at presentation was 20.2 years. The authors found the males to have a premorbid tendency to obesity. The maximum weight loss during the illness amounted to 42% matched population mean weight (MPMW). Bingeing and vomiting were also commonly found in around half of the males alongside depressive and obsessional symptoms. There was also a strong family history of affective disorders and alcohol abuse was reported in over one-third.

Bruch (1974) and others have commented on the early, pre-pubertal age of onset in the male anorectic, whereas others have reported no difference between the two sexes. As with the female, the male deems he is ill. When he does eventually seek help it is most likely to be for an endocrine or gastrointestinal problem that is a consequence of his anorexia nervosa. The physical symptoms may conceal the eating disorder. It could therefore be the case that more anorectic males are in fact receiving treatment for the physical consequences of their anorectic state but that they have not yet been diagnosed with anorexia nervosa.

It is likely that the male suffering from anorexia nervosa will begin to diet just to lose a few pounds. Then he begins to exercise as well. As his weight reduces he sets himself a lower and lower weight target, while still arguing that he is too fat. Before his illness, the male anorectic will have been reported as being successful in schoolwork and perhaps also in athletics. This results in praise and encouragement from family and friends. His family is one with high expectations of perfection. The effort to constantly seek approval results in the male anorectic suffering from low self-esteem and a feeling of inadequacy. However, despite his emaciated state, his drive for achievement continues.

In our culture masculinity is seen as a strong and muscular physique. By dieting, the male anorectic's physical appearance changes in contrast to this cultural expectation. Through a pattern of dieting and excessive exercise the male anorectic's body alters and what we see is a pre-pubertal boy who will often look much younger than his years. It is argued that male anorectics have a more marked disturbance of gender identity, which can reflect itself in their relationships and in their homosexual concerns.

The issue of homosexuality in male patients with anorexia nervosa has been raised frequently. Homosexuality was reported by several authors (Taipale et al., 1972; Herzog et al., 1984; Burns and Crisp, 1984) but while it does occur in male anorectics it is not common. Effeminate features are more common. It could be argued that the gay male subculture imposes strong pressures on gay men to be physically attractive. Gay men can experience extreme pressure to be eternally slim and youthful looking and are therefore just as likely to be dissatisfied with their bodies as women can be. Physical attractiveness is highly valued by gay men, but since anorexia nervosa is so widely acclaimed as an illness of females it could be that gay males are overlooked as a group at risk of the disorder.

Touyz et al. (1993) looked at demographic and clinical features of 12 male patients with anorexia nervosa. While the clinical characteristics of male patients were found to be remarkably similar to female patients, they did, however, note that there was a greater tendency to exercise excessively. Exercise was in fact the most frequently used behaviour to bring about weight loss. This is similar to the findings of Oyebode et al. (1988) who reported that 10 out of their 13 male patients had exercised excessively. Overactivity is a common feature of anorexia nervosa in males and it has also been shown to reduce testosterone levels (Beumont et al., 1972).

Some anorectic males will describe themselves as living a life lived under the control of other people such as domineering or overprotective parents. They see their anorectic behaviour as a way of taking control of their lives. Most males with anorexia nervosa are unmarried. Burns and Crisp (1984), in their male sample, found 93% to be still single. Other features found in the males are the presence of prior obesity, reported as 44% and 80% respectively by Beumont et al., 1972 and Taipale et al., 1972, and a lower prevalence of laxative abuse and pre-morbid sexual fears as reported by Sharp et al. (1994). Childhood sexual abuse, widely studied in women, is common in men with anorexia nervosa (Olivardia et al., 1995).

The prognosis for male patients is poorer than for females as males appear generally to be more resistant to treatment.

Chapter 5
Treatments used in anorexia nervosa

The traditional medical approach to the management of anorexia nervosa involves the use of techniques to correct malnutrition and cachexia, these being the visible end products of a disturbed eating pattern. The main goal of the clinician is the preservation of life with the restoration of hydration, correction of any electrotype imbalance, the alleviation of any other medical complications and the restoration of normal weight. It is necessary, in the first instance, to eliminate the possibility that the condition may be something other than anorexia nervosa. Once the diagnosis is confirmed, the initial goal of treatment is to prevent death by starvation.

It would appear that we are moving away from single-treatment methods to more multi-model treatment methods. The combination of family therapy and a cognitive-behavioural approach is just one example. Treatment for a patient with anorexia nervosa usually includes individual or group psychotherapy, often with cognitive-behavioural components. Adjunctive treatment approaches, in addition to pharmarcotherapy, may include group psychotherapy, family therapy and nutritional counselling. Treatments for anorexia nervosa have changed from being primarily single – focus based on one particular theory of etiology – to being more integrative. An integrated approach that incorporates medical, psychological, nursing and occupational therapy intervention can help restore patients to a healthy weight while improving abnormal eating behaviour and improving many of the central psychopathological attitudes and behaviours so characteristic of the disorder. The treatment setting, whether it be an in-patient or out-patient environment, or a combination of both, is based on the needs of the patient. This will include not only the amount of weight to be gained but also the need for family therapy or individual therapy.

The complexity of the illness requires a co-ordinated multi-disciplinary approach to treatment, focusing on the combined biological, social, behavioural and psychological needs of the patient. Licavoli and Orland (1997) see the key to the success of the team approach as being communication, respect and openness to sharing expertise and ongoing thoughts about the patients. This also has the advantage of reducing the chances of the patient 'splitting' staff. Patients with anorexia are notorious for their resistance to accepting therapy. Since therapeutic interventions are almost always directed at weight gain, anorectic patients are reluctant to respond to these efforts. This can cause a clash between patients and clinicians. Most importantly patients must be educated that their eating disorder has significant medical complications.

There is a scarcity of specialist centres in the United Kingdom, partly due to frequent lengthy in-patient stays, which are very expensive, and also due to lack of specialists working in the field. If a patient is admitted weighing approximately five stone and is given a target weight of eight stone, then that will take some time to achieve. Staff experience and understanding of the nature of eating disorders is essential for optimal care. Re-feeding works best in an environment in which caregivers provide a safe, firm, caring environment. Adolescents should be treated within facilities where staff have expertise in treating adolescents. However, a survey conducted in the United Kingdom in 1990 dealt exclusively with public services for eating disorders. The report found that only 58 National Health Service beds were specifically designated for eating disordered patients and, of these, 40 beds were in the London area. The only comprehensive day patient programme was in Scotland. There would therefore appear to be a considerable demand for treatment beds that cannot be met.

Following referral the anorectic patient will be assessed for her physical wellbeing, her personal psychopathology and the family system. Patients with chronic illnesses or recurrent episodes need to be referred to specialist eating disorder units. Emergency admission to a medical or general psychiatric ward is indicated in the event of a life-threatening physical deterioration or where there is concern about suicide if there is accompanying depression. Compulsory admission under the Mental Health Act may also be used on occasions, but this should be prevented if at all possible, since the patient could see it as coercion and this could, in fact, do irreparable damage to the long-term therapeutic relationship with such a patient.

Admission is indicated if any of the following are present:

* weight is less than 70% of that expected;
* marked dehydration;
* electrolyte imbalance;
* circulatory failure;
* uncontrolled vomiting;
* gastro-intestinal bleeding;
* severe depression or suicidal behaviour;
* failed outpatient treatment. (Bryant-Waugh and Lask 1995)

However, many clinicians recommend hospitalizing patients who have lost 20–25% of their ideal or pre-illness body weight, especially if they are still on a downward spiralling path.

It is preferable to admit patients to a specialist eating unit as the staff are experienced in the assessment and management of anorexia nervosa. The Royal College of Psychiatrists (1992) found that treatment outcome is substantially better if provided in a specialist facility than in a non-specialist service. It should be recognized that, for many of these patients, treatment involves a long-term commitment from both the patient and treatment provider since many patients will have lived with their illness for years. A treatment programme is required that will assist these patients to experience life without the burden of constant preoccupation with food and weight. Treatment for anorexia nervosa requires a balanced approach to managing both the physical and psychological aspects of the disorder. This can at times also include pharmacotherapy but, because anorexia nervosa follows a chronically relapsing and remitting course, it will be necessary to offer some patients different treatment interventions during different phases of their illness.

Anorectics can be treated as in-patients or out-patients depending upon the severity and chronicity of both the medical and behavioural components of the disorder. Young adolescents who have lost a higher percentage of body weight, and whose growth therefore may be retarded, should be admitted earlier. It is also hoped that the sooner the weight loss is stopped, the better the chance of a more complete recovery.

In-patient status

In-patient stays have been greatly reduced due to financial constraints imposed on the healthcare system. However in-patient treatment of anorexia nervosa has been shown to promote lasting change even though its path may at times be difficult and complex. It is preferable to provide treatment in a special unit, otherwise if the patient is admitted to a general ward or medical ward, Beumont et al. (1993) argue that she is given either special status or she is rejected because her illness is viewed as self-inflicted. Crisp et al. (1992) report that the long-term mortality of patients treated in a specialist unit is significantly less than that of patients treated in a general psychiatric setting. Sometimes contracts are drawn up that include weight goals and expectations. Patients, their families or spouses and the treatment team members, will sign these. Licavoli and Orland (1997) see contracts as representing goals that have been negotiated with the patient and the expectations are not only the patient's goals, but also the means of achieving these as agreed with the team.

The structure of the ward should be orderly, with unambiguous communications and strategies firmly implemented to prevent splitting. In-patient treatment of anorexia nervosa can be difficult and taxing for staff and patients as these patients often have serious underlying character pathology that manifests itself during hospitalization as regression, hostile dependency unstable mood and impulsive behaviour including self-harm. Anorectics can often view external control as punitive so they are compelled to oppose therapeutic manoeuvres by 'splitting' staff. Hospitalization is only one part of a much more comprehensive long-term treatment process. In-patient treatment of anorexia nervosa is not intended to replace out-patient treatment but to precede and prepare for long-term recovery. Its goals are multifaceted.

Medical management of anorexia nervosa

The anorexia nervosa patient needs a direct and immediate modification of her acute, life-threatening, non-eating behaviour. The time-honoured treatment of persuasion and meticulous supervision of the patient's diet, practised so successfully by early physicians (Ross, 1936 and Hurst, 1936) has now proved to be much less satisfactory in the treatment of anorexia nervosa. The forms of physical treatments that are now used to treat this disorder include naso-gastric and intravenous feeding, medication and occasionally electroconvulsive therapy (ECT).

The primary goals of treatment are to restore weight, normalize eating behaviour, treat co-morbid medical and psychiatric conditions, change overvalued beliefs about thinness and prepare for long-term outpatient care (Bowers and Andersen, 1994). However, the arrest of further physical deterioration and reversal of weight loss are the first priority in any treatment programme. The state of starvation accounts for many of the psychological characteristics of the ill anorectic, such as her preoccupation with food, obsessionality, irritability and apathy. This state of starvation needs to be corrected before any form of psychotherapy can begin.

Naso-gastric and intravenous feeding

In the case of severe anorexia, naso-gastric or intravenous nutritional intervention may be necessary. Such measures of feeding are used only in extreme situations, as a life-saving measure, not only because rapid refeeding can have life-threatening complications, but also because of its effect on other more interpersonal forms of treatment. Some patients react vehemently to having control taken away, even though they may be near death. It would appear that neither of these methods of enforced feeding positively effect the long-term maintenance of weight restoration.

Pharmacotherapy

Controlled pharmacotherapy trials in anorexia nervosa have for the most part been conducted in an in-patient setting. This allows the researchers to evaluate the efficacy of intervention in the most acute phase of the illness.

The literature on the benefits of antidepressant medication for anorexia nervosa is mixed. Extensive studies of tricyclics such as amitriptyline and imipramine have yielded mixed results. Hudson et al. (1985) tested several antidepressants, including imipramine, desipramine, trazodone and nortriptyline, in various combinations in a group of nine anorectic patients with some benefit to seven of the group. The findings highlight the difficulties associated with using these drugs for this patient group. Anorectic patients have a low tolerance for the anticholinergic side effects of tricyclic antidepressants, and the extremely low weights of these patients makes the management of such pharmarcological regimes difficult.

Leach (1995) has found that whereas as many as 30% of anorectic patients can have obsessive-compulsive disorders, anti-obsessional agents do not appear to be useful unless there is evidence that obsessive-compulsive behaviours involve non-eating disorder symptomatology. These drugs do not seem to address the ritualistic, perfectionist behaviours that are centred around eating and body shape.

Although some neuroleptic drugs such as chlorpromazine were used initially for anorexia nervosa in an effort to disrupt the delusional cognitions toward body and food, they have not been found to be effective in inducing cognitive changes or weight gain (Hoffman and Halmi, 1993).

The use of sedatives, either benzodiazepines or major tranquillizers, can be used during weight restoration to decrease anxiety regarding food and body shape. They can also be helpful in alleviating anxiety around mealtimes.

Drugs that are used to promote food intake and weight gain, such as cyproheptadine, amitriptyline, clonidine and opiate antagonists, have all provided disappointing results (Kennedy and Goldbloom, 1989).

Bakan et al. (1993) argue that since 50% of anorectics are practising vegetarians, they are at a greater risk of zinc deficiency. The authors suggests that such vegetarian anorectics should be identified as a subgroup of anorexia nervosa and given zinc supplementation and nutritional management to improve the quantity and bio-availability of zinc intake as a useful therapeutic intervention. This is a view supported by Birmingham et al. (1994) who found that zinc supplementation of anorectic patients increased weight gain and they argue that it seems reasonable to consider this supplementation as an adjunct to standard treatment.

It would therefore appear that the role of drugs in the treatment of anorexia nervosa is somewhat limited. Johnson et al. (1996) firmly state that no medication has been shown to change eating behaviour reliably, assist with weight gain, modify fear of weight gain or alter body image disturbance.

Electroconvulsive therapy (ECT)

The use of ECT has been prescribed less in recent years in the treatment of anorexia nervosa. Ferguson (1993) has suggested that it could be used in

cases of intractable anorexia nervosa or when it is a
depression. It can be useful in those anorectic pati
pressants have failed to improve their depression. H
Garner (1982) argue that it contributes nothing
maintenance of weight and in their view is not sh
other non-pharmacological therapies.

Nutritional management

The normalization of nutritional status is the first goal of treatment. The
traditional hospital-based refeeding regimes involve a high-calorie diet
with modified bed rest in a controlled and supportive environment.
Treatment can be difficult and complex. Teamwork is essential if success is
to be ensured. The need for consistency among staff demands constant co-
ordination, as this group of patients can be very manipulative, both
individually and collectively.

The patient is given a target weight, which is usually a matched population weight for her height and age at onset of the disorder, and not her
present age as it is thought that biological growth actually stops at the
onset of the condition. It is expected that the patient will reach this weight
before discharge. Target weights are not negotiable.

Patients' diets before hospital admission will often reflect individual
idiosyncratic patterns. Some eat food at certain times of the day and in a
particular way. They see foods as good or bad or safe and forbidden.
Except for patients who adhere to particular religious traditions, or in
some cases where patients have been vegetarian from birth, vegetarianism itself is not allowed during weight restoration as it symbolizes an
avoidance of foods that are high in calories or that contain fat. Patients
may be allowed to exclude two or three individual foods from their
daily diet but not food groups. For example, they can exclude baked
beans, liver or bananas, but not bread, biscuits and meat. Apart from
this one concession, anorectic patients cannot determine their food
preferences.

Appropriate meal management is essential in an in-patient programme.
This needs to be structured in order to restore weight, but also to bring
some control back into the patient's meal times and food intake. This is
usually done in one of two ways. Positive and negative reinforcement is
used to gain privileges for either weight gained or food consumed. The
alternative is that food is prescribed in certain quantities to be eaten at
certain times in the day. The meals should be well balanced and with
enough calories to promote a healthy diet. Sometimes it is necessary to
have an adult sit beside the patient when she is eating, not only as a means
of support and encouragement, but also to provide firmness and
discipline.

...oural management

...avioural approach has been the treatment of choice for anorexia ...osa for some clinicians, as weight can be gained rapidly without the ...npleasant effects of drugs or tube feedings. Operant conditioning procedures have been used to directly promote weight gain. Specifically, the amount of food eaten or weight restored may be rewarded with preferred privileges (such as television, telephone or visitors). Eckert and Mitchell (1989) found that reinforcing food intake is more advantageous than rewarding weight restoration during in-patient treatment. Although positive reinforcement is preferred, negative reinforcers (room isolation or reduction in privileges) play a rational part in behavioural programmes.

Behaviour therapy programmes can seem unnecessarily harsh and increase the patient's isolation. It is important to ensure that the programme itself does not become the focus of treatment rather than therapy to resolve the underlying psychological problems. Bruch (1974), while speaking on behavioural techniques, warns against simply letting the patient gain weight to 'eat her way out of hospital'.

Systematic desensitization has also been employed to treat the fear of gaining weight as anorexia nervosa is seen by some as a weight problem. Systematic desensitization has been used to reduce this phobia. This treatment procedure, like the operant conditioning procedure, only addresses one feature of this complex illness. It is necessary to introduce broader coping skills if long-term improvement is to be made.

Behavioural techniques have proved useful for immediate weight gain but the long-term benefits are not so impressive. Bhanji and Thompson (1974) reported follow-up data at two to 72 months for seven patients treated on a behavioural programme. Three were found to have achieved normal weight, four were considered to be eating normally, whereas two had resumed normal menstruation. One was considered to be good, three were fair and three were rated as poorly adjusted.

Behaviour therapy given as a sole means of treatment seems to be gradually being discarded in preference to a combined treatment programme. Bryant-Waugh and Lask (1995) argue that behavioural techniques should not be used with children who are not in a position to give informed consent to a treatment that requires their co-operation. So, while behaviour therapy is useful to promote weight gain, it is not comparable to a comprehensive treatment for anorexia nervosa. Behaviour therapy is best seen as one aspect of a total treatment programme that also includes psychosocial and medical intervention. Behaviour therapy does nothing to alleviate fundamental emotional problems and unresolved family conflicts. Immediate weight gain does not imply long-term cure. The ultimate goal for any treatment of this disorder must include maintenance of normal weight and eating habits over an extended period with a return to adequate functioning in daily life.

Psychodynamic approaches

Family therapy

It has been recognized that disturbances exist within the family network of the anorexia nervosa patient. Family therapy is useful in helping the anorectic whose eating symptoms are seen as an indicator of family or parental marital distress. There is a large body of theoretical literature in the area of family therapy. Perhaps the most well known theorists are Minuchin and his colleagues at the Philadelphia Child Guidance Center and Palazzoli in Milan.

Palazzoli (1974) is one of the earliest writers on the subject of family therapy for anorexia nervosa. She views family pathology as comparably severe and lists a number of family characteristics seen in the anorectic's family:

- there is a willingness to communicate;
- every family member of the system generally defines himself in the relationship in a coherent manner;
- every family member frequently rejects the messages of others;
- all family members have great difficulty in playing the role of leader overtly;
- all open alliances of any two against the third are proscribed;
- no one member will take the blame for anything.

Minuchin et al. (1978) strongly argue that treatment based on family interventions would be more likely to be beneficial than the traditional psychotherapeutic methods. They identified five predominant characteristics of family interaction that were seen to be excessive in families with an anorectic member. These characteristics are enmeshment, overprotectiveness, rigidity, lack of conflict resolution and involvement of the anorectic member in unresolved parental conflict.

Shugar and Krueger (1995) evaluated family communication during systemic family therapy with 15 hospitalized anorectics using the Family Aggression Scale developed by them. The findings suggest that family aggression is a significant index of pathology in anorectic families and that it is a clinically meaningful measure of improved conflict resolutions during family therapy. The authors found a high level of covert aggression (62% of interactions) and a low proportion of overt confrontation (5.1% of interactions). This could partly explain the observation that anorectic families can present such a strong facade of togetherness, rigidity and over-protectiveness. The authors found that, by the end of treatment, the style of communication had shifted dramatically with covert aggression having increased from 5.1% to 63.9%. While all subjects gained some weight, the greatest gain was found in those subjects whose families had low levels of covert or indirect aggression.

It is generally accepted that a family assessment is essential as part of the initial assessment of a younger patient, while a marital assessment is essential for those married or cohabiting anorectic patients. Russell et al. (1987) states that family therapy should be used in every case where the patient is still living at home because the anorexia creates distress that reverberates among all family members. Vandereycken (1987) argues that family therapy should be viewed as one component within a multi-dimensional approach to eating disorders that is guided by a construc-tivist, positive attitude toward the family.

A study comparing family therapy versus individual treatment was carried out by Russell et al. (1987). They used 80 eating disorder patients whose illnesses were of varying degrees of severity. The study was carried out following weight restoration as in-patients. The authors found that family therapy produced more improvement than individual therapy on weight, menstrual functioning and global psychosocial adjustment ratings for adolescents with restricting anorexia nervosa whose illness began before 18 years of age and was of less than three years' duration.

Robin et al. (1995) also examined the relative impact of family therapy versus individual therapy on family interactions. The results indicated that both treatments produced significant reduction in negative communica-tion. The authors found that the improvements in eating-related conflict were maintained at one-year follow up and they argue that such structured therapies for adolescents do have a bearing on family relations, even though the family may never have been seen as a unit during the therapy.

Crisp et al. (1974) provide evidence of the complexity of the relation-ship between family interventions and family processes in anorexia. The authors found that, by using a combined family/individual therapy, improvements were seen in the adolescent's weight and health status, but a worsening of parental pathology especially maternal anxiety and paternal depression, became apparent.

Family therapy is not recommended as the sole initial treatment for anorexia nervosa. However, it is now being used increasingly during after-care following discharge from hospital.

Marital therapy

It would appear to be the case that, for an anorectic in a marital relation-ship, a considerable amount of distress exists. Some believe that marital distress tends to increase with the resolution of symptoms and it would therefore seem appropriate to use marital therapy as an essential part of treatment for married eating disordered patients.

Cognitive-behavioural therapy

There are various factors that could contribute to the anorectic's impair-ment in cognitive function. They could be the disordered effect associated with anorexia and the neurological effects of starvation. Food deprivation can be associated with a wide range of impairments in cognitive functioning. Green and Rogers (1995) found that even normal weight dieters can display poorer immediate recall, vigilance performance and simple reaction times during dieting.

Garner and Bemis (1982) formulated a cognitive-behavioural approach to the etiology and treatment of anorexia nervosa. This cognitive model involves educating the patient about the illness, teaching the patient and family about weight regulation and caloric intake and teaching the patient to identify and focus on thoughts and emotions associated with maladaptive behaviours and distorted beliefs regarding weight, body shape, nutrition, exercise and other aspects of the disorder. The specific treatment techniques used in this model include (a) behavioural rehearsal, such as a role play of the patient's reaction to increasing weight, (b) scheduling pleasant events in an attempt to extend the patient's set of reinforcers, (c) behavioural exercises to help the patient develop an awareness of typical anorectic behaviour, (d) other behavioural techniques that can be used to treat specific problems such as assertiveness or social skills training. These techniques are used alongside other procedures that are aimed at modifying the patient's beliefs and attitudes.

Cognitive behavioural therapy (CBT) is based on two core assumptions. One is that anorexia nervosa develops as a means of coping with adverse experiences often associated with developmental transitions and distressing life events. The other is that food restrictions and rituals of food avoidance become entrenched habit patterns, independent of the events or issues that provoked them (Kleifield et al., 1996).

Cognitive behavioural therapy is collaborative, using the patient's phenomenological world to change thoughts, feelings and behaviours. It emphasizes an equal partnership between the patient and therapist in establishing therapeutic tasks. The structure of CBT is systematic and it begins with behavioural interventions before shifting to more cognitive interventions, as the patient is able to handle them. It aims to identify factors that contribute to anorexia nervosa. These can include early life experiences and anti-personal situations (such as teasing by schoolfriends for being overweight, or domineering parents). At the same time it attempts to alter the patients interpretation of these factors and this leads to an improvement in symptoms. Developing the ability to become more self-aware and self-observant is a critical aspect of cognitive-behavioural approaches and thus such treatments usually include food diaries and other types of recording activities.

Cognitive behavioural therapy is used with the anorectic to help promote healthy eating attitudes, behaviour and activity levels. The anorectic's cognitive sets are examined and challenged, while healthier replacements are sought, for a new cognitive set is adapted in which the importance of a thin body shape is reduced and more value is given to other aspirations. The aim of CBT is to modify abnormal cognitions regarding the personal significance of body shape and weight and to replace dysfunctional eating patterns with a more normal eating and activity pattern.

Fairburn (1985) suggest a variety of procedures to be used in CBT, including the presentation of the cognitive view of the disorder, self-monitoring of relevant thoughts and behaviours, education, cognitive restructuring, the use of self-control measures to establish regular meals and activity and the introduction of 'feared' and avoided foods into the diet. Cognitive behavioural therapy is generally accepted as a helpful adjunct both in the initial and later phases of treatment. Initially, cognitive behavioural techniques are helpful in promoting a change in the anorectic's attitude towards food and eating, whereas in the later stages, these techniques are useful in helping to address such issues as body weight and social pressures to be thin. However Garner and Bemis (1982) believe that a cognitive-behavioural approach should not be used in isolation with the cognitive distortions being seen as the sole focus of intervention. They argue that family therapy, pharmacotherapy and operant conditioning are not incompatible with CBT. As relapse prevention is another element common to anorexia nervosa, cognitive behavioural intervention can help to restructure attitudes and beliefs that will encourage healthy behaviours and thought patterns.

Individual psychotherapy

Garner (1985) reports that individual psychotherapy is the most commonly used psychotherapeutic intervention in in-patient treatment for anorexia nervosa. It can be useful for promoting good long-term outcomes. Various types of individual psychotherapy have been used to deal with crucial development issues of anorexia nervosa, however, a supportive and educational pychotherapeutic approach is more helpful in the early stages of in-patient care.

All anorectics need psychotherapy to reverse their entrenched ideals and distorted body image and to help them achieve other life goals. Patients should also be taught ways to prevent relapse. While ongoing psychotherapy during all phases of treatment is necessary, it is essential that it is tailored to the patient's abilities and needs. In young patients the psychotherapy should be tailored to their level of cognitive development and to their emotional needs, whereas in adolescents, empathetic support, problem solving, educative and cognitive restructurings and insight should also be used to achieve the greatest benefits from treatment. If this is continued following discharge, it may prevent the occurrence of relapses.

Psychotherapy is used to encourage expression of feelings and the tolerance of uncertainty and change while encouraging a realistic appraisal of personal strengths and weaknesses. It is important to provide

a secure relationship that permits the patient to develop indep
The therapist needs to be mindful of how these patients are ex
vulnerable to shame, criticism and judgement and to remember that
anorectic patients are afraid to change and this automatically limits their
motivation to change.

Group therapy

Current research on eating disorders supports the use of group
psychotherapy as an effective treatment strategy. The value of this therapeutic intervention is the peer support given, the decreased isolation and
interpersonal learning that a group provides. Group treatment provides
an atmosphere of mutual support. The sense of isolation experienced by
the anorectic as a result of disturbed eating patterns is alleviated by mutual
sharing of what they had previously felt to be humiliating and degrading
behaviours. Anorectics are frequently unaware that there are many other
people who share their difficulties. Being with other anorectics provides
an environment that allows these isolated individuals to share their shame
and secrecy and to begin to express their frustration or helplessness about
their relationship with food. This can provide a sense of hope while the
group itself allows participants to recognize each other's problems and to
become involved in their resolution and at the same time begin to understand themselves.

The research on the use of successful group treatment of anorectics
supports both the use of psycho-educational (Fairburn, 1985) and insight-
oriented approaches (Laube, 1990; Tubin and Johnson, 1992). Riess and
Rutan (1992), however, feel that not all patients are ready for group
psychotherapy. They argue that patients can be too absorbed in their
persistent symptoms and are not ready to examine causative issues,
whereas those who are ready to explore the meaning of their symptoms
can prefer to move beyond eating behaviours to deeper aspects of
themselves.

Group psychotherapy is frequently used as part of in-patient and out-
patient treatments as it is seen as a useful means of enhancing weight
restoration and producing a healthy, psychological and social change.
Group therapy can be an effective and economic psychotherapeutic tool
in the treatment of anorexia nervosa.

Out-patient status

A growing number of in-patient and out-patient programmes have
emerged in response to the increasing needs associated with eating disorders and to the treatment options. Beumont et al. (1993) are of the view
that a substantial number of patients do well as out-patients if their emaciation is not severe, they have no medical complications, they are
motivated for change and they have supportive friends and relatives.

The advantages of out-patient treatment is that it is cheaper, avoids the stigma of admission to a mental health unit and it limits the effects of being negatively influenced by other patients as well as causing as little disruption to the person's life as possible. Sometimes out-patient treatment is offered on a trial basis, if only to convince the anorectic that she is unable to alter her behaviour by going it alone. Out-patient treatment is generally offered to those who have been ill for less than one year, have lost less than 25% of ideal body weight, do not binge or purge, have a well-functioning and intact family and have access to clinicians experienced in the treatment of the disorder (Eckert and Mitchell, 1989). Even with these good prognostic indicators, many patients with anorexia nervosa fail to recover with out-patient care. If care is provided on an out-patient basis and the patient falls below her stated target weight, then treatment is given to facilitate re-feeding and the adoption of patterns of eating that will result in weight gain. Weight gain is always much slower in an out-patient environment.

Treasure et al. (1995) compared two forms of out-patient treatment: educational behavioural treatment and cognitive analytical therapy for adult anorectics. Thirty patients were randomly allocated to the two treatments. The groups consisted of older patients whose prognosis was thought to be poor. The results indicated that out-patient treatment in older patients with a longer history of anorexia nervosa can lead to a substantial improvement in symptoms after one year. The severity of weight loss was the only predictor of outcome. The greater the loss of weight, the poorer was the response to treatment. The authors were unable to find many significant differences between the two forms of treatment, although self-reported improvement was greater with cognitive analytical therapy. In keeping with the anorectic's ambivalence about treatment, only two-thirds of the group completed the full course of treatment.

Crisp et al. (1991) also reported difficulties with compliance. They found it to be worse for in-patient treatment, but, as well as that, only six out of 20 out-patient sessions that were offered were attended. The Royal College of Psychiatrists Working Party on Eating Disorders (1992) recommended a stepped care approach in the management of anorexia. They suggest that a proportion of patients respond to a brief out-patient intervention of a non-specific nature while others, particularly those with severe weight loss, require more specialized treatment of longer duration. There will always be a clinical need for in-patient treatment to avert death or serious complications.

Out-patient treatment has proved to be effective in several studies (Hsu, 1987; Le Grange et al., 1992). However, most of the studies have involved young patients with a short duration of illness and this is in fact the group with the best prognosis. It is not so certain if the same out-patient treatment would be as effective in older more chronic patients.

Out-patient anorectics have also used day-treatment programmes, which allow the therapeutic milieu of the in-patient unit to extend to an out-patient programme. The anorectic will still have her meals supervised and will join in psychotherapeutic groups, including occupational therapy, but she will be allowed home in the evenings and at week-ends. This arrangement has the advantage of easing the anorectic gradually back into the 'real' world, but it also provides her and her family with a little 'breathing space' away from each other.

Future planning

With the changing climate in the National Health Service and the financial constraints that it imposes, it is necessary to find the most efficient and effective model of treatment that will not only reduce hospital in-patient times but will prevent the 'revolving door' scenario caused by frequent relapses due to premature discharges. The anorectic requires a comprehensive treatment strategy that usually involves the services of the multidisciplinary team with its specialist skills. A few central facilities may be able to cater for the needs of those patients who require in-patient care, whereas well co-ordinated out-patient and day hospital programmes would be able to deal with the milder cases. Long-term medical and nutritional care must be provided to monitor and treat common complications such as growth failure, pubertal delay, menstrual irregularities and decreased bone mineral density.

Health education needs to be provided regarding energy metabolism, medical complications and nutrition. It needs to be given at an appropriate level for the age of the sufferer. Long-term guidance and advice are necessary to provide recovering anorectics with nutritional information that will last them their lifetime.

Chapter 6
Risk factors complications and outcomes

Risk factors

It could be useful to know the risk factors attached to anorexia nervosa in order that we may be able to influence a reduction in the prevalence rates. By increasing awareness of the risk factors and underlying dynamics of eating disorders, women can begin to change their unhealthy behaviours and adopt a more nurturing, self-accepting view of themselves.

Katz (1985) has usefully tabled the risk factors in the culture, family and individual that predispose to the development of anorexia nervosa.

Culture risk factors

– Westernized and contemporary,
    (a) Equates thinness with both beauty and happiness,
    (b) Emphasizes attention to self and body,
    (c) Demands varied and at times conflicting, roles of women.

– Capable of readily disseminating cultural values and styles through visual media (such as movies, television, and magazines).

– Other?

Family risk factors

– Achievement-oriented.

– Intrusive, enmeshing, overprotective, rigid, unable to resolve conflicts.

– Frugal with support, nurturance, encouragement.

– Over-invested in food, diet, weight, appearance or physical fitness.

– Known to have members with a formal history of eating disorder or affective disorder.

– Other?

Individual risk factors

- Female.
- Adolescent.
- Slightly overweight.
- Subject to feelings of ineffectiveness and low self-esteem.
- Subject to conflicts and doubts about sense of personal identify and autonomy.
- Subject to bodily perceptual disturbances (eg, distorted body image, uncertain feelings of satiation after meals).
- Subject to overgeneralization and other cognitive distortions.
- Subject to an obsessional style.
- Other?

(Katz, 1985)

Prevention

Health education in schools today emphasizes the need for healthy eating, thus making children more conscious of the problems of obesity and society's disapproval of it. The ideal body now is not only thin (fat free) but also healthy (fat free). The route to perfection through low fat, low cholesterol, low carbohydrate diets can be particularly dangerous. The growth in this advice could also account for the growth of anorexia nervosa in the population. What these approaches fail to address is the social and psychological aspects of food in our society. Health professionals can become involved in primary prevention of eating disorders by providing accurate information about weight and shape to children, adolescents and parents. This information should include a description of what is a normal weight range, the determinants of normal weight and the information and consequences of dieting strategies.

School curriculums need to include information on how to manage weight, exercise and proper nutrition. The detrimental effects of anorexia should also be included in this education programme as classmates are usually the first to recognize the illness in their friends. School friends will be able to observe the anorectic's eating behaviour at the lunch table while her low body weight will be particularly highlighted in the sport's changing room and when wearing her game's attire. If peers can tell a teacher or counsellor then early intervention steps can be taken.

Neumark-Sztainer (1996) described a useful framework for involving schools in primary and secondary prevention of eating disturbances. They suggest that a comprehensive school programme should be devised that would include staff training, classroom interventions, integration of relevant material into existing curriculum, individual counselling and small group work with high risk students, referral systems and opportunities for healthy eating. The physical education programme would also need to be modified and outreach activities provided. School children should also be helped to look critically at the messages given out by women's magazines. Schools should place more emphasis on helping children to resist these cultural pressures for a thin, lean figure. They should be given advice on the dangers of dieting.

Teachers are often very observant about their pupil's eating patterns but they should be educated about the risk factors and early signs. A misleading factor is that while anorexia is seen as a female disorder, cases amongst males go undetected. Males, as well as females, need to be targeted as males are now becoming part of the greater culture emphasizing thinness.

Prevention programmes for anorexia nervosa attempt to prevent cases arising while simultaneously encouraging students with symptoms of the disorder to seek early treatment. Some programmes may use 'recovered' anorectics to educate others on the negative aspects of the disorder by describing their own experiences and providing information on anorexia nervosa. However this approach can sometimes have a detrimental effect in that the 'recovered' anorectic can inadvertently be teaching the non-anorectics how to develop the disorder rather than how to prevent it. This was found to be the case in the Mann et al. (1997) study. They concluded that encouraging such open communication reduces the stigma of the anorexia and inadvertently normalizes it.

Research has failed adequately to address the issue of prevention of anorexia nervosa and how the topic of prevention could best be approached. It may perhaps be helpful if the social, family and personal significance of puberty and personal maturation should occupy a more central role in our education system. Since many of our most prevalent diseases are stress related, then perhaps more time should be invested in teaching ways of coping with stress rather than through food.

Early detection and intervention would in fact reduce the severity of the disorder and there is evidence to support the view that, with early treatment, the disorder is associated with a good outcome.

Complications of anorexia nervosa

Complications of anorexia nervosa are numerous, involving almost every organ system in the body. However, many of these complications can be corrected through adequate nutrition and gradual weight restoration to more normal and healthy levels.

Most of the complications of the disorder are directly related to the body's attempts to conserve energy in the face of an inadequate food supply. Woodside (1995) has listed these complications clearly.

Table 6.1: Complications of anorexia nervosa

Dermatological	Cardiovascular	Gastrointestinal
Dry skin	Bradycardia	Delayed gastric
Thinning hair	Hypotension	emptying
Lanugo hair	Dependent oedema	Bloating
Cyanosis	Arrhythmias	Early satiety
Carotene		Constipation or
pigmentation		diarrhoea
Pale skin		Reduced taste

Musculoskeletal	Endocrine	Cognitive and behavioural
Amenorrhea	Weakness	Depression
Hypothermia	Osteoporosis or	Poor concentration
Abnormal laboratory	osteopenia	Food
findings		preoccupation
		Impaired sleep
		Decreased libido

Metabolic complications may be numerous and varied, depending on whether the patient engages in purging behaviours. Hypokaelemia is especially common in patients who vomit or take diuretics or laxatives and may acutely cause life-threatening arrhythmias and muscle cramping.

Cardiac complications are fairly common and are the most frequent cause of death in anorexia nervosa. Bradycardia as low as 40 beats per minute occurs in the body's attempt to conserve heat by reducing the work of the heart.

Gastrointestinal complications are related to starvation and purging behaviour and the experience of bloating, which is very uncomfortable, improves fairly quickly with the reintroduction of regular amounts of food.

Dry skin and thinning scalp hair are caused by starvation and decreased collagen. There is a growth of lanugo hair usually on the face, upper arms and back in a desperate attempt by the body to keep warm. The cyanosis reflects a peripheral vascular shutdown by the body in an attempt to conserve energy. Hypothermia develops secondary to the depletion of body fat stores. This accounts for patients who will often be seen, even on sunny days, wearing layers of clothing in order to keep warm.

The carotene pigmentation is due to the starved liver being unable effectively to metabolize carotene pigments. Pale skin signifies an iron deficiency.

In those patients who regularly vomit, the erosion of teeth enamel is very common. Swollen parotid salivary glands, resulting from irritation of the gland by stomach acid can also occur in those patients who routinely vomit.

Disturbed zinc metabolism has been suggested as a potential factor in the etiology of anorexia nervosa and to explain some of the symptoms of the disorder such as skin lesions, irritability, alopecia and nausea. Oral supplementation with zinc sulphate has been reported by some to be successful in treating this (Varela et al., 1992).

Constipation is caused by dehydration as the result of starvation, plus the absence of having eaten any food.

Osteopenia and osteoporosis

Anorectic patients with six months or more of amenorrhea can have significant osteopenia and also develop characteristic pathological fractures. The cause of osteopenia in anorexia nervosa is not completely understood. Diminished bone mineral density is most closely correlated with length of amenorrhea and is inversely correlated with the amount of weekly exercise, suggesting a balance between bone diminishing and augmenting effects. Other skeletal complications of anorexia include delayed skeletal maturation, short stature, osteoporotic fractures of the hip, spine and vertebrae.

Kotler et al. (1994) describe the case of a young female with severe anorexia that included prolonged exposure to both low body weight and amenorrhea. Bone mineral density (BMD) measurement during the acute stage of her illness revealed severe osteopenia. Six years after recovery from anorexia, follow-up studies showed only modest gains in BMD. It could therefore be argued that those patients who develop anorexia in childhood or early teens have not had the chance to reach the maximum expected peak bone mass density and, should the anorexia continue, they are particularly susceptible to osteoporosis as they age. Bone mass increases with age until it reaches its peak in early adult life for both sexes.

Osteoporosis is less common in men who are protected by various reasons not least that they have a higher bone density than women at any given age. Men are less prone to osteoporosis because of their higher testosterone levels. This testosterone has an anabolic effect on muscle, which, in turn, increases the stress on bone during exercise, resulting in more bone deposition. It could therefore be argued that those anorectics who use high levels of physical activity to control their weight could have a greater bone density as a result. Scurlock et al. (1997) described the case of a 38-year-old male with a 23-year history of anorexia, who developed severe osteoporosis.

This was discovered when he presented with a spontaneous crush fracture of his first lumbar vertebra. It could therefore be argued that there is a need to consider osteoporosis in male as well as female patients as a potential serious complication of chronic anorexia nervosa. A search of the literature found another similar reported case by Rigotti et al. (1986) of a 22-year-old man.

It is essential to recognize the complications of anorexia nervosa since changes in clinical practice appear to be shifting towards the treatment of the disorder on an out-patient basis, as opposed to the traditional intensive in-patient regimes.

Course and outcome

The data on the outcome of the disorder do, for the most part, paint a picture of the seriousness of anorexia nervosa. However outcome studies can differ in definitions of outcome. Common domains of measurement include body weight, eating attitudes, eating behaviour, menstruation, mortality and psychological and social functioning. Recovery rates are difficult to compare, as differing methodologies have been used. However, a significant number of patients do recover. Rates of full recovery vary from 71% to 32% at 20 years.

Hsu (1987) has suggested six criteria that could be adopted to assess 'good' anorexia nervosa outcome studies. These are:

* explicitly stated diagnostic criteria so that atypical cases can be excluded;
* more than 25 subjects in the study;
* minimum follow-up of 4 years from onset of illness;
* rate of failure in tracing patients less than 20%;
* the use of direct interview at follow-up for over half of the patients;
* the use of multiple well-defined outcome measures.

The identification of prognostic factors can influence the decision to treat patients and the choice and duration of treatment. No single factor has been found to be consistently predictive of outcome. Commonly observed predictors of poor outcome include longer duration of illness and the presence of vomiting. **Poor prognostic indicators** include:

* pre-morbid obesity;
* complications during pregnancy;
* high initial weight loss;
* repeated in-patient treatment for anorexia nervosa;
* late onset of illness (older than 30 years);
* long duration of illness;
* pre-morbid personality difficulties;
* previous admissions to psychiatric hospitals;
* strained family relationships;

- low weight at discharge;
- poorer adjustment in childhood;
- compulsiveness;
- social class III or IV.

However, the most frequent predictors for an unfavourable course of the disorder are a long duration of the illness, disturbed family relationships, a low body weight, and purging behaviour. These are in contrast to **good prognostic indicators**:

- early age at onset;
- a lesser amount of denial;
- hysterical personality;
- a lesser degree of psychosexual immaturity;
- conflict-free parent–child relationship;
- short interval between onset of symptoms and treatment intervention;
- a greater acceptance of body image;
- a short duration of in-patient treatment with no re-admissions;
- social class I or II;
- high level of education.

Bruch (1974) observed many years ago that expert intervention soon after the onset of anorexia nervosa is crucial for preventing a protracted course and a poor outcome. Outcome results provide strong support for the claim that, with treatment, complete recovery from anorexia nervosa is possible for a significant number – some might even say the majority – of patients. Hsu (1996), however, argues that if outcome studies can identify indicators of poor prognosis consistently, then it should be possible to improve outcome by targeting intervention at those indicators.

Eating disorders can be long lasting, but rarely do they change into other diagnoses. Sometimes anorexia nervosa can progress into bulimia but not the other way round. Schork et al. (1994) reported on a 10-year follow-up of 59 women with anorexia focusing on the relationship between eating disorder and general psychopathology. The 18 women who did not suffer from the disorder at follow-up had the least general psychopathology, whereas, those with full syndromes had the most. Participants in their study did tend to improve over the 10-year period, although most of them still showed some symptomatology of the disorder. Five women (8.5%) died. While some moved towards bulimia nervosa, none developed other psychiatric illnesses.

Srinivasagam et al. (1995) looked at persistent perfectionism, symmetry and exactness after long-term recovery from anorexia nervosa. They found that the recovered anorectic patients still had a need for order and precision that persisted after good outcome and recovery. The authors argue that this raises the issue as to whether these behaviours are in fact traits that contribute to the pathogenesis of this illness.

Windauer et al. (1993) looked at eating behaviour, nutritional intake and psychopathology in a group of 16 weight-recovered anorectic patients. While body fat and overall psychosocial adjustment had returned to normal in most patients, 12 still had a restricted eating pattern with nutritional intake below 90% of their energy requirement. The authors therefore argue that weight, menstruation and psychosocial criteria are not enough when determining a full recovery from anorexia.

In an effort to characterize the psychopathology of anorexia measured 10 years post-treatment, Sunday et al. (1996) looked at a sample of 51 women who had an adolescent onset of anorexia. Approximately half of their sample had a good outcome from their anorexia and 31% had a poor outcome. They found no relationship between age of onset of anorexia and long-term outcome and neither did the age of onset lead to any increased psychopathology 10 years after initial treatment.

Herpertz-Dahlman et al. (1996) also carried out a prospective longitudinal study to examine outcome, psychosocial functioning and prognostic factors in adolescent anorexia. The authors investigated factors in adolescent anorexia. They investigated 34 (88%) out of a consecutive series of 39 in-patients, three and seven years after discharge. At the seven-year follow-up, five patients (44%) still fulfilled the conditions for a diagnosis of anorexia, whereas 21 (62%) had some other psychiatric diagnosis. Patients with a poor outcome experienced more problems in most cases of psychosocial functioning than the good outcome group. The authors found that only a low weight during the course of illness was proved to be of any predictive value.

In an effort to elucidate the process of recovery for anorexia nervosa, Beresin et al. (1989) asked 13 recovered anorectics to describe helpful or harmful therapy and non-therapy related experiences that led to their recovery. The majority of subjects were able to pin-point a specific turning point in their lives when they felt bored with, and tired of, the disorder. It was at this time that they felt they could 'let go' of their symptoms. The factors that the group found to be helpful included distance from the family, group therapy and a positive job or school experience. They also saw having a meaningful relationship with either a therapist, friend or partner as important.

Steinhausen et al. (1991) reviewed outcome studies from four decades and found little difference between the results of earlier or more recent decades. The studies indicated that approximately 50% of patients were in the good outcome category, with 30% in the medium category and 20% in the poor outcome categories respectively.

Several studies of anorexia nervosa have found early onset of illness to be a positive predictor of outcome. Bryant-Waugh et al. (1996) reported on a prospective follow-up of 22 children (mean age at onset 12.1 years). The outcome was good in 10 (55.5%), intermediate in five (27.8%) and poor in three (16.7%). None had died. They found that no prognostic factors could be identified. Walford and McCune (1991) also looked at children with the disorder. They studied 15 children who developed anorexia nervosa at 13 years and under. They followed them up for at least three years and found the general outcome to be good in seven, intermediate in four and poor in four, with one having died. Early onset anorexia nervosa is potentially a very serious illness, with major physical complications accompanying starvation and weight loss. The prognosis is generally unsatisfactory with many children continuing with abnormal eating attitudes, eating problems and psychosocial and psychosexual dysfunction. Long-term problems were also highlighted by Theander (1985), who carried out a long-term study in Sweden investigating outcome in patients with different ages of onset. He found that, although there was a general trend of early onset being a good predictor of outcome, the long-term course is not so favourable in many early onset cases. He found a significant risk of short stature in anorectic patients with an early onset if they are allowed to run a long, or chronic, course of the illness.

Patient dropout is an important issue in treating anorexia nervosa. The proportion of patients who begin treatment, but then terminate prematurely can be significant. Clinton (1996) found that dropping out among anorectics appear to be related to the patient–therapist relationship. He argues that it is therefore essential for therapists to openly discuss patients' expectations of treatment from the outset, thus focusing on particular areas of discrepancy between them, in order to minimize this.

Relapse rates are significant for anorexia nervosa, which would support the view that the disorder can be a chronic one. The chronically ill patient can, despite all the best efforts being made, fail to recover. This may be due to many reasons ranging from an unwillingness to change to difficult treatment experiences. Individuals who are still unwell are usually underweight, not menstruating, are preoccupied with weight or shape and experience difficulties in their social and sexual relationships.

The prognosis for patients with anorexia nervosa is, in general, not very good. An outcome study by Hsu (1996a) found that only 35% of patients ate normally four years after the onset of the illness as well as being free from their neurotic fixations with body weight. It is necessary to view the outcome of this disorder as a continuous process as opposed to a definite, easily measurable end product. Outcome measures should take into account a multifaceted psycho-sociological model of eating disorders. Various outcomes need to be examined, including the overall physical and psychological wellbeing of the patient, irrespective of absolute changes in weight. Follow up studies of ex-patients do have their limitations. Eating disorders are associated with shame, but so too is the link with mental illness. Some patients and their families also do not wish to be reminded of the past and the associated painful memories.

Anorexia nervosa can be a chronic illness, with patients taking years to recover, undergoing several hospital admissions and relapses. Herzog et al. (1997) carried out a 12-year follow up study of the occurrence and timing of first recovery in 69 hospitalized patients with severe anorexia nervosa. The results indicated that the anorexia did not improve until after six years following the first in-patient treatment in 50% of the patients.

So, although the majority of studies indicate that a sizeable majority of anorectics remain impaired in physical, psychological and social functioning even after normal weight and menstruation have been restored, the course of the illness varies. An individual may suffer from a single or several episodes of starvation or the illness may be unremitting until death.

Mortality

The accounts of mortality in the literature vary depending on the length of follow up and date of onset. The incidence of death has been reported as varying from less than 1% to as high as 18%. Typically the longer the follow-up period, the more patients have died. Mortality in anorexia is among the highest of all psychiatric disorders. Sullivan (1995) assessed the mortality rate for anorectic subjects to be substantially greater than that reported for either female psychiatric in-patients or the general population. Death is not always directly due to the disorder. Complications from starvation are significant causes of death among this patient group, but suicide and other causes account for a significant number. Herzog et al. (1988) found that of the 88 reported deaths in 13 outcome studies, complications from anorexia accounted for 50%, suicide for 24%, unknown causes for 15%, lung disease for 6% and other disorders or accidents for 6%. Death is more commonly caused as a result of starvation, electrolyte abnormalities or suicide.

Higher mortality rates are found with longer duration of illness, extremely low weight, poor family support, purging behaviours and multiple relapses. Mortality rates vary from between 1% after six years (Morgan et al., 1983) and 18% after 33 years (Theander, 1985). However, due to the protracted nature of anorexia, it is felt that outcome studies should allow for a minimum follow-up period of four years. Crisp et al. (1992) reported on two cohorts of adult patients with anorexia at 20 years follow up. The authors estimated a crude mortality rate of 40% (St George's cohort) and 13% (Aberdeen cohort). Apart from suicide, the accompanying illnesses included bronchopneumonia, chronic bronchitis, emphysema, carcinoma, coronary artery disease, acute cardiac dysrhythmia, myotonia dystophica, plus the anorexia-related complications. The authors concluded that appropriate medical treatment with the aim of quickly alleviating the nutritional deficit and reducing the number of early deaths due to anorexia is essential and that the psychotherapeutic intervention should aim to reduce the number of late deaths.

Lucas et al. (1991) also carried out a long-term study covering a 50-year period. They reported a mortality rate of 5% when the disorder is of four to five years' standing, with the rate increasing to 15 to 20% when the illness is of 20 to 30 years' duration.

A study carried out in Denmark by Moller-Madsen et al. (1996) examined mortality among in-patient anorectics in a mental health setting. The patients had been admitted between 1970 and 1986. They found 50 deaths recorded during a mean follow-up period of 7.8 years. In the male patients, five of 63 died and the mean age of death was 24.5 years. In the female subjects, 45 of 79 died and the mean age at death was 36 years. There was no mortality among childhood-onset female subjects, but in the males one death was found in this group. Suicide was the dominant cause of death among subjects who died from unnatural causes, otherwise anorexia was the main cause of death followed by other medical conditions. These findings are in fact in contrast to those of Norring and Sohlberg (1993) in Sweden who reported a mortality rate of 6.25% in 30 adult anorectic patients at a follow-up of over six years. The authors found that none of the deaths were attributable to starvation but that they were attributable to suicide and alcohol abuse. In fact, rates of death due to alcoholic complications among anorectics have not been particularly addressed in the literature.

Anorexia nervosa is a very severe disorder with a mortality rate well above that for most severe mental illnesses. It has a suicide rate comparable to that seen in schizophrenia. The data on suicide are usually precise, but other causes from complications of the eating disorders are inadequately defined or, in the case of sudden death, are reported as unknown. There are problems of methodological assessment in determining true mortality rates, but what does appear to happen is that rates generally increase with longer follow-up periods. However mortality does also seem to be particularly high in the first year after initial diagnosis, which would warrant a vigorous treatment programme, especially in this first year after presentation, to deal with these individuals, who are very vulnerable. Recovery is a long process in anorexia nervosa. Treatment planning should anticipate this because, without treatment, anorexia nervosa remains potentially fatal. It is often chronic, persisting for decades in some patients, resulting in death in others.

PART 2
Bulimia nervosa:
an overview

Chapter 7
Bulimia nervosa

History

The word 'bulimia', derived from Greek, means ox-like hunger, although current usage always suggests compulsive or binge eating. It mostly affects teenage females or young women. It is not possible to write a truly historical account of bulimia nervosa since the diagnostic term has only been used since 1979. Unlike anorexia nervosa, whose history can be traced for many centuries, bulimia is an illness limited to contemporary society. The use of the term bulimia is confusing as the term has acquired two meanings. It has been used firstly to describe a symptom (binge eating) and secondly, to describe a syndrome of which bingeing is only one component. It is this syndrome to which the name bulimia nervosa has been applied.

The idea of binge eating is not new but has been seen since antiquity. Historically, during periods of uncertain food supply, consuming large quantities of food and subsequent purging was an expression of social superiority. The Romans were known for their gorging on delicacies, which led to the use of vomiting rooms adjacent to their banqueting rooms. They were able to tickle their throats with feathers after each meal to induce vomiting, thus allowing them to return to their gluttonous feasting. Such behaviour is in contrast to today's society, which interpret bulimic eating as an expression of self-control deficits.

Physicians around the turn of the century (Osler, 1892) were familiar with bulimia as a symptom, although Casper (1983) claims that the history of bulimia only began in the 1940s and that earlier observations are non-existent. It was around 1940 when the first cases of compulsive overeating and induced vomiting evolved in connection with anorexia nervosa. This occurred around the time that patients first voiced their concern over body shape. Bruch (1957) described the case of a female patient who binged and vomited but was neither obese nor anorectic. Since these patients did not have an obvious weight disturbance, it was thought necessary to define a new disorder. Stunkard (1959) was another early researcher who identified binge eating as a feature of a number of eating disorders. The term 'bulimiarexia' was used by Boskind-Lodahl (1976) to describe an eating disorder, usually in young women at a normal weight, in which the patient alternates between bingeing and strict fasting. Boskind-Lodahl saw bulimarexics as having low self-esteem, poor body image and a fear of not being successful in heterosexual relationships.

The modern history of bulimia first appeared in connection with patients who also suffered from anorexia nervosa. Although many authors were aware of overeating, laxative abuse and self-induced vomiting in anorexia nervosa, bulimia was seen as a variant of anorexia nervosa rather than a distinct syndrome. In the 1970s, when the idea of thinness was seen as a virtue symbolizing independence, autonomy, self-control and moral grace, the rapid emergence of bulimia nervosa began. This could also have been precipitated by cultural, economic and psychological factors. Since these patients did not seem to have an obvious weight disturbance it seemed necessary to define a new syndrome that would encompass this disorder.

Russell (1979) first described bulimia nervosa as a variant of anorexia nervosa in his paper 'Bulimia nervosa: an ominous variant of anorexia nervosa'. This paper provided the first full description of the disorder. He described the disorder as comprising of an irresistible urge to overeat, followed by self-induced vomiting, purging or both. The other feature was a morbid fear of becoming fat. Only two of his thirty patients, whose ages ranged from 15 to 37 years at the onset of the disorder, were males. Seventeen (57%) patients had a previous history of anorexia nervosa and a further seven (23%) had experienced milder forms of the illness. Russell stated the prognosis to be poor. However, bulimia that occurs only in the course of co-existing anorexia nervosa should be diagnosed as anorexia nervosa/bingeing/purging. In the early reports of the condition, the behaviour was always associated with anorexia nervosa. Authors reporting on this population have used terms including 'thin fat' (Garner and Garfinkel, 1980) 'dietary chaos syndrome' (Palmer, 1979) 'compulsive eating' (Ondercin, 1979), while Crisp (1981) labelled the condition the 'abnormal normal weight control syndrome'.

Bulimia nervosa – the condition

Bulimia nervosa was only formally recognized as a clinical entity by the American Psychiatric Association in 1980. It is a disorder in which the individual rapidly consumes an unusually large amount of food. This 'binge' is terminated by vomiting, laxative abuse, abdominal pain or sleep and is experienced by the individual as abnormal and distressing. Before 1980, only a small number of cases were described; however, after the DSM III in 1980, when bulimia was included, there was a sharp increase in detected cases. However, some of these cases may have originated many years earlier. Between 1979 and 1987, the criteria used to diagnose bulimia nervosa were very different in North America and the United Kingdom. These differences largely disappeared with the introduction of the DSM-III-R criteria in the United States.

There is remarkably little consensus as to the origins of this disorder. The theories that have been put forward vary from those that support a primarily biological approach (Mitchell et al., 1985) to the more sociocultural approach of Irving (1990). Although bulimia was once considered a rare disorder, it has begun to attract a lot of attention in the past 15 years in both professional and popular literature, with estimates suggesting that 4% to 10% of high school and college women have bulimia in severe forms, whereas only less than 0.4% of men are affected.

Garner et al. (1980) showed how shifting cultural norms for contemporary young women has forced them to face multiple, ambiguous and often contradictory role expectations. Such role expectations include accepting more traditional feminine expectations such as physical attractiveness and domesticity, while incorporating more modern standards for vocational and personal achievement. Changes in cultural and economic conditions, such as increased prosperity after the Depression, promoted an increased concern over body weight. The pursuit of thinness achieved through restrictive dieting then emerged in our culture as a means whereby women can compete among themselves and show that they have self-control. Some bulimics also use dietary restriction to assert control over non-weight-related aspects of their life while others use their eating disorder to avoid conflicts about sexual issues. Even though feeling too fat and dieting have become a way of life for most women, only a small minority develop bulimia nervosa.

Classification of bulimia nervosa

Much of the overt bulimic symptomatology revolves around a dysfunctional relationship with food. Although bulimics share many characteristics with anorectics, such as concern with body weight and a fear of becoming fat, bulimics will normally fluctuate in their weight, whereas anorectics show a continuing pattern of lower weight levels.

DSM-IV (1994) Diagnostic Criteria for Bulimia Nervosa

(a) Recurrent episodes of binge eating. An episode of binge eating is characterized by both of the following:
1. Eating, in a discrete period of time (for example, within any two-hour period), an amount of food that is definitely larger than most people would eat during a similar period of time and under similar circumstances.

    2. A sense of lack of control over eating during the episode (for example, a feeling that one cannot stop eating or control what or how much one is eating).
(b) Recurrent inappropriate compensatory behaviour to prevent weight gain, such as self-induced vomiting, misuse of laxatives, diuretics or other medication; fasting or excessive exercise.
(c) The binge eating and inappropriate compensatory behaviours both occur, on average, at least twice a week for three months.
(d) Self-evaluation is unduly influenced by body shape and weight.
(e) The disturbance does not occur exclusively during episodes of anorexia nervosa.

There are two types:

* Purging type: the person regularly engages in self-induced vomiting or the misuse of laxatives or diuretics.
* Non-purging type: the person uses other inappropriate compensatory behaviours, such as fasting or excessive exercise, but does not regularly engage in self-induced vomiting or the misuse of laxatives or diuretics.

(Diagnostic and Statistical Manual of mental Disorders IV 1994 by the American Psychiatric Association)

The typical bulimic will be a female in her early twenties who will be more sexually active than her anorectic counterpart. It is likely that she will be married and have children. She will come from a family in social classes I or II and will be well educated or still in higher education. The majority of bulimics weigh within the normal range for their height, weight and sex or are slightly above or below normal. In most bulimics there is a discrepancy between their desired weight and their healthy weight. Russell (1979) found that their desired weight is usually significantly less than the healthy weight.
    Bulimia nervosa would appear to be multi-determined with cultural, psychological and biological factors playing their part in the development and maintenance of the disorder.

Differential diagnosis

What separates bulimia nervosa from other food disorders is the bingeing, vomiting, purging cycle and its importance in maintaining the desired body weight of the individual. It is necessary to separate vomiting in other psychosomatic or organic conditions with that used in bulimia. However, the absence of bingeing with the excessive concerns with weight loss and body image is what distinguishes this disorder from those with a physical basis.

Chapter 8
Epidemiology

The true incidence of bulimia is difficult to assess owing to the nature of the disorder. It is often not identified because the bulimic individual is of normal weight and appearance and also because the secrecy surrounding binge eating and purging means that her eating habits appear normal to friends and family members (Martin, 1989). Evaluating studies of the prevalence of bulimia is not easy as the syndrome was recognized more recently than anorexia nervosa. The diagnostic criteria have also been significantly revised and are more stringent than earlier diagnostic criteria. The more stringent the criteria applied to the diagnosis, the lower the prevalence rates will be, so those studies using the DSM IV criteria tend to report lower rates than studies using early DSM III, DSM III-R criteria.

After bulimic disorders were first formally described by Russell in 1979, and after they were introduced in DSM in 1980, the referral rates to specialist treatment centres went up, giving the impression of a rising incidence. It can be the case, however, that once the incidence of a disorder has been recognized then increased numbers of cases are subsequently identified in the community or clinical samples.

For most bulimics the onset of symptoms does not occur until middle to late adolescence. This has resulted in most researchers targeting their investigations at these age groups rather than perhaps examining early childhood precipitating factors. The majority of prevalence studies have tended to focus on adolescent and young adult women or those seeking treatment, rather than on large community-based epidemiological samples. Rates tend to be higher for the 15-to-40-year-old group; bulimia does still clearly occur in older individuals as well, but little attention has been given to investigating those who are 40 years or older.

College populations

Many studies have used samples that are biased in one way or another toward higher incidences, such as high school, college or other defined populations of Caucasian women between the ages of 14 and 40 years.

Soundy et al. (1995) found a rate of 125.1 per 100 000 for 15-to-19-year-old girls and 82.7 per 100 000 for 20-to-25-year-old young women. The authors argue that their findings are the highest incidence recorded up to that time. The estimates of the frequency of bulimia nervosa in college age women varies from 3.8% to 19%, depending on how binge eating has been defined. In schoolgirls it is reported as ranging from 3% to 8.3%. Ondercin (1979) attempted to characterize eating disorders in college women. She reported that, in a college population of women, compulsive eating was unrelated to hunger and was used as a tool to blunt unpleasant affect states, such as anxiety, depression and anger. The author concluded that binge eating could be a normal part of college life for a significant number of women.

Allowing for the discrepancy in the interpretation of the term binge, research does reveal a disproportionately high prevalence rate for bulimia nervosa in college women (Pope et al., 1984; Pyle et al., 1991). It could be that academic life increases stress and social pressure but it could also be that college females experience a greater focus on appearance relating to social activities, parties and dieting.

Community

According to community studies, approximately 1–2% of women report a lifetime prevalence of bulimia nervosa (Fairburn and Beglin, 1990; Kendler et al., 1991; Garfinkel et al., 1995). The disorder is less common in men (Rathner et al., 1995; Bushnell et al., 1990) with Garfinkel et al. (1995) finding a prevalence rate for men in a Canadian community sample to be 0.1%. Bulimia is not commonly found among minority populations, but rates in these groups are thought to be rising (Hsu, 1987).

Two large studies that have been carried out to assess the prevalence of bulimia in a community were those of Soundy et al. (1995) and Hoek (1991). Hoek reported an annual incidence rate of 9.9 per 100 000 during the years 1985 to 1986 for bulimia. This study was carried out through morbidity records of 58 general practices in the Netherlands and by applying the DSM III criteria for the disorder. This survey accounted for 1.05% of the total Dutch population. Soundy et al. (1995) aimed to determine the incidence of bulimia nervosa in those residing in the community of Rochester, Minnesota, using 777 medical records. They identified 103 Rochester residents (100 female and three males) who fulfilled the criteria for bulimia. For many patients, bulimic symptoms were not the principal reason for seeking help, but were in fact an incidental finding. It could therefore be assumed that there might be more who simply do not disclose their symptoms. The authors concluded that bulimia nervosa is a common disorder in adolescent girls and young women from 15 to 24 years. In addition to bulimia, histories of alcohol or drug abuse, depression or anorexia nervosa were also higher than expected in the general population.

King (1989) carried out a prevalence study in the United Kingdom in a general practice population based in south London and found 1% of women between 16 and 35 years old had bulimia nervosa.

Minority groups

A lower incidence of bulimia has been found in non-Caucasian subjects and in developing countries, compared with Western industrialized countries (Dolan, 1991). Bulimia is scarcely known in the countries of Central and Eastern Europe; however, a two-stage survey was carried out by Szabo and Tury (1991) in Hungary and they reported the prevalence to be 1.3% for females and 0.8% for males in a college sample. Few attempts have been made to compare directly bulimic patients in different cultures, but those who have argue that the features of the disorder are very similar between cultures.

Mangweth et al. (1995) compared 33 college women meeting the diagnostic criteria for bulimia nervosa in Austria, with 33 bulimic women in Boston (USA). The disorder showed striking similarities across the two cultures. Both groups reported similar demographic features, bulimic symptoms, severity and chronicity of illness, associated personal and familial psychiatric disorders, upbringing and family environment and frequency of childhood abuse. There were only two variables – substance abuse and satisfaction with body image – which differed markedly between the two groups. Alcohol and substance abuse were more common among American subjects than among Austrian subjects. American subjects were also significantly fatter, although they wished to be slightly thinner than their Austrian counterparts, as well as being more dissatisfied with their bodies than the Austrians. Some studies have focused upon particular subgroups in society and some have included men in their samples. Non-white populations are also now being examined as they appear to be under-represented in prevalence studies. The evidence would indicate that there is an increased number of cases in the black population.

Warheit et al. (1993) looked at the prevalence of bulimic symptoms and bulimia in a sample of 1736 whites and 339 blacks (of whom 1040 were females and 1035 were males) in north central Florida. Their results indicated that females had significantly higher rates than did males on nine of the 10 bulimic symptoms. Blacks had symptom rates equal to, or greater than, whites on eight of the 10 items and those in the lowest socio-economic groups had rates greater than those in the highest socio-economic groups on nine of the 10 symptoms. Eight persons (0.4%) of the total sample fulfilled the diagnosis of bulimia. These included six white females and two black males. Five of the females were in the lower middle socio-economic group and one was in the upper middle socio-economic group. The two black males were aged 30 and 44 and both were in the lowest socio-economic group. As well as providing a comparison in the prevalence rates for bulimia in black and white populations, this study also highlights the need to distinguish between bulimic type symptoms and bulimia the syndrome when estimating the prevalence of eating-related problems in the general population.

Males

The symptomatolgy and demographic characters have been found to be similar in males and females. Robinson and Holden (1986) examined nine male patients with bulimia – that is, one in 24 bulimic patients attending for treatment – and found a history of either anorexia nervosa or obesity to also be present, whereas in six patients the condition was seen to be chronic. Five of the men also showed atypical sexuality. These findings are similar to those of Gwirtsman et al. (1984) who reported on a series of three male bulimic patients and found one to have a history suggestive of anorexia nervosa and another who had been premorbidly overweight. The males were maintaining their weights between 84% and 88% of premorbid weight. All vomited after bulimic episodes and all had episodes of strict dieting, while two used purgatives.

A significant number of men with bulimia nervosa are gay males, suggesting that gay men could be more at risk of developing the disorder than heterosexual men. Herzog et al. (1984) examined 27 patients with eating disorders, 14 of whom had bulimia. Nine of the 14 had been previously overweight. In contrast to female controls with eating disorders, the bulimic males were more likely to report homosexuality and sexual inactivity. Silberstein et al. (1989) carried out a study using college students and compared gay men with heterosexual men. They found that gay men showed more body dissatisfaction and considered appearance very essential to their sense of self. They also indicated that exercise in gay men was motivated by a desire to improve physical attractiveness whereas overweight gay men were found to have more disordered eating attitudes and behaviour.

The subject of food-related attitudes and behaviours was examined by Schneider et al. (1995) as they contrasted the attitudes of heterosexual men and women to those of lesbians and gay men. Their study consisted of comparable groups of 25 lesbians, 5 gay men, 75 heterosexual women and 75 heterosexual men. The authors aimed to determine whether gay men could be a population at risk for developing eating disorders. The results showed that heterosexual women and gay men shared many unhealthy attitudes to patterns of eating and food-related behaviours that differed from the other two groups. They were more likely to binge eat, have less control over eating, binge frequently, engage in weight-control activities and experience an excessive concern with their body shape and weight. Both groups feel themselves to be fat. Gay men, however, did not report as much concern at being fat or overweight as did the heterosexual women. The authors argue that this could be due to the way they compensate for their compulsive eating by exercising. Although gay men binged more than the other groups the authors found that they also did more exercise than the heterosexual women or heterosexual men. Only the lesbian group did more exercise than the gay men. Gay men see exercise not only as a means of weight control but also as a way to help with their body appearance. The authors found that while the lesbians and heterosexual women did not differ in obesity, the lesbians were less concerned with weight. They also binged less than heterosexual women, although the heterosexual women were more concerned with using restraint over their eating than lesbians. These findings are in contrast to those of Striegel-Moore et al. (1990), who found lesbians to diet less but binge eat more than heterosexual women, whereas Bradford and Ryan (1982) found lesbians to be three times more likely to binge eat than dieters.

Family and twin studies

Studies have shown that considerable disturbance can exist in the families of both anorectics and bulimics. Hudson et al. (1987) carried out a family history study and found the prevalence of bulimia in relatives of bulimic probands to be 3.4%. This is in contrast with the findings of Kassett et al. (1989) who, by using direct interviews with relatives, found that the risk for bulimia nervosa in relatives of hospitalized bulimic probands was 9.6% versus 3.5% of relatives of normal control subjects. There is no conclusive evidence to demonstrate that family dysfunction causes eating disorders, although there is strong evidence to suggest that eating disorders may lead to family dysfunction.

Kendler et al. (1991) was the first to assess lifetime prevalence of an entire epidemiological sample and found 2.8% of female twins received a lifetime diagnosis of bulimia. The authors found significantly higher rates of bulimia among younger than among older members of a sample of 2163 female twins. They speculated that older subjects could have forgotten episodes or else been simply unaware of bulimia as a disorder. However, they also found that most of those with symptoms of bulimia also suffered from other disorders. Only 22.8% of cases of bulimia had no other lifetime history of mental illness, such as phobias, anxiety disorders, panic disorders and alcoholism, whereas over a half had a history of depression. Based on this genetic epidemiological twin study, Kendler et al. (1991) argue that one in 25 women is at risk for developing the full syndrome of bulimia nervosa at some time during her life.

Hsu et al. (1990) and Fichter and Noegel (1990) have also carried out twin studies with varying results. In the Hsu study, subjects included 11 twin probands with bulimia, who had been referred to an eating disorder's clinic. The co-twin was personally interviewed in six of the pairs and the results indicated that two of the six monozygotic female–female pairs (33%) were concordant for bulimia compared to none of the five dizygotic pairs (two female–female and three male–female pairs). The Fichter and Noegel (1990) study was larger than that of Hsu et al. and included 27 twin pairs with bulimia nervosa gathered from volunteers to a press survey (17 pairs) plus two clinical services (10 pairs). They reported that, after excluding the one male monozygotic pair and the five opposite sex dizygotic pairs, they found pairwise concordance for bulimia nervosa in five of six female monozygotic pairs (83%) and in four of 15 female dizygotic pairs (27%).

The disparate findings on the prevalence rates are undoubtedly related to methodological differences between studies – sample sizes, methods of data collection, prevalence periods, the populations being studies but especially the definition and criteria for bulimia that were applied. This view is also supported by Fairburn and Beglin (1990) who analysed the incidence data on bulimia in more than 50 publications. They found the prevalence in adolescent and young adult women to range from 1%–35%. The authors feel that such marked discrepancies must be due in part to non-standard diagnostic criteria, self-report data and sampling procedures. They conclude that a true estimate is probably about 1% of the population of adolescent and young adult women.

King (1989) argues that, despite anecdotal claims, there is no unequivocal evidence that bulimia nervosa is becoming more prevalent. Increased recognition by physicians as well as a greater willingness on the part of the bulimic to admit to the problem may be important factors in creating the impression of an increase in the disorder.

Chapter 9
Etiology

There appears to be a consensus among investigators that bulimia nervosa originates from psychological stress and is a multi-determined disorder that serves a variety of biological, psychological and sociocultural adaptations. Boskind-Lodahl (1976) developed one of the early theories of etiology when she argued that an over-acceptance of the feminine stereotype was causal in bulimia. The feminist etiology would hypothesize that the pursuit of thinness is an expression of perfectionist strivings to achieve an exaggerated ideal of femininity. Early in their development, bulimics learn a passive and accommodating approach to life, which is reinforced by parents and society. Assertiveness and independence are discouraged, whereas submissiveness and goodness are rewarded.

Sociocultural influences

There are, of course, the sociocultural expectations concerning thinness alongside the anti-fat prejudice that has become more pronounced. According to Stice (1994), various sociocultural influences are involved in the development of bulimia, including the thinness ideal for women, the importance of appearance in the female gender role and the importance of appearance for women's societal success. Bulimic women are often seen as more achievement oriented than others, while striving to be the smartest, most popular and the most successful among their peers. Mason and Claney (1996) argue that in our culture, where success and achievement equate with beauty and thinness, the bulimic feels compelled to pursue thinness with the same vigour, leading many young women to develop dangerous eating patterns to meet this idealized standard. Society's emphasis on thinness helps the individual to see weight loss as a solution to her problems as the external pressure to be thin is transformed into self-imposed pressure.

The emphasis on feminine attractiveness has continued despite the changing social roles, expectations and opportunities for women that have occurred in the last 25 years. It could be argued that these social changes have contributed to increased stress for women as a result of the conflict between many of the competing role demands in both their personal and professional lives. Thorton et al. (1991) suggest that women who strongly adhere to a superwoman ideal are at an increased risk of eating disorders.

Familial variables

Studies suggest that individuals with bulimia do perceive their families as more conflictual, disorganized and non-nurturing than do control subjects. Family studies of bulimia have generally used relatively small sample sizes ranging from an investigation by Stern et al. (1984) of 27 families to one of 69 families by Hudson et al. (1987). As secrecy is a hallmark of bulimia, it is unlikely that bulimic individuals will permit inclusion of their family in a study of the disorder. This was the case with Herzog et al. (1992a), who found that seven out of 15 bulimic women did not want to involve their families in any study of the illness.

Familial variables have been examined to uncover the origins of bulimia. These have revealed that low levels of cohesion, disorganization and non-expressiveness are to be seen in the bulimic's family (Attie and Brookes-Gunn, 1989). Parents of bulimics can be more belittling, less helpful and nurturing and restricting than parents of non-bulimics (Strober and Humphrey, 1987). Bulimic young women do report high familial conflict and low family cohesiveness. The families can also exert direct pressure (by teasing or control of food intake) on young bulimics in an effort to cajole them into pursuing the thin ideal.

Family studies have been useful in examining the relationship of bulimia to major affective disorders and other psychiatric disorders. The majority of family studies on bulimia did find an increased risk of psychopathology among relatives of case probands compared to control probands. The risk has essentially been linked to major depressive disorder. Reports of family histories of alcoholism or other addictive behaviours, as well as the presence of depressive and anxiety disorders, would support the view that the condition had possible biological origins. However, the empirical data supporting a purely biological basis for the disorder are very limited.

Boumann and Yates (1994) associated parental psychiatric illness with high rates of divorce in families of probands with bulimia nervosa. Parental psychiatric illness and divorce were also associated with a trend toward lower ratings of paternal relationships, but not with maternal relationships. Actual studies of divorce rates in parents of bulimic sufferers are few in number. Dolan et al. (1990b), however, carried out such a study and found the rate to be insignificant in a sample of 50 probands with bulimia. They reported the divorce rate to be 12% compared to a control rate of 7.5%. There is a need for more investigations into the effect of parental divorce on bulimic patients as it is evident that it affects a large number of bulimic sufferers.

Wonderlich et al. (1994) aimed to identify perceptions of non-shared childhood environmental factors associated with bulimia and the co-morbid personality traits associated with this disorder. They compared 27 individuals with bulimia and 27 normal controls. The researchers found that the bulimics were more likely than the controls to rate their fathers as showing less affection and more control toward them than toward their siblings. Also in the bulimics, borderline personality disorder ratings were associated with the perception that both mother and father showed less affection toward the bulimic individual than toward her sibling.

A larger study by Woodside et al. (1996) aimed to examine 91 bulimic families for family functioning. The average age was 24.8 years and 82% were single. They found that the measurements before and after therapy showed improvement in virtually every case, confirming the authors' clinical observations that these families are, on the whole, relieved at their daughter's improved condition or recovery. The authors showed that improvement in family functioning could also be due to the fact that the bulimics in their group were older and could have undergone some life-cycle changes.

Relationships

Pruitt et al. (1992) suggest that fear of intimate relationships, especially with the opposite sex, is a control dynamic in bulimia. Their study consisted of 11 women who met the criteria for bulimia and 23 women who denied bingeing and/or purging. The authors measured the fear of intimacy in both groups and found that bulimic subjects exhibited significantly greater fear of intimacy than did the control subjects.

Bruch (1974) also states that bulimics have difficulty in establishing intimate relationships with men. Bruch argues that bulimics overemphasize, idealize and exaggerate romantic relationships as their need for love and acceptance is not met by their families. This overemphasis results in failed relationships.

Pruitt et al. (1992) also found that, on less complex measures of psychosocial functioning, such as being involved in a dating relationship, and the number of male and female friends of bulimics, that no significant group differences were found. This would therefore suggest that although bulimics do not differ from controls in the quantity of their interpersonal relationships, they do differ from controls in the quality of these relationships. Thelen et al. (1990) asserts that an important focus on treatment of bulimics may be the assessment and treatment of their functioning within intimate relationships.

When bulimics are married, or live with a partner, the question arises as to the impact that the disorder has on their relationship, or even the influence that the intimate relationship has on the course of the illness. Homogamy (where like marries like) was investigated by Lacey (1992) using 112 consecutive patients with bulimia. Seventy-three patients (65%) had a current sexual partner. They came from a similar social background although they were slightly older. Twenty-seven per cent of partners reported having an eating problem, with a quarter having been treated for a psychiatric or emotional disorder. Twelve per cent had a mother or sister with an eating disorder. Heavy drinking was also found in over 40% of partners. Lacey concluded that heavy drinking partners and multi-impulsive bulimics seek each other out.

Food as an etiological factor

Miller et al. (1993) examined correlates of bulimia with early family mealtime experiences. They found that bulimics reported more negative early mealtime and food-related experiences than did women who were non-bulimic. The bulimics related high levels of stress and conflict during meals, the use of food as a tool for punishment or manipulation and an emphasis on dieting and weight. Mealtime was also likely to be the only time when the family was together. Interpersonal grievances and hostilities were frequently raised, parents tended to dominate or control the conversation, and a great deal of attention was also paid to eating habits. The authors also found that food was used as an instrument of reward or punishment. The bulimics said that food was likely to be given as an important part of a celebration, or to be offered as a treat when the child was hurt or upset. There is the case of the girl whose bulimia started at the age of 10 years as a result of her self-imposed secretive eating of sweets as her mother was very strict regarding staying slim and avoiding carbohydrates. The girl felt so guilty about eating the sweets that she vomited to ease the guilt. However, many bulimics complain about a carbohydrate craving that some have linked to biological factors playing a part in increasing appetite for sweet foods.

Johnson and Larson (1982) have conceptualized bulimia as an addictive disorder with food being the abused substance. Food they argue is used for tension release, whereas purging is used to avoid the social problems associated with obesity.

Compulsive eating as an etiological factor

Kagan and Squires (1983) looked at teenagers' feelings of failure as related to their (1) dieting and concern about weight and (2) their compulsive eating. They used 405 high-school students who indicated how successful they felt they were in living up to their own expectations and to the perceived expectations of their parents. For the boys, dieting and compulsive eating were both directly related to feelings that they had failed to meet the perceived expectations of their parents. This was in contrast to the girls whose compulsive eating was dependent upon the perceived power structure of the family. Girls from families perceived to be mother dominated reported more compulsive eating and a feeling of failure

Heatherton and Braumeister (1991) suggest that an escape theory could provide an explanatory model for binge eating. They argue that bulimics tend to set unrealistically high expectations for themselves and experience negative self-awareness and affect while exhibiting impulsive behaviour and irrational beliefs. The authors argue that binge eating followed by purging is engaged in to escape from self-awareness of these aversive factors.

The alternating cycle of binge eating and purging becomes the means through which the individual attempts to avoid open and direct expression of emotion, lest she should displease others. As the bulimic's emotions become suppressed, tension and anxiety build up so that the bulimic sees no way out other than bingeing and purging to release this pent-up emotion.

Risk factors for bulimia nervosa

Family factors have been seen as important risk factors by several authors. Halmi et al. (1981) have suggested that the bulimic patient may be part of a generally disturbed family, whereas Hudson et al. (1983) have demonstrated an increased incidence of alcoholism in close relatives of bulimic patients with Collins et al. (1985) finding alcoholism to be 2.5 times more common in families of bulimic patients than in the general population. Boumann and Yates (1994) studied 25 women with normal weight bulimia and compared them with 25 age- and weight-matched women without bulimia on measures of parental psychiatric illness. The authors argue that parental psychiatric illness may be a risk factor for bulimia and may contribute to environmental effects through increased rates of divorce and impaired paternal relationships. Fairburn et al. (1997) have also strongly associated parental problems, obesity risk, parental psychiatric disorder, sexual or physical abuse and pre-morbid psychiatric disorder with risk factors for bulimia nervosa. Pope et al. (1992) considered the issue of sexual abuse on its own as a risk factor for bulimia nervosa and examined controlled and non-controlled studies of bulimia in order to carry out their investigation. However, the authors concluded that there is insufficient evidence to support the hypothesis that childhood sexual abuse is a risk factor for bulimia nervosa. This is not supported by Welch and Fairburn (1996) who found that sexual and physical abuse are both risk factors for the development of bulimia, even though they are not present in the majority of cases.

Kendler et al. (1991) aimed to clarify the major risk factors for bulimia from both an epidemiological and genetic perspective. They carried out interviews on 2163 female twins and their results indicated risk factors for bulimia to include (1) birth after 1960, (2) low paternal care, (3) a history of wide weight fluctuations, dieting or frequent exercise, (4) a slim ideal body image, (5) low self-esteem, (6) an external locus of control and (7) high levels of neuroticism. The authors suggest that bulimia is substantially influenced by both epidemiological and genetic risk factors.

Garner and Bemis (1982) have suggested a number of distorted attitudes that could predispose an individual to develop and maintain an eating disorder. They included (1) striving for perfection, (2) scepticism being superior to self-indulgence, (3) thinness being admirable whereas fat is seen as disgusting, and (4) weight gain being seen as making one bad or out of control.

Chapter 10
Clinical features

Bulimia is recognized by an abnormal eating pattern, showing uncontrolled episodic binge eating, often accompanied by self-induced vomiting or laxative abuse. Bulimics feel out of control and depressed while also suffering guilt and shame at their behaviour. These patients tend to set high self-expectations as well as being perfectionistic. They will set unrealistic goals for themselves both in their personal lives and with regard to how much they should weigh. Many have high expectations for themselves in their academic or career life. Bulimics have been found to be less liberated in both sex role attitudes and behaviour. They report less enjoyment of sexual relationships and have more difficulty expressing their sexual wishes, while also feeling they do not meet their partners' sexual expectations.

The bulimic patient's weight can fluctuate and, unlike the anorectic, a bulimic may not necessarily be underweight. Studies have shown that 70% of bulimics are within the normal weight range, whereas about 15% are overweight and about 15% are underweight. Russell (1979) reported a history of anorexia nervosa in 80% of bulimics in his study. However, some clinicians refuse to make a diagnosis of bulimia if there is a present or previous history of anorectic symptoms.

Bulimics have a fear of becoming obese and, whereas a dissatisfaction with body shape is seen as a prominent feature of the psychopathology of bulimia, it is not of diagnostic significance as it is not always present in those with bulimia, but can also be seen in some people with no eating disorder. This is in contrast with the overvalued ideas about body shape and weight that are central to both bulimia and anorexia nervosa. These are closely related to the patient's low self-esteem and are an essential diagnostic feature for both disorders. Cooper and Fairburn (1993) found that, during the course of treatment, a change in body shape dissatisfaction was closely associated with a change in the mood of the bulimic, whereas a change in the overvalued ideas was closely associated with a change in self-esteem. The authors argue that this highlights the distinction between these two aspects of the core psychopathology of bulimia.

As the bulimic loses weight she becomes more dissatisfied with her body and this behaviour is in contrast to the 'normal dieter' who will usually find that their body image is improved with weight loss. The bulimic will then find herself more socially isolated as her life revolves around eating, dieting, studying, exercising, vomiting and purging. So the disorder cannot be viewed simply as a problem of binge eating as these patients frequently engage in other eating-related behaviours in their attempt to lose weight.

The DSM IV criteria have differentiated the disorder into purging and non-purging types. The 'purging type' is when the individual engages in regular self-induced vomiting or laxative abuse and the 'non purging type' is when other inappropriate compensatory behaviours such as severe dietary restriction, or excessive exercises are used.

Binge eating

The major clinical feature of bulimia is bingeing. However, the term 'binge' is not always clearly defined or understood. It means different things to different people in different cultures and can differ markedly from the clinical use of the term. It is also difficult to establish the criteria by which people define a binge, such as loss of control and/or the amount and type of food. This was attempted by La Porte (1996) who looked at the influences of gender, amount of food and speed of eating to determine external rates of binge eating. The results indicated, as expected, that eating by females is more often labelled as a binge, even when they eat exactly the same amount as a male, in the same amount of time and under the same circumstances. The author found it particularly surprising that it was the female subjects who decided this to be, but only for females. For males to be labelled as having had a binge they needed to eat twice as much and twice as fast. As predicted, a female eating doughnuts was labelled as bingeing to a significantly greater extent than a male. The majority of women labelled eating three doughnuts as a binge, even though this would amount to only 600 calories eaten at a rate of one doughnut in 3.9 minutes and even though this would fail to meet the diagnostic criteria for a binge.

Striegel-Moore (1995) argues that, in our culture, where beauty equates with thinness and femininity, a woman is seen to be more feminine if she makes an effort to enhance or preserve her beauty. Women know the importance of eating and how others perceive them. This view is also supported by Pliner and Chaiken (1990) whose study indicated how women who eat small meals are rated as significantly more feminine, less masculine, more concerned with their appearance and more attractive as compared with women who reportedly eat large meals.

Binge eating involves the ingestion of a large amount of food in a discrete period of time accompanied by a sense of loss of control over eating. The act of bingeing is often carried out in secret and may follow a stressful event or feelings of anxiety, depression, boredom or loneliness. Food consumed in a binge will often consist of sweet or salty carbohydrates, which require no cooking, are easily accessible and easily digestible. The amount of food consumed during a binge is described in terms of calories. Abraham and Beumont (1982) found that bulimics consumed three to 27 times their recommended daily food allowance in a binge, whereas Russell (1979) reported 20 000 calories and Johnson et al. (1982) 41 800 calories per binge. The type of food eaten during a binge may also depend on availability and may include inappropriate foods such as raw or frozen foods or scraps from rubbish bins (Abraham and Beumont, 1982). The foods that are most frequently consumed include ice cream, bread, sweets, doughnuts, soft drinks, sandwiches and biscuits. If the bulimic intends to follow this binge with vomiting then large amounts of liquid will also be consumed at the same time.

Most bulimics binge at least once a day, usually in the evening, with most reporting the frequency of their binge eating to range from between two to 20 times a week. One third report bingeing several times every day. Some patients will virtually starve whereas others will spit out food and some may regurgitate and ruminate. Binges can follow in a chain reaction fashion after eating just a small amount of a favourite fattening food, or the binge could be planned and shopped for in a ritualized manner.

It is essential to distinguish binges from episodes of overeating. The first issue therefore is the amount of food involved. Walsh et al. (1989) assessed, in laboratory conditions, that a binge should consist of over 4000 calories. Therefore one extra piece of pizza, a second helping of pudding, or a small amount of 'forbidden' food is not an episode of bingeing. It could also be said that large amounts of food eaten rather slowly over a prolonged period of time are also not a binge.

Weltzin et al. (1991) described the naturalistic feeding characteristics of a large number (54) of bulimics by direct observation and compared them with matched controls over a 24-hour period in a feeding laboratory. Bulimic women consumed a wide range of caloric intake with 44% overeating and, 19% undereating in comparison to the range of controls. The study also confirmed that bulimic women choose sweet desserts and snacks with a high fat content when overeating. Another study examining the relationship between actual caloric intake and subjective perceptions of amount eaten was undertaken by Gleaves et al. (1993) using self-monitoring data for 20 bulimics and 20 normal controls. They found that the bulimics tended to overrate the amount consumed and this effect increased as their caloric intake increased. Bulimics' ratings were influenced by the type of foods eaten and also by their mood prior to eating.

Bulimia nervosa sufferers frequently do not eat for more than 24 hours after a binge and they then find themselves hungry, which sparks off the bingeing–fasting cycle again. Very few bulimics eat three meals a day even on those days when they do eat. The binge–purge cycle is an all encompassing symptom and pervades almost every aspect of the bulimic woman's daily life. It affects her work, social and family relationships and ultimately affects her health. The financial considerations involved in bulimic behaviour are enormous as the cost of a single binge can be as much as £40. This involves the bulimic in a lot of expense and could also drive her to steal either food or money.

Binges are usually terminated when the patient or her food supply are exhausted or because of pain, sleep, vomiting or the arrival of company. This is followed by the patient feeling guilt, shame and unhappiness. Thoughts of suicide following a binge are not uncommon (Abraham and Beumont, 1982). Despite feeling shameful and humiliated by bingeing, the actual binge eating itself can offer a number of compensatory adaptations that become quite reinforcing, and for some, binge eating serves as a mechanism for tension regulation.

Vomiting

About 75% of bulimics vomit to rid themselves of food. This is usually achieved by inserting a finger or toothbrush into the throat, or some can just do it at will or by putting gentle pressure on the abdomen. Russell (1979) describes the major cutaneous manifestation of bulimia as the callous or sore on the dorsum of the hand, usually over the knuckle, this having been caused by abrasion of the back of the hand on the upper front teeth during the manual induction of vomiting.

The incidence of daily vomiting in most studies is around two vomits per day (Mitchell et al., 1981). Once the stomach is empty, the pain also decreases and the bulimic can then continue eating if she so wishes. While vomiting may have begun as a substitute for dieting, this rather benign habit then becomes malignant in that it completely controls the individual's life (Martin, 1989). Attempts have been made to explain the functions of vomiting in bulimia and Rosen and Leitenburg (1982) postulate that it can serve as an anxiety-reducing function similar to the various rituals in obsessive-compulsive neurosis. Vomiting can also be seen as a rather violent act and the physical process of vomiting can be cathartic of aggressive feelings.

Vomiting leads to electrolyte loss, resulting in alkalosis with associated hypoglycaemia, which is characterized by muscle weakness, constipation, abdominal pain and heart palpitations. Vitamin deficiencies may also occur as a result of the disruption to the diet.

Laxatives

Laxative use is very common in Western culture, with 4.9% of adult women reporting regular use of laxatives (Fairburn and Cooper, 1984). However, in bulimia their reported use is eight times or more common than in the general population. Authors report that laxatives are used in 43% to 75% of normal-weight bulimics (Russell, 1979; Abraham and Beumont, 1982; Mitchell et al., 1985).

The quantities of laxatives ingested range from three times the daily dosage to handfuls of tablets at a time with Hsu (1983) having reported one patient who took up to 900 laxatives a week. Bulimics report using laxatives to help counteract the effects of binge eating and to help lose weight. However Lacey and Gibson (1985) argue that laxatives do not have an effect on either binge eating or weight loss.

Weltzin et al. (1995) conducted anxiety ratings of 23 bulimics who purge with laxatives and 17 who purge by vomiting. They found that the laxative-abusing group had higher levels of anxiety and they were also more likely to be treated with medication for anxiety during hospitalization. The authors therefore suggest an association between laxatives and anxiety in bulimia nervosa. Anxiety levels are also increased if there is an abrupt discontinuation of laxative use. What is also apparent, however, is that high levels of anxiety do make treatment difficult in many cases, especially when working in a structured treatment programme.

Laxative abusers are also reported as having an increased prevalence of suicide attempts, self-injurious behaviours and in-patient treatment for depression (Mitchell et al., 1986). Like binge eating, purging also serves a variety of different adaptive functions. It provides a sense of relief from the anxiety that is created by binge eating and for those patients who feel especially guilty and self-critical around binge eating episodes. Purging is seen as self-punishment. Johnson (1984) reported by clinical observations that patients who regularly use laxatives are often masochistic and have fragile ego boundaries and that the painful distress that is associated with the repeated episodes of diarrhoea provides a psychological function similar to other forms of self-mutilatory behaviour.

Chewing and spitting of food

Chewing and spitting out food without actually swallowing it is a behaviour that has received little attention even though it is apparently quite common in bulimic patients. It has been reported by Mitchell et al. (1988) as an alternative to laxative abuse and vomiting. They describe a series of 25 patients who use this method regularly for weight control. It has also been reported by Robinson and Holden (1986) who found that patients used chewing and spitting of food in conjunction with appetite suppressants and exercise to control weight. Abraham and Beumont (1982) found that some bulimics used this activity in an attempt to resist the urge to binge. Other diversion methods included keeping no money in their purse, planning to be occupied at every moment or by not cooking.

Multi-impulsivity

Individuals with bulimia nervosa have been portrayed as displaying problems with impulsivity. Lacey and Evans (1986) proposed the term 'multi-impulsive form of bulimia', which they defined based on the existence of at least one of the following behaviours: alcohol or drug abuse, suicide attempts, repeated self-harm, sexual disinhibition or shoplifting.

As a result of the current research on eating disorders and the possible associations between self-mutilation and bulimia, Parry-Jones and Parry-Jones (1993) considered this from a historical perspective and examined 25 bulimic cases reported from the late seventeenth to the late nineteenth century. The authors found four examples of self-mutilative behaviour in three males and one female. Their historical evidence would lend support to the view that there is a connection between eating pathology and self-mutilation.

Fahy and Eisler (1993) also looked at this question of multi-impulsivity in their sample of 39 patients with bulimia and found that 20 of the 39 patients exhibited at least one of the behaviours indicative of impulse problems: drug abuse, self-harm and shoplifting. However, only three patients indicated more than one impulsive behaviour. McElroy et al. (1995) reported on kleptomania and compulsive buying in bulimia, and argued that it is more common than realized, especially in women, while also causing substantial morbidity.

Wiederman and Pryor (1996) investigated potential relationships between multi-impulsivity and other clinical variables. They compared 40 bulimics who displayed multi-impulsivity with 177 who did not. They looked at symptom history and presentation, eating-disordered attitudes and sexual experience. The authors found that women in the multi-impulsive group reported earlier onset of binge eating and sexual intercourse, a greater incidence of laxative abuse and the use of a greater number of different substances.

A study by Fichter et al. (1994) examined multi-impulsivity in two groups of women – one group of 32 women with multi-impulsivity compared to a group of 32 bulimic women with no impulsive behaviour. The authors defined multi-impulsivity as having at least three of the following six behaviours – suicide attempts, self-harm, shoplifting, alcohol abuse, drug abuse or sexual promiscuity. The groups differed with regard to their general level of functioning with the multi-impulsive groups showing a greater co-morbid psychopathology and lower psychosocial functioning. Such findings led the authors to suggest that the multi-impulsive bulimics should be seen as a distinct subgroup of patients presenting with bulimia. They are indistinguishable with regard to disordered eating, but they do exhibit greater pervasive psychopathology.

A follow-up study of 35 adult patients who had either anorexia nervosa or bulimia was carried out by Sohlberg et al. (1989). They examined the role of multi-impulsivity in predicting long-term outcome. The authors defined multi-impulsivity as the sum of four possible impulsive behaviours – bingeing, drug abuse, stealing and suicide attempts, and reported increased impulsivity as being the best predictor of poor outcome at both two-to-three year and four-to-six year follow-ups. Taken as a whole, these women who display multi-impulsivity leave themselves vulnerable not only to medical complications but also to legal ramifications.

Addictive behaviours – alcohol, drugs, smoking

A reported higher incidence of substance abuse among eating disordered patients has been found. Some investigations have looked at this relationship while examining abuse, both by the type of substance (alcohol versus non-alcohol) and in both anorexia and bulimia. Moderate rates of substance dependence have been found in anorexia, but Herzog et al. (1992b) reported that this difference could be attributed to the significantly lower rate of alcohol use among the anorectic group. This finding would support previous views that a link exists between impulse-related behaviours and bulimic symptoms.

It has been reported (Mitchell et al., 1985) that bulimics in large proportions (14% to 36%) have either a history of problems with alcohol and drugs or are experiencing such problems concurrently. Wiederman (1996) compared bulimia with anorexia nervosa for substance use. They found that women with bulimia were more likely than those with anorexia to have used alcohol, amphetamines, barbiturates, marijuana, tranquillizers and cocaine. The severity of binge eating was predictive of tranquillizer use and the severity of purging was predictive of alcohol, cocaine and cigarette use.

Susuki (1995) investigated the co-prevalence of bulimia with alcohol abuse and smoking by surveying 2597 male and female Japanese high-school students. They found a group of bulimic students and compared them with a control group that reported no binge eating experience. The results indicated significantly more alcohol abuse for both male and female bulimic students than for the non-bulimic control group. The incidence of smoking was significantly higher among the bulimic females than among the female control group, although there was no significant difference between the male groups' smoking experiences. The results clearly indicate a strong association between bulimia and alcohol abuse in both female and male Japanese adolescents.

The bulimic's difficulties with alcohol can be related to her indirect approach to managing emotions in general and perhaps her depression in particular. Abuse problems can also arise from the bulimic's low frustration tolerance and their need for immediate gratification. Some have linked the severe craving that is found in both bulimia and alcoholism. There could also be a link with the 'loss of control' that is experienced by both bulimics and excessive drinkers. Some have also drawn a link between bulimia and alcoholic parents (Strober and Humphrey, 1987; Collins et al., 1985; Kassett et al., 1989).

Susuki et al. (1995) offer explanations for the high co-prevalence of bulimia and alcohol among young bulimic females as being (1) those who binge eat can readily shift to heavy drinking, (2) drinking is known to mask depressive and guilt feelings which the bulimic experiences following binge eating, (3) alcohol consumption can be chosen as a means of avoiding being overweight and (4) there could also be a genetic basis for the association of bulimia with alcohol.

Tordjman et al. (1994) found the presence of nicotine dependence as an extremely sensitive and specific predictor of bulimia. Smoking has also been reported in females with bulimia by Lavic et al. (1991). Since some bulimics use smoking to decrease food intake, this will help account for the co-prevalence.

Combination of methods

The compensatory behaviour that occurs subsequent to binge eating can be either purging behaviour, which includes mechanical or chemical self-induced vomiting, ruminatory regurgitation and laxative and diuretic abuse, or non-purging behaviour, which includes prolonged abstinence from food, extreme vigorous exercise and the use or abuse of medication. Excessive exercise is a commonly used form of behaviour by the bulimic and is seen by the patient and her family as a healthy pastime activity. However, it is often the hardest of all the bulimic's activities and behaviours to alter.

Mitchell et al. (1985) presented data on the characteristics of 275 patients with bulimia. The mean age of the patients was 24.8 years and the average duration of illness was approximately seven years. The patients reported a variety of abnormal eating-related behaviour including binge eating (100%), self-induced vomiting (88.1%), laxative abuse (60.6%), diuretic abuse (33.1%) and chewing and spitting out food (64.5%). Over one-third reported a history of problems with alcohol or other drugs, whereas most also indicated substantial social impairment.

Psychopathology

Seasonal affective disorder (SAD)

A large percentage of the population shows seasonal changes in mood, energy and appetite, but there has emerged a subgroup whose symptoms are sufficiently severe in the winter months to be considered as having a seasonal affective disorder (SAD). The relationship between mood and eating disorders has always been considered a controversial issue.

Affective symptoms frequently accompany dysfunctional eating and patients with bulimia often have concurrent or past experience of depression. Patients with SAD regularly become depressed in the winter months, with remission of depression or hypomanic symptoms in the spring and summer.

Fonari et al. (1989) found that patients with bulimia reported feeling worse and eating more in the winter than at other times of the year. It is suggested that binge eating in bulimia may follow a seasonal pattern as patients with bulimia and those with SAD share the same common symptoms, especially that of carbohydrate craving and binge eating. However, the high levels of depression consistently reported in bulimia could not be accounted for by SAD alone.

Symptoms of bulimia such as carbohydrate craving and weight gain are also characteristic of winter depression. It has been suggested that bulimia peaks during autumn and winter and that those with this disorder may respond to treatment with artificial light. Such a view is supported by Blouin et al. (1992), who studied 31 patients with bulimia over a four-year period to determine whether a seasonal pattern to symptoms of bulimia could be identified. They reported that 35.5% of the subjects with bulimia met the criteria for seasonal effective disorder whereas only 6.5% of the 31 subjects in a comparison group met the criteria for this disorder. The bulimic's bingeing behaviour was found to be highly associated with the number of daylight hours. The authors suggest, therefore, that winter depression or some vulnerability associated with it predisposes people to develop bulimia.

Lam et al. (1991) offer some explanations as to the prominence of seasonal mood symptoms in bulimia. The condition may worsen in winter due to environmental and social variables such as seasonal dietary changes but the Christmas festivities are also associated with large meals and provide a societal focus on food. As more time is spent indoors during the winter months, the bulimic has a greater opportunity to engage in her secretive behaviour and eating patterns. It is also the case that winter does not lend itself easily to outdoor exercise, such as walking or jogging.

Two cases are reported on by Del Medico et al. (1991) concerning bulimic patients whose symptoms were linked to SAD. These two individuals experienced worsening bulimia with the onset of major depression in September and a spontaneous recovery in April. The authors report that the symptoms of both disorders responded well to tranylcypromine. Blouin et al. (1992), however, suggest that seasonal changes in bulimia may be due to the effects of changing light availability on appetite, weight and mood. They could also be due to their sensitivity to cold and the need to increase their food intake to produce body heat.

It could be argued that there is now mounting evidence for some common biological mechanisms in the pathogenesis of SAD and bulimia. Lam et al. (1991) have shown that bulimic patients, like SAD patients, exhibit a reduction in their binge eating behaviour when treated with full spectrum bright artificial light or serotonergic medications.

Co-morbidity

Co-morbidity may be exaggerated in clinical populations as those individuals with two disorders are more likely to present for treatment than individuals with one disorder. Kendler et al. (1991) found that for those with a lifetime diagnosis of both major depression and bulimia, the onset of bulimia followed rather than preceded the major depression. They also found a significant co-morbidity with alcoholism and anxiety disorders. Schwalberg et al. (1992) also found the presence of anxiety disorders in 80% of bulimics and substantial prevalence rates of depression. Impaired psychological development has also been implicated by Russell (1979) who noted associations between eating disorders and depression in his study of 30 bulimic patients. Symptoms of depression were found in 87% of the subjects. Robinson and Holden (1986) found atypical features of psychosexual histories to be present in five out of nine patients in their study, with three being homosexual.

Bulimic individuals share a low self-esteem, low tolerance for frustration and anxiety and affective instability. These features may play a role in the development of bulimia but they can also help to maintain the disorder as well.

Chapter 11
Abuse in bulimia nervosa

It has been suggested in recent years that a history of sexual abuse may be more prevalent among women with eating disorders than in the general population and may be linked to anorexia nervosa or bulimia nervosa. Clinicians treating survivors of childhood sexual abuse have noted that the rate of eating disorders seems higher than would be expected by chance (Courtois, 1988). Studies have shown that there is an association between the nature of abuse and bulimic symptomatology (Hastings and Kern, 1994; Pribor and Dinwiddle, 1992; Waller, 1992). However a surprisingly low rate of sexual abuse has been reported among restrictive anorectics relative to either bulimic anorectics or normal weight bulimics (Waller et al., 1993; Steiger and Zanko, 1990).

Early clinical reports of apparently high rates (30% to 66%) of childhood sexual abuse among bulimic patients (Oppenheimer et al., 1985; Root and Fallon, 1988; Sloan and Leichner, 1986) have been followed by more controlled investigations. However, Pope and Hudson (1992) having reviewed six studies comparing rates of sexual abuse among bulimics and normal control subjects concluded that there is not sufficient evidence to support the view that child sexual abuse is a risk factor for bulimia nervosa. This viewpoint is not supported by Connors and Morse (1993), who reviewed the literature on the relationship between sexual abuse and eating disorders and concluded that about 30% of patients with eating disorders had been sexually abused.

It is true to say that prevalence rates vary substantially across studies and this variation is partly due to differences in the diagnostic criteria used, but principally it is due to different methods of inquiry and definition of abuse. Perhaps the most important methodological limitation has concerned the definition of child sexual abuse. Abuse is usually broadly defined to include anything from non-contact sexual experiences such as an invitation by a stranger to do something sexual, to repeated penetration by adult family members. Pope and Hudson (1992) suggest that a more narrow definition of abuse, restricted to more severe negative experiences, may allow for the emergence of significant group differences.

Welch and Fairburn (1996) also looked at the area of definition and for their investigations defined sexual abuse as any sexual experience involving physical contact that was against the subject's will. This therefore included the subject being touched or being made to touch the abuser in any sexual way, including oral sex and rape. They defined physical abuse as any deliberate physical contact resulting in injury such as bruising (including physical punishment by parents or teachers). Severe physical abuse was to include more severe injuries such as burns or fractures as well as any injury to the subject's head or face.

Much of the research in the area of child sexual abuse and eating disorders is plagued by methodological problems such as the reliance on clinical samples and the lack of control groups. Since much of the information on child sexual abuse is collected retrospectively from adult women who are receiving treatment for well-established eating disorders, the accuracy and validity of the reported sexual abuse is uncertain as it can also be influenced by treatment.

In a comprehensive review of the growing literature on the relationship between sexual abuse and bulimia, Pope and Hudson (1992) highlighted certain methodological problems. These included (a) the lack of control groups, or the use of inadequate control groups, (b) an unsatisfactory definition of sexual abuse, (c) poor evaluation of sexual abuse, (d) lack of attention to the timing of the abuse in relation to the onset of the eating disorder and (e) the absence of comparison control groups with other psychiatric disorders in order to examine specificity.

Sexual abuse

Hastings and Kern (1994) investigated 786 female college students and found that bulimia was strongly associated with self-reports of significant sexual abuse during childhood and/or adolescence. Furthermore, among abuse victims, the severity of the abuse was also related to the severity of the bulimic disturbance. Bulimics reported growing up in relatively chaotic families and to a lesser extent in relatively restrictive families.

Abramson and Lucido (1991) looked at the relationship between childhood sexual experiences and bulimia and found that it is not the childhood sexual experience per se but rather the nature of this experience that differentiates bulimics from non-bulimics. The bulimics had a significantly greater number of sexual experiences with their fathers and brothers. These findings are consistent with those of Russell (1986), who reported that childhood sexual experiences with fathers and stepfathers were the most traumatic followed by sexual experiences with brothers. Russell suggests that feelings of betrayal, powerlessness and guilt may be responsible for the severity of the trauma. Abuse severity and traumatization are, of course, likely to be related to one another, whereas repeated contact abuse by familiar individuals could be said to increase the probability of trauma resulting in bulimia. Hastings and Kern (1994) found a link between severity of bulimia and reported severity of sexual abuse.

In the study by Welch and Fairburn (1996) they compared the prevalence rates of reported sexual abuse among (1) community and clinical bulimics, (2) a psychiatric control population and (3) a matched group of normal controls. The authors reported that there was only one significant difference between the groups, and that is of sexual abuse involving physical contact. This was reported to be more common in the community bulimics than in the control women.

A retrospective study of 184 female out-patients with bulimia was carried out by De Groot et al. (1992). The authors found that 25% reported previous sexual abuse. They also found that previous sexual abuse was associated with greater psychological disturbance. Since the study did not reveal any differences in sexual functioning in those who did or did not report sexual abuse, the authors therefore concluded that sexual abuse may affect the severity rather than the type of eating disorder.

Most of the research into sexual abuse in bulimia has been conducted in the United Kingdom or America but Ono et al. (1996) investigated the subject in Japan. They looked at the childhood abuse histories of 50 Japanese female bulimic out-patients and found that 16 reported a history of physical abuse and 20 reported a history of sexual abuse. The authors suggest that, although the abuse experiences themselves do not seem to be a cause of bulimia, these experiences can affect the style and level of adaptive functioning in later life and the type of abuse may influence the nature of future psychological difficulties.

Waller (1992) looked at a clinical series of 40 bulimic patients and found a reported history of unwanted sexual experience was associated with more frequent bingeing and (to a lesser extent) vomiting. The authors found these symptoms to be more marked when the abuse was intrafamilial, involved force, or occurred before the victim was 14 years old.

In order to understand the nature of any relationship between sexual abuse and bulimic symptomatology it is necessary to examine the purpose that the bulimic behaviours serve. It has been suggested that, for a bulimic individual with a history of sexual abuse, the binge/purge cycle could serve a number of distinct functions that are directly related to the abuse. Some of these functions include expression of anger, relieving stress and tension, regaining a sense of self, establishing control, ensuring predictability and personal space and 'cleansing' oneself of the abuse experience (Root and Fallon, 1989; Schupak-Neuberg and Nemroff, 1993). It would also appear that vomiting is a response to the self-denigratory cognitions and emotions following abuse, rather than to the abuse per se or to a generalized decrease in self-esteem. Vomiting is seen to have a functional role in responding to negative cognitions.

Oppenheimer et al. (1985) have also looked at the links that might exist between sexual abuse and eating disorders. They suggested that those women who had been abused were likely to feel disgust or inferiority with regard to their own femininity and sexuality. Such feelings, the authors argue, are likely to manifest themselves as concern about weight and body shape and size. However, the authors do not draw a causal link between sexual abuse and eating disorders.

Abuse and psychopathology

Some clinical reports have examined the association between childhood sexual abuse and various types of psychopathology, such as depression, anxiety, sleep disturbances, excessive guilt, sexual problems, substance abuse and other types of self-destructive behaviour.

Tobin and Griffing (1996) explored rates of sexual abuse in different diagnostic subgroups of eating-disordered patients and the extent to which sexually abused patients presented with a higher incidence of disturbed behaviour, affective distress and personality disturbance. The authors assessed sexual abuse in 103 eating-disordered patients and found that abused patients were not only more disturbed on co-morbid psychiatric symptoms but were also more likely to have engaged in self-injurious behaviour (80%) and attempted suicide (75%).

Some studies (Rorty et al., 1994; Waller, 1993) have found a relationship between sexual abuse, affective disorders and personality disorders in eating disorders, but only the study of Pitts and Waller (1993) has demonstrated that self-denigratory beliefs and attitudes can differ among sexually abused and non-abused eating-disordered patients. Self-criticism and self-denigration have a role as both a symptom and a coping response.

Wonderlich et al. (1996) looked at the relationship between reported history of incest and the subsequent development of bulimic behaviour by comparing a group of 38 women receiving treatment for reported incest abuse with a group of 27 control subjects who were also receiving treatment for other psychiatric disorders but who denied any history of sexual abuse. Their results indicated that incest victims were significantly more likely to binge, vomit, experience a loss of control over eating and report body dissatisfaction than the control subjects. The incest victims also showed more co-morbidity with other maladaptive behaviours such as alcohol abuse, suicidal gestures, self-mutilation and cigarette smoking. The authors argue that incest may increase the risk for the development of bulimic behaviour and that such eating problems may be part of a larger pattern of dysfunctional efforts to regulate trauma-related emotional distress.

Zlotnick et al. (1996) examined whether patients with histories of sexual abuse reported a higher degree of pathological eating behaviours and attitudes as compared to a non-sexually abused control group. The subjects in the study were 134 psychiatric in-patients and the findings support an association between sexual abuse and an overall pattern of eating disorder symptomatology. Those patients with histories of sexual abuse compared with those patients without such histories obtained higher scores for drive for thinness, interpersonal distrust, perfectionism and interceptive awareness. The authors also found an increased drive for thinness (not usually associated with sexual abuse) in patients with a history of sexual abuse and suggest that an excessive concern with diet, body weight, shape and size is a defence against out-of-control feelings experienced as a result of a violation of the body.

Some studies have shown that the rates of sexual abuse in eating-disordered patients were comparable to those in other psychiatric patients, suggesting that sexual abuse is not a critical factor in the development of an eating disorder (Pope and Hudson, 1992; Folsom et al., 1993). However, Everill and Waller (1995) argue that such a view is based on an inappropriate level of analysis of the phenomena of sexual abuse and diagnosable eating disorders. They found that there was a more complex link between the nature of sexual abuse and specific bulimic symptomatology.

Abuse and the family

Studies have attempted to clarify how family background and childhood sexual abuse are associated and linked with the development of an eating disorder. Kinzl et al. (1994), in a study of 202 female university students, found that 44 (21.8%) were victims of childhood sexual abuse. However, those who reported an adverse family background displayed significantly higher eating-disordered scores than did those who assessed family background as a secure base. The authors concluded that childhood sexual abuse is neither necessary nor significant for the later development of an eating disorder, although an adverse family background may be an important etiological factor.

Mallinckrodt et al. (1995) looked at childhood attachment, family environment and adult social competencies in order to explain the association between sexual abuse and eating disorders. Their study investigated 102 female college students and 52 female sexually abused patients. Incest survivor patients had a higher eating-disordered rate (46%) than did sexually abused patients (22%), student incest survivors (24%), or non-abused students (17%). The authors found significant associations between family environment, incest, social competencies and eating disorders. Incest survivors had more dysfunctional families and lower social competencies than did non-abused women. Among incest survivors, those with the lowest levels of social competencies and poorest bonds with their mothers had more eating disordered symptoms.

Physical abuse

Studies of child abuse in eating disorders have concerned themselves primarily with child sexual abuse, but some studies have examined other forms of trauma in the histories of eating-disordered women and have reported high rates of physical abuse, psychological abuse, the witnessing of intrafamilial violence and other adverse events (Schmidt et al., 1993; Rorty et al., 1994).

Rorty et al. (1995) examined aspects of childhood parental physical punishment and its family environmental correlates among women with a lifetime history of bulimia nervosa and women with no history of eating disorders. They found that the women in the bulimic group reported significantly more physical punishment and perceived their discipline to have been more harsh and capricious than women in the control group. However, the groups did not differ significantly in the extent to which they believed that they deserved their punishment, or in their belief that they were 'physically abused.' The bulimic subjects, however, perceived themselves to be no more deserving of punishment than their non-eating disordered peers, despite having received harsher and more arbitrary punishment. The authors also found that the bulimics tended to underestimate their physical abuse whereas more than one-third of the bulimic women who met stringent criteria for abuse failed to identify themselves as 'physically abused'.

Rorty et al. (1994) looked at child sexual, physical, psychological and multiple abuse in women with a lifetime history of bulimia and those with no history of eating disorders. The subjects were 80 women with a lifetime history of bulimia and 40 females who had an eating disorder. The women with bulimia reported higher levels of childhood physical, psychological and multiple abuse. However, contrary to the authors' expectations, rates of sexual abuse did not distinguish the groups except when combined with other forms of abuse. The authors suggest that child abuse, especially physical and psychological abuse and the endurance of multiple forms of abuse, could constitute a risk factor for the development of bulimia.

Crime victimization

There has in recent years been increased interest regarding the role of crime victimization in the development and/or maintenance of eating disorders, particularly bulimia. The first study to systematically assess the relationship between crime victimization, post-traumatic stress disorder and eating disorders, is the study by Dansky et al. (1997). They examined the relationship between assault, bulimia and binge eating in a national representative sample of 3006 women who completed structured telephone interviews. The results indicated that lifetime prevalence of completed, forcible rape for respondents with bulimia was 26.6% as compared to respondents without bulimia. Aggravated assault history was also significantly more prevalent in women with bulimia (26.8%) as was a lifetime history of post-traumatic stress disorder (36.9%). Such results, the authors argue, support the hypothesis that victimization can contribute to the development and/or maintenance of bulimia. The overall results demonstrate that, when compared to non bulimics, those with bulimia had a significantly higher prevalence of rape, sexual molestation, aggravated assault, direct victimization as well as current and lifetime diagnoses of post-traumatic stress disorder. The prevalence of sexual assault was almost twice as high among those bulimics who used two or more methods to compensate for a binge, as compared with those who used one method. It was also found that a higher degree of loss of control over eating was associated with a higher prevalence of sexual assault.

Abuse in males

Investigations using male samples are greatly lacking, although Olivardi et al. (1995) did find that, relative to a non-eating disordered control group, eating-disordered men reported higher rates of being beaten in childhood (36% versus 8%), mother–child abuse (32% versus 4%) and sexual abuse (20% versus 0%). Further research is required to establish the causal links between the phenomenon of abuse and bulimic symptoms in both male and female patients. It is also necessary to begin to develop a treatment programme that would address both the abuse and the bulimia in an effective manner, while appreciating that the professionals' inquiry into any history of abuse needs to be sensitive and sympathetic.

Chapter 12
Treatments

The prevalence of bulimia nervosa presenting for treatment has been rapidly increasing. In contrast to anorexia nervosa, most bulimia nervosa sufferers state clearly that they would like help and treatment. A significant number of patients, particularly the more complex, may require in-patient treatment to provide symptom management and internal change. Hospitalization needs to be considered when symptoms interfere with the patient's ability to function on a daily basis, or when there is medical necessity such as dehydration or other complications. The need for in-patient treatment is also suggested by a poor response to out-patient treatment in the form of failed appointments, or if the patient is suicidal. Russell (1979) emphasizes the importance of hospitalization as the external controls of the hospital setting are required to break the unending cycle of starvation, bingeing and vomiting. He reports that admission for two to three weeks considerably reduces the urge to vomit. This is controlled in hospital by the patient being prevented from using the bathroom for one to two hours following a meal, unless accompanied by staff. Russell (1979) also recommends antidepressants or electroconvulsive therapy (ECT) if depressive symptoms are severe. A multi-dimensional, interdisciplinary focus is essential in the treatment of these complex cases.

However controlled studies of the treatment of bulimia nervosa have demonstrated that the great majority of patients can be managed as out-patients, whereas those patients with co-morbid psychopathology such as substance abuse, personality disorders and multi-impulsivity syndromes are likely to need longer treatment or require more specific attention. Several alternative strategies have been employed in the treatment of bulimia nervosa. Patients in many treatment programmes receive some form of nutritional or dietary counselling designed to emphasize the importance of resuming a pattern of appropriately sized and balanced meals to be consumed on a regular basis. Other treatments used include pharmacotherapy, usually antidepressants, psychotherapy (both individual and group), cognitive-behavioural therapy or behaviour therapy techniques.

96

Pharmacotherapy

No pharmacological agent has been found to be a panacea for bulimia nervosa and pharmacotherapy is not usually recommended as an initial treatment for the condition. Antidepressant medication may be indicated when there is evidence of a concurrent major depressive disorder that preceded the development of the disorder or for individuals whose depressive symptomatology does not diminish as the eating disorder symptoms subside. Carbamazepine, antidepressants and lithium have been prescribed on the basis of a possible relationship between bulimia and the affective disorders. Anticonvulsants have also been used in view of the EEG abnormalities found in some individuals with compulsive over-eating.

Treatment with an antidepressant medication represents the most widely studied psychopharmacological intervention for patients with bulimia nervosa. Initial trials of antidepressant medication for bulimic patients were prompted by observations regarding the high prevalence of major depression in patients and their first degree relatives (Jimerson et al., 1990; Kassett et al., 1989).

Pope and Hudson (1987) support the view that antidepressant therapy has been shown to be efficacious in the treatment of bulimia nervosa, arguing that in all of the positive studies of this treatment modality, antidepressant agents appeared effective even in bulimic subjects who did not display concomitant depression. They suggest that antidepressants should not be reserved for depressed bulimics only.

There are numerous studies which have examined the effectiveness of antidepressants in bulimia nervosa (Pope et al., 1985; Russell et al., 1988). Consistently a substantial minority of patients will experience a reduction in their urge to binge as a consequence of antidepressant administration. Many antidepressants have been investigated and all appear to show similar anti-bulimic activity. In general, most antidepressants appear to reduce bulimic symptoms. A large majority of patients decrease binge eating by at least 50%, with a corresponding decrease in vomiting and with remission rates ranging from one-third on imipramine to about two-thirds of patients on desipramine or fluoexetine over a minimum period of six to 10 weeks.

Walsh et al. (1988) conducted a double-blind, placebo-controlled trial to examine the efficiency of the monoamine oxidase inhibitor phenelzine in the treatment of bulimia. In 50 women who completed the trial, phenelzine was found to be significantly superior to placebo in the reduction of binge frequency (64% versus 5%) in the proportion of patients who had ceased bingeing at the end of the trial (35% versus 4%) and in several measures of psychological state. The authors argue that this study provides strong evidence that phenelzine is superior to placebo in the short-term treatment of normal weight women with moderate to severe chronic bulimia.

However, some studies suggest that fluoxetine hydrochloride (Prozac) in daily doses of 60 mg lessens the number of binge episodes and the dysphoria accompanying bulimia (Mickley, 1994). Goldbloom and Olmsted (1993) examined fluoxetine and demonstrated that drug-induced improvements in patients with bulimia nervosa were not limited to decreased frequency of bulimic behaviour but were also significantly associated with clinically meaningful improvement in attitudinal variables. They also found that the severity of depression and the degree of carbohydrate craving were decreased.

Schwitzer et al. (1993) suggested that bulimic patients who experience symptoms similar to seasonal affective disorder have reported a good response to the serontonin agonists fluoxetine and fenfluramine. Fenfluramine is associated with helping to decrease the meal size in patients with bulimia nervosa.

Earlier placebo-controlled studies of antidepressants in bulimia nervosa patients focused on the short-term reduction in the frequency of binge eating and measures of depression. However, more recently, greater emphasis has been placed on comparisons with psychotherapeutic interventions and measurement of more diverse and long-term aspects of outcome. There are virtually no studies that have examined the long-term effects of pharmacological treatment except for that of Agras et al. (1994), which indicated that six months of treatment with desipramine produced lasting improvement even when the medication was withdrawn.

Cognitive-behavioural therapy (CBT)

The rationale underlying a cognitive-behavioural approach is that dysfunctional beliefs and attitudes regarding weight and shape, which characterize bulimia nervosa, are of primary importance in the development and maintenance of the disorder (Fairburn et al., 1993b). Treatment therefore focuses on modifying these cognitions through a combination of behavioural and cognitive procedures in order to promote a change in patients' behaviour, their attitudes to shape and weight and other cognitive distortions such as low self-esteem and extreme perfectionism. Treatment is designed to shift attitudinal disturbances and to disrupt the cycle of restraint, binge eating and compensatory behaviour. Cognitive-behavioural therapy (CBT) has been shown to produce significant reductions in the symptomatology of depression and general psychopathology in addition to improving eating disorder psychopathology (Wilson et al., 1991). Cognitive-behavioural therapy combines a variety of procedures, which include the presentation of the cognitive view of the disorder, self-monitoring of relevant thoughts and behaviours, education, cognitive restructuring, the use of self-control measures to establish regular meals and activity and the introduction of forbidden or avoided foods into the diet (Fairburn, 1981).

Fairburn (1981) was the first to describe CBT for binge eating in bulimia nervosa. His approach to this subject was described in a treatment manual, which was later extended and published in 1993 (Fairburn et al., 1993b). Many have implemented this approach, albeit in varying clinical and research settings. The current manual (Wilson et al., 1996) is now widely accepted not only for out-patient treatment of bulimia nervosa, but also in major clinical research centres.

A CBT model proposes that there are two types of cognitive dysfunction that contribute to the development and maintenance of the disorder. Firstly, there are irrational beliefs, attitudes and values about eating, weight and shape and, secondly, there are cognitive distortions or rigid thinking styles and structures that underlay the disorder. According to this model it is essential that dysfunctional cognitions change if the patient is to recover completely. Fairburn (1985) presented a CBT programme that consisted of 19 sessions over 18 weeks, carried out in three stages. The first stage consisted of a treatment rationale being provided and behavioural techniques being introduced to establish regular eating habits and restore normal dietary intake. In the second stage, maladaptive and dysfunctional attitudes, thoughts, beliefs and values about food, eating, weight and shape are discussed and challenged, whereas the third stage emphasizes the maintenance of change.

Cognitive-behavioural therapy has broad effects. Apart from reductions in binge eating and purging, it has also been shown to consistently reduce dietary restraint and improve attitudes to shape and weight. Garner et al. (1993) compared the effectiveness of CBT and supportive-expressive therapy for bulimia nervosa and found that both treatments led to significant improvements in specific eating-disorder symptoms and in psychosocial disturbances. Supportive-expressive therapy was equally effective as CBT in reducing binge eating. Treatment differences were found, but they favoured CBT. Cognitive-behavioural therapy was superior in reducing the frequency of self-induced vomiting, as 36% of the CBT patients and 12% of the supportive-expressive therapy patients abstained from vomiting in the last month of treatment. Cognitive-behavioural therapy was also significantly more effective in modifying disturbed attitudes towards eating and weight, depression, poor self-esteem, general psychological distress and certain personality traits. However, long-term follow-up is required of both treatment modalities in order to determine the durability of outcome.

Smith et al. (1994) state that CBT is the most extensively studied psychotherapeutic intervention for bulimia nervosa and is generally regarded as the treatment of choice by many. Studies have consistently demonstrated that most bulimia nervosa patients improve considerably following CBT and maintain their improvements for the year following treatment (Fettes and Peters, 1992). Cognitive-behavioural therapy has also been shown to improve the over-concern with weight and shape

(Fairburn et al., 1993b). Wilson (1996), however, argues that CBT has not demonstrated unequivocal superiority to other forms of psychotherapy.

With CBT, what is clear is that no more than 50% of patients cease binge eating and purging whereas the remainder shows partial improvement and a small number derive no benefit at all. However, it would appear that CBT seems to be more acceptable to patients and may therefore result in fewer dropouts during treatment. The advantage of this approach is that the patient retains responsibility for change.

Behaviour therapy

A behavioural approach to the treatment of bulimia nervosa focuses on increasing control over eating, eliminating food avoidance and changing maladaptive attitudes. This is done by positive reinforcement of abstinence from bulimic symptoms, or indirectly, by modifying one or more of the proposed reinforcers. Behaviour therapy focuses exclusively on the normalization of eating habits. It is aimed at regaining control over eating by establishing a regular pattern of eating. Any form of dieting is discouraged since dietary restraint is thought to promote overeating in this patient group.

Behavioural interventions for bulimia nervosa attempt to alter environmental antecedents and consequences thought to control critical responses in the binge/purge cycle. A prominent example of behavioural treatment of bulimia nervosa is exposure–response prevention (Rosen and Leitenberg, 1982). This intervention is based on the hypothesis that purging is maintained by the reduction of anxiety generated from fear of weight gain subsequent to binge eating. Exposure–response prevention involves the systematic delay or prevention of purging following binge eating. A large number of the studies using behavioural approaches have been based on the anxiety-reduction model of bulimia nervosa. This model proposes that self-induced vomiting is an escape response and by inducing vomiting the patient reduces anxiety. This response occurs after bingeing or after eating foods that are seen as fattening. However, this model suggests that bingeing is a consequence of vomiting rather than vomiting a consequence of bingeing. The treatment proposed based on this model has been exposure to the anxiety-provoking stimulus of food and prevention of the avoidance or escaping response or self-induced vomiting, otherwise known as exposure with response prevention.

Rosen and Leitenberg (1982) reported the first empirical evaluation of exposure techniques with women suffering from bulimia nervosa. According to this model, eating (especially bingeing) elicits anxiety in the bulimic woman due to fear of weight gain. Subsequent vomiting then negatively reinforces binge eating by reducing the fear of weight gain. Once vomiting has become established as an escape response, it becomes the force behind the sustained binge eating. It therefore follows that in this model, treatment focuses on reducing the frequency of vomiting rather than bingeing. Exposure treatment therefore involves exposing the bulimic woman to cues associated with vomiting and then preventing that response. For example, the bulimic is invited to eat as much as she can until she has a strong urge to vomit (exposure) and then to refrain from doing so (response prevention). The patient is not permitted to vomit for at least two-and-a-half hours following exposure. A therapist stays with the patient until the urge to vomit has passed. During this time the therapist discusses and challenges the patient's distorted beliefs regarding the effect of food on her body, feelings of fatness, interpersonal issues and self-esteem.

Thakwray et al. (1993) compared behavioural and cognitive-behavioural treatments for bulimia nervosa. Their study examined the relative efficacy of the two approaches for the treatment of bulimia nervosa. Female bulimics were randomly assigned to CBT, behaviour therapy or attention placebo conditions. At follow-up, 92% of the CBT group and 100% of the behavioural therapy group were abstinent from binge eating and purging. At six months' follow-up, 69% of the cognitive-behavioural group and 38% of the behavioural group were abstinent from binge eating and purging. The authors argue that such results would support the conceptualization of bulimia nervosa as a multifaceted disorder that is best treated with an approach that directly addresses maladaptive cognitions, problematic behaviours and the development of more adaptive coping skills.

Behaviour therapy is seen to be helpful in treating bulimia, especially if it is part of a comprehensive treatment programme, because it can be successful in breaking the vicious cycle of bingeing and purging. The disadvantage of this approach is that it places minimal emphasis on the patient's body image, low self-esteem, feelings of helplessness and the loneliness and shame felt as a result of their maladaptive behaviour (Martin, 1990). However, Martin argues that deficits in these areas can be examined in occupational therapy.

Psychodynamic approaches

Psychodynamic theories of bulimia see a basic deficit in self-regulation in which the patient uses her bingeing, vomiting and dietary restrictions to help internal tension regulation and self-definition. Schwartz (1986) argues that food is viewed as the semi-symbolic equivalent of the oral mother and that for the bulimic individual, the bingeing/vomiting syndrome is an expression of the introjection-projection struggles of early infancy.

Group therapy

The rationale for this psychodynamic approach in the treatment of bulimia nervosa is that insight is gained, defences are neutralized and underlying conflicts can be explored. However it is generally agreed that group therapy may be best suited to those patients who have established some degree of control over their eating problems. Group therapy is becoming more popular as a treatment approach in bulimia nervosa primarily because of the need to provide quicker and more cost-effective services. The advantage of the group is that it helps to reduce the shame, isolation and emotional disconnection associated with bulimia nervosa.

Group therapy is one of the earliest treatments for bulimia nervosa and came about through the work of Boskind-Lodahl and White (1983) using a feminist perspective. The authors reported a reduction in bingeing and purging by the end of treatment, with group members also reporting improvements in social competence, self-esteem and emotional stability. Given the intensity of group treatment, results are slow to show improvement. However, the maintenance of these results over a longer period is more impressive.

Groups have many advantages. They decrease the desperate isolation and loneliness typical of eating-disordered patients. They allow members to be helpful as well as to be helped and they offer relative anonymity for those reluctant to come to treatment. They are also useful in that members often confront other members about their behaviour and their feelings of basic worth. They gain a lot from sharing with others who have experienced the same isolation and secrecy that they have endured for many years. Groups usually have a fixed membership, follow a structured programme and meet for a fixed number of sessions. The group approach may also include keeping detailed food diaries, goal setting, group feedback, cognitive restructuring, support, discussing relationships, educating about bulimia nervosa, nutrition and medical complications. Relaxation training or assertiveness training may also be incorporated by the occupational therapist.

McKisack and Waller (1997) examined the factors that influence the outcome of group psychotherapy for bulimia nervosa. Their results indicated that no obvious advantage could be attached to any single therapeutic orientation or to the gender of therapists. The authors did, however, find that other aspects of group psychotherapy do seem to influence outcome. Better outcomes are associated with longer, more intensively scheduled groups and with the addition of other treatment components, such as individual work. Mitchell et al. (1990) reviewed the controlled studies of psychotherapeutic treatments and noted that the percentage of subjects free of binge eating and purging at the conclusion of treatment ranged from 8% to 80% with a mean of 35% to 37%. Their 12-week course of intensive group psychotherapy produced an abstinence rate of 51%.

Lacey (1983) reported on a combination of group and individual therapy used in treating bulimia nervosa. The treatment consisted of half an hour of individual therapy and one-and-half hours of group therapy per week over 10 sessions. The author found that 80% of patients had stopped bingeing and vomiting by the end of treatment, whereas 93% had stopped within four weeks of the end of treatment. There seems to be general agreement that by adding hours to therapy and by combining therapies, both can have a positive effect on treatment outcome. However, this can also make evaluating the effectiveness of group work complicated especially if patients are receiving other treatments while the group is running. Cox and Merkel (1989) comment that the majority of studies in their review failed to document or to control for such concurrent treatment. They identified twice as many studies of group treatment as of individual treatment for bulimia nervosa arguing that the group approach may be more popular due to an increasing client demand for treatment accompanied by limited treatment resources.

It could be argued that group therapy provides a unique therapeutic experience for bulimic patients to explore their difficult social and interpersonal fears. Such an approach may be particularly appropriate in working with bulimia nervosa patients owing to the secrecy and isolation that surrounds the condition. This form of treatment, however, does tend to have a high dropout rate, whereas therapists often find the sessions very frustrating and extremely hard work.

Interpersonal psychotherapy

This is a specific form of short-term focal psychotherapy with the focus on the patient's current interpersonal functioning. It was originally developed by Klerman et al. (1984) for the treatment of depression, but has since been used with some success in the treatment of bulimia nervosa (Fairburn et al., 1993a). The techniques used include focusing on current life situations, particularly interpersonal conflicts, losses, role transition and interpersonal deficits, while exploring thoughts and emotions and generating practical solutions. So whereas this treatment targets interpersonal problem areas, it does not directly address eating habits or beliefs about shape and weight. Fairburn et al. (1993a) have found that it does help to modify the underlying over-concern with shape and weight in addition to improving binge eating and purging.

Fairburn et al. (1993a) compared CBT, behaviour therapy and interpersonal psychotherapy used in the treatment of bulimia nervosa for 18 weeks. At one-year follow-up, patients receiving behaviour therapy had by far the poorest outcome, with a high dropout rate. In contrast, patients in the other two groups made equivalent, substantial and lasting changes across all areas of symptoms, although interpersonal therapy took longer to achieve its effects.

Combination of treatment approaches

Two treatments that have attracted particular attention are pharmacotherapy and CBT. Koran et al. (1995) have shown that 15 sessions of

CBT combined with desipramine for 16 weeks are superior to both CBT alone and desipramine alone in producing abstinence from binge eating and purging at 16 weeks. Agras (1994) also found a combination of CBT and psychopharmacological treatment to be more effective on eating variables. Combining drugs and other treatments are now beginning to emerge as being valuable in the treatment of bulimia.

Brambilla et al. (1995) treated 15 women suffering from bulimia nervosa with a four-month course of combined CBT, nutritional and antidepressant therapy. They found that with this combination of treatments, the eating-disorder symptoms improved and scores for depression and anxiety decreased. Combined treatments have shown substantial benefits, particularly in the short-term, but their ability to produce lasting change is the key issue particularly as bulimia nervosa tends to run a chronic course.

Self-directed manuals

Self-help manuals are becoming more popular. Schmidt et al. (1993) provided a patient-administered handbook proposing that it may be a useful first intervention in the treatment of patients with bulimia nervosa. This problem-orientated handbook incorporated nutritional education, self-monitoring, goal setting, assertiveness skills, problem solving and relapse-prevention strategies. The results of those twenty-eight patients provided with this cognitive-behavioural handbook were favourable. On a clinician-rated global improvement scale, 12 patients had much improved and eight patients had somewhat improved. Fifteen patients were free from vomiting or laxatives at reassessment as opposed to only five patients before treatment. Of the 21 patients who were bingeing before treatment, seven had a 75% to 100% reduction in binges and five had a 50% to 75% reduction in bingeing. The authors state that the patients' nutritional knowledge also increased significantly through this form of treatment.

Cooper (1993) and Treasure and Schmidt (1993) have produced two manuals which contain a guided self-help strategy, which can be used with or without professional help, and it could be that these manuals prove to be helpful for mild or uncomplicated cases. Treasure et al. (1994) carried out a controlled trial of their therapeutic manual. The 81 subjects in their study were randomly assigned to one of three groups: the manual group, the CBT group or a waiting list group. Results indicated that CBT produced a significant reduction in the frequency of binge eating, vomiting and other behaviours used to control weight. The manual group showed significantly reduced frequency of binge eating and weight control behaviours (other than vomiting) and there was no change in the group on the waiting list. Full remission was achieved in 24% of the group assigned to CBT, 22% of the group who used the manual and 11% of the waiting-list group.

Cooper et al. (1994) presented findings on eighteen patients treated with a therapist-administered CBT self-help manual and found that, at four-to-six months follow-up, 50% of patients had ceased bulimic episodes and self-induced vomiting and the remainder had significantly improved. The frequency of bingeing and vomiting decreased by an average of 85% and 88% respectively. What is of interest is that the patients felt that this self-help format of treatment was highly appropriate to their needs. The authors argue that since loss of control is central to bulimia nervosa, then a therapeutic approach that directly places responsibility for treatment in the hands of the patients, has the dual effect of immediately addressing the issue of control and receiving credibility with patients.

A self-directed treatment manual may be a useful first intervention in the treatment of bulimia and, for some, it could prove to be all that is required. Alternative forms of treatment now need to be examined since specialist treatments, which are very time consuming, are not always available. This, coupled with an increasing number of referrals of patients with bulimia nervosa, is putting a strain on clinical services.

Psycho-educational treatment

This approach is based on the understanding that bulimic behaviours can be reduced by giving the patient a comprehensive understanding of issues relating to the disorder, such as weight regulation, dieting, obesity, cultural factors and medical complications. This treatment also offers practical recommendations and techniques for controlling bingeing and vomiting, normalizing eating habits, addressing difficulties with self-esteem and self-image and relapse prevention. Psycho-educational groups are now being used more frequently and are found to be effective. These groups often include assertiveness training, self-monitoring, relaxation training, goal setting, increasing awareness of negative thoughts as well as providing practical advice.

Nutritional education is an integral component of CBT. Meal planning, encouraging a pattern of regular eating and discouraging dieting are all part of the first stage of this intervention, in addition to educating about body weight regulation and the adverse effects of dieting. The patient's ability to establish a pattern of regular eating is seen as the central element of the programme. This would normally consist of three planned meals, plus two or three planned snacks per day. Patients would also be encouraged to limit the quantity of binge food in the house and not to go shopping when they are hungry. It is also important that they sit down to eat and do not become distracted by doing other activities while still eating. Patients are discouraged from eating too little as this results in hunger, thus encouraging binge eating. However they are asked to incorporate some of their forbidden foods into their diet.

A psychoeducational approach is frequently incorporated in behavioural procedures. Olmsted et al. (1991) compared a brief four-week group using a psychoeducational approach with a longer individual CBT programme. The educational components of the two approaches were the same. The results indicated that the CBT approach was associated with a significantly greater reduction in vomiting frequency (81%), the psychoeducational approach indicated a reduction of 55% and both were associated with significant reductions in bingeing and vomiting.

Katzman et al. (1986) describe an educational programme which consists of exercises that the authors see as 'helping women to feel better about themselves'. Their programme consists of seven weekly 90-minute group sessions focusing on a particular topic, such as coping strategies, self-esteem, perfectionism, depression, anger, cultural expectations of thinness for women and enhancing body image. The authors encourage the developing of new skills rather than focusing on the eating behaviour. Each group member receives a treatment packet containing reading materials, exercises and homework. The purpose of this book is that it can also be used as a self-help guide at the termination of the programme. The authors propose that by emphasizing building skills, they encourage women to take responsibility for their own behaviour that in turn helps to promote change.

Psycho-educational principles are, on the whole, used as an adjunct to treatment rather than as a separate therapeutic approach. They are also more likely to be effective for bulimia nervosa patients with less psychopathology.

Family therapy

Very few studies have examined the use of family therapy to treat patients with bulimia nervosa. Russell et al. (1987) carried out a major study of the treatment of anorexia nervosa and bulimia nervosa and found that patients showed little improvement with family therapy. This study was marked by a high dropout rate (44%) and an unusually poor outcome (only a 9% abstinence rate), especially in adult patients. However the treatment had previously been advocated for anorectics and it is true to say that patients with bulimia nervosa differ in many important respects from anorectics and consequently their treatment needs will also probably differ. It should not be assumed that effective treatments for anorexia nervosa will automatically prove to be effective for bulimia nervosa.

Studies in family therapy are very small in number, despite the fact that a great deal of psychopathology has been noted in the families of bulimic patients. Schwartz et al. (1985) used a structured out-patient family treatment programme for 30 bulimic patients and their families. The programme was divided into three stages for an average of 33 sessions over nine months. The goals of the family therapy were to create a context for change, challenging patterns and expanding alternatives, while consolidating change. The authors found that by the end of treatment 66% of the 29 patients who completed the study were seen to have improved in controlling their symptoms and were bingeing or vomiting either not at all or once per month.

Dodge et al. (1995) suggest that family therapy is effective in alleviating the symptoms present in adolescent bulimia nervosa especially for laxative abuse and self-induced vomiting. The authors argue that symptom changes in bulimia nervosa go hand-in-hand with an improvement in the patient's psychological wellbeing and social adjustment. They describe family therapy for eight adolescent sufferers of bulimia nervosa. Dodge et al. (1995) measured change by assessing symptomatic behaviour and global measures of family and social function prior to treatment and again one year later. At reassessment there was a significant reduction in bulimic behaviours, although some individuals still had continuing symptoms.

Family therapy aims to reduce the enmeshment of family members while enhancing the individualization of the bulimic member. It provides the opportunity to discuss the issues of appearance, style and body image with mother and daughter (Martin, 1990). These issues are also reflected in the occupational therapy programme.

Light therapy

Winter worsening of mood and eating symptoms similar to seasonal affective disorder is reported in patients with bulimia nervosa. Lam et al. (1994) assessed the effectiveness of light therapy for treating bulimia nervosa in a study of 17 patients. They found that bright white light therapy was an effective short-term treatment for both mood and eating disturbances associated with bulimia nervosa, although the therapeutic effect may be greater in those patients with a seasonal pattern.

Dropouts

Group CBT is becoming a very popular form of treatment for bulimia since it has been seen to be a highly cost-effective method of treating the disorder. Unfortunately the dropout rate from group CBT is relatively high ranging from 0% (Schneider and Agras, 1985) to 47% (Lee and Rush, 1986). This dropout rate is higher than that found in individual CBT for bulimia nervosa where Garner (1987) reported an average dropout rate across studies to be 15.3%.

Blouin et al. (1995) have also examined dropout rates in CBT group treatments. The purpose of their study was to identify predictors of dropout rate in a structured time-limited educational and CBT group programme for bulimia nervosa. The dropout rate was found to be 28.7%. The only factors that the authors found would discriminate dropouts from completers was the bulimic's difficulties in trusting and relating to others. The authors did not find the dropout rate was affected by depression.

There is also a problem of dropouts in psychopharmacological studies in bulimia nervosa ranging from 57% in an eight-week trial of phenelzine reported by Walsh et al. (1984) to 14% in a comparable six week trial of imipramine conducted by Pope et al. (1983). Several other authors have reported on the high dropout rates (Walsh et al., 1997; Sabine et al., 1983). This high rate is argued by Margitta et al. (1986) to be greater than that seen in other psychopharmacological studies conducted on out-patients with depression

McKisack and Waller (1996) examined dropouts among 15 women who attended group therapy for bulimia nervosa and who completed measures of their eating psychopathology and other characteristics at the outset of the group. The women who completed the group were compared with those who did not and the proportion of sessions attended was correlated with the women's pre-treatment characteristics. The results indicated that poor attendance appeared to be related to the group not addressing the women's immediate wishes (weight loss) whereas good attendance was associated with more severe levels of bulimic pathology.

The subject of premature dropout poses a problem for the whole group in group therapy. Patients who terminate prematurely do not benefit from the therapy but it also affects the cohesiveness of the group (Martin, 1990). Merrill et al. (1987), in looking at dropouts, indicated that certain demographic information, feelings of tension and anxiety and self-statements of subjects could be useful in predicting those patients who would remain and those who would drop out of group treatment. They also found that other measures, including binge/purging frequency and depressive symptoms were not useful in discriminating between the dropouts and persisters. The authors found that the dropout subjects tended to be younger than persisters, were less likely to be employed and less likely to be married or sexually active and had less obvious physical tension and more positive cognitive beliefs than the persisters. The dropouts' lack of commitment to the therapy process could be a reflection of their lack of commitment in other spheres of their lives. However, the level of experience of the therapist was also associated with persistence, and those groups that had the highest level of therapist experience also had the lowest dropout rates. Patients' reasons for premature termination were that they did not feel they could be helped and that they did not feel they belonged in the group.

Methodological limitations

Pharmacotherapy studies have been shown to be beneficial in treating bulimia but few of the studies have systematically examined the mainte-nance of the patients' improvement. No one has reported on the effects of drug discontinuation, although the side effects, poor compliance, suicide risks or preference for other treatments often preclude the use of medica- tion with these patients. Some drug trials fail to include a pill placebo and some treatments, when being compared, can be unequally weighted in terms of global amount of therapist contact. There can also be ethical constraints against randomization to inactive treatment versus treatments of established efficacy. High dropout rates, especially in treatments were patients feel they are not improving, can also significantly compromise the data collected.

When looking at the data on treatment approaches it is necessary to view some with caution since a lot of the data rely heavily on self-reports. Independent outcome measures and control groups are not always used. Small sample sizes, the differing populations from which subjects are drawn, the possibility of subjects receiving other concurrent treatments, the varying follow-up periods and the comparability of treatments are all methodological limitations that need to be considered when examining the research regarding the effectiveness of group treatment. It is very diffi- cult to compare group studies accurately as there will be differences not only in patient populations but also in measuring improvements while allowing for subtle differences in treatment approaches. It could be argued that there is a significant role for group therapy in treating bulimia because behaviour can be measured and seen to improve in terms of a reduction in bingeing/purging episodes. However psychological improve- ment is harder to measure when looking at improvements in self-esteem and attitudes to food, eating, mood and body image.

Little attempt has been made to study long-term maintenance of change and this is important since bulimia nervosa tends to run a long and chronic course. The current state of the National Health Service and the need for fund-holders to feel they are getting value for money means that some form of cost-effectiveness of treatments needs to be implemented for bulimia.

Chapter 13
Complications and outcomes

Bulimia nervosa is viewed as a serious disorder as it can lead to potassium depletion and other physical complications such as swollen salivary glands and deterioration of tooth enamel. The resulting loss of body fluids and electrolytes may lead to muscle weakness or even paralysis, ECG abnormalities, tetanus or epileptic seizures. Bulimia nervosa patients have died from cardiac arrest induced by a severe depletion of potassium. Bulimia nervosa differs from anorexia nervosa in that medical complications result from different sources. Most complications in bulimia nervosa occur as a result of bulimic behaviours, most notably binge eating and purging. Problems and complications of the disorder can be found in all the body's major systems.

Endocrine system problems often involve disturbance of menses. Some patients may experience amenorrhea and others may have menstrual irregularity, which can occur even when the individual's weight is within a normal range.

Gastrointestinal side effects are very common and relate mostly to the direct effects of vomiting or laxative abuse. Swollen parotid glands, abdominal cramps, bloating, constipation and diarrhoea are all common. Other more serious, but less frequently found problems have been described by Woodside (1995). These include the loss of the gag reflex, oesophagus-related difficulties such as ulceration or perforation and stomach-related difficulties such as slowed gastric emptying, spontaneous or reflex regurgitation, gastric and duodenal ulcers and even stomach rupture. Laxative abuse may lead to loss of normal bowel function with consequent constipation and bleeding.

Cardiovascular side effects are very serious as they probably represent the most common causes of death in bulimia nervosa. Purging either by vomiting, laxatives or diuretics causes a significant loss of potassium, which can cause severe arrhythmias. Direct myocardial damage can result from nutritional deficiencies.

Electrolyte abnormalities and dehydration are frequent complications of purging. Electrolyte balance is essential for the proper functioning of the body's major systems – particularly the cardiovascular system. Abuse of diuretics is serious as it can be accompanied by eventual renal impairment. Dental problems and gum diseases occur frequently in the bulimic nervosa sufferer who vomits. Erosion of tooth enamel and increased cavities are also common due to the gastric acid that is found in the mouth from vomiting, but is also due to the increased intake of sweets. These dental problems can all develop within six months of the onset of bulimia nervosa (Harwood and Newton, 1995). The dental practitioner can potentially be the first healthcare worker to make a diagnosis of bulimia due to the characteristic dental signs of tooth substance loss.

Other easily recognized complications found following vomiting include a very sore throat, swelling of the lateral parts of the cheeks and calluses over the dorsum of the hand as a result of the repeated friction of skin against the incisors. However, many of the medical problems (except the dental erosion) can be corrected and reversed if the bulimic behaviour ceases and a more normal eating regime is instigated.

Outcome and predictors

Outcome data on bulimia nervosa vary tremendously, making any comparison of results across studies very difficult due to difference in outcome definitions, diagnostic criteria, duration of follow-up intervals and methods of assessment. The definitions of recovery used in studies of bulimia nervosa vary greatly. Some researchers consider a patient who binges and purges once per month as recovered, whereas others define recovery as complete abstinence from bingeing and purging. Improvement does not always equal cure since a patient can improve from bingeing ten times a day to ten times a week but, although she is 85% better, she cannot be classed as 'cured'. The nature of the illness can result in the patient having long periods of normal eating in between long episodes of bingeing and purging (Martin, 1991).

The most commonly assessed outcome domains in bulimia have been mortality, weight, eating behaviour, menstruation, psychological functioning and psychosexual functioning. Treatments for bulimia are more promising than for anorexia nervosa. What is apparent is that bulimia nervosa patients do tend to improve over time, both in clinical and non-clinical settings. The overall recovery rates range from 13% to 71% (Herzog et al., 1988; Keller et al., 1992; Lacey, 1983; Theander, 1985). However most bulimics have a fluctuating road to recovery with full relapse occurring in 30% to 40% of individuals.

Follow-up studies of bulimia first appeared in the literature in, 1983 and indicated varying rates of recovery. Swift et al. (1987) carried out their follow-up study of 30 hospitalized patients who were assessed for outcome in terms of bulimic symptomatology, nutritional status, menstrual status, psychiatric outcome, psychosexual outcome and psychosocial outcome. The subjects were followed up for two to five years using semi-structured interviews and psychometric measures. The results indicated that the majority of the patients continued to report bulimic behaviour at follow-up, although the intensity of the symptoms was greatly reduced. The authors argue that the outcome in bulimia is heterogeneous in that, while some patients are symptom-free, others remain severely afflicted.

The treatment undertaken can also influence the outcome of the disorder. Fairburn et al. (1995) carried out a prospective study of outcome in bulimia nervosa and the long-term effects of three psychological treatments. They concluded that the longer term outcome of bulimia nervosa very much depends on the nature of the treatment received. Patients who receive a treatment such as behaviour therapy, which only has a short-lived effect, tend to do badly, whereas those who receive treatments such as cognitive-behavioural therapy or interpersonal therapy have a better prognosis. Cooper et al. (1996) measured the progress of 67 patients who completed a course of self-help. Three-quarters of those who persisted with the programme of supervised self-help were followed up a year after commencing treatment. The authors found that clinical gains were well maintained with almost two-thirds being abstinent with respect to both bulimic episodes and self-induced vomiting. For those subjects who had a poor outcome or dropped out of treatment, the authors found they were more than twice as likely to have had anorexia nervosa in the past and were somewhat more likely to have a personality disorder.

Keel and Mitchell (1997) reviewed 99 studies that conducted follow-up assessment with bulimic subjects at least six months after presentation. They found that the mortality rate due to all causes of death in the 88 studies varied between zero and 3%, or seven deaths in 2194 subjects. Five to ten years following presentation, approximately 50% of subjects were fully recovered from their disorder, while nearly 20% continued to meet the full criteria for bulimia nervosa. Approximately 30% of women experienced relapse into bulimic symptoms although risk of relapse appeared to decline four years after presentation. The authors found few prognostic factors that could be consistently identified although personality traits, such as impulsivity, may contribute to poorer outcome. While treatment intervention may hasten eventual recovery, the authors argue that they do not seem to affect outcome five years or more following presentation.

Fallon et al. (1994) examined the relationship between three factors: childhood trauma, family environment and parental psychopathology on the long-term outcome of bulimia nervosa. The 52 subjects were followed up from two to nine years after hospitalization. The results indicated that childhood physical abuse and a family environment characterized by low cohesion and high control were significantly associated with poor outcome. Characteristics of the family environment did appear to have a greater influence on outcome than physical abuse alone. Sexual abuse, the authors found, was not associated with co-morbidity and they concluded therefore that aspects of the family environment of childhood may contribute to the course of the disorder.

Most studies include follow-up of at least one year and show a consistent rate of relapse usually in the 30% to 50% range, with no clear pattern of predictors of relapse. Factors cited range from poor self-esteem, to binge frequency, to disturbed attitudes toward weight and shape. Co-morbidity with alcohol or drug abuse is also quoted as an adverse risk factor. However, perhaps the most interesting result from all of the studies is the lack of clearly identifiable predictors of outcome despite exhaustive examination of rather large samples. Olmsted et al. (1994) reported a substantial relapse rate of 31% in a two-year follow-up study of 48 patients who had participated in an intensive day treatment programme. Moreover, the majority of relapses occurred by the end of the sixth month following discharge. Those patients who were younger had a higher vomiting frequency and were less trusting of others and were more likely to experience a relapse, whereas those who had a high binge-eating frequency were more socially maladjusted, more depressed, had lower self-esteem and were not as likely to have a relapse.

Collings and King (1994) carried out a 10-year follow-up of 50 patients with bulimia nervosa. They reported that 52% had recovered fully and only 9% continued to suffer the full syndrome, whereas 39% continued to experience some symptoms. Significant predictors of favourable outcome were younger age of onset, higher social class and a family history of alcohol abuse. The authors argue that outcome for the disorder continues to improve over ten years with the majority of patients eventually making a full recovery or suffering only moderate abnormalities in eating attitudes.

Prognostic indicators

Blouin et al. (1994) looked at the prognostic indicators of short-term outcome in 69 women with bulimia nervosa. They found that the only significant predictor of improvement in binge frequency and bulimic cognitions was family environment. Conflicted, controlling and over-organized family environments appeared to impede both reductions in binge frequency and changes in bulimic cognitions. A greater reduction in vomit frequency was attained by patients who were less likely to use laxatives or diuretics and by patients with lower past and present weights. The experiences of having used laxatives or diuretics and having been at a higher weight appear to be directly associated with poor prognosis in terms of reducing vomit frequency.

A group of 39 patients with bulimia nervosa was studied by Fahy and Russell (1993), who assessed them at the end of an eight-week course of CBT and again at one-year follow-up. The patients who had a poor clinical response at the end of treatment had greater pre-treatment symptom severity, a lower body mass index and were more likely to have personality disorders. Poor response after one year was associated with personality disorder, pre-treatment symptom severity and a longer duration of illness. Authors concluded that patients without the poor prognostic indicators were more likely to respond to brief psycho-educational intervention, whereas those with poor prognostic indicators were more suited to intensive psychological, pharmacological and experimental treatment approaches.

The ability to identify variables that are predictive of outcome can influence the type, intensity and duration of treatment. Commonly assessed prognostic factors include age at onset, the presence of co-morbid disorders, psychosocial functioning, weight at referral and eating and weight loss behaviour. However, no single factor has been shown to be able to consistently predict outcome. Davis et al. (1992) found several clinical variables that are associated with outcome in their five session psycho-educational groups. They noted that greater depression, higher frequency of vomiting and a history of low adult bodyweight predicted poorer outcome as measured by changes in bingeing and purging frequency. Turnbull et al. (1997) found that a longer duration and lower binge frequency at the beginning of treatment were predictive of a better outcome both at the end of treatment and at 18 months follow-up. The authors suggest that those with more frequent bingeing may require a more intense intervention, whereas those who have been ill for longer may be more motivated to respond to treatment.

In summary, those factors that have been found to be predictive of poor outcome include:

- frequency of vomiting;
- severity of eating pathology;
- extreme weight fluctuations;
- impulsivity;
- existence of co-morbid disorders;
- low self-esteem;
- suicidal behaviour;
- abuse of alcohol;
- having previously suffered from anorexia nervosa;
- high level of personality disturbance.

Factors that are predictive of a good outcome include:

- earlier age of onset of bulimia nervosa;
- higher social class;
- motivation for change;
- friendships.

It would also appear that by extending the follow-up period it seems to increase the probability of achieving a good outcome, particularly since bulimia nervosa can follow a rather fluctuating path before full and lasting recovery is achieved. Sohlberg et al. (1989) also found this to be the case in their study. At two-to-three-year follow-up, 45% of the group had improved, whereas, at four-to-six-year follow-up, 85% had improved. This would suggest that extending the follow-up duration allows for the improvement of slower recovery patients.

The chronic patient

Bulimia nervosa is often a chronic disorder characterized by multiple episodes of relapse and remission. Keller et al. (1992) found a bimodal pattern of relapse, with an increased probability of relapse at nine to 18 weeks and again at 36 to 46 weeks following recovery. Olmsted et al. (1994) found that the variables contributing to relapse were older age, frequent pre-treatment vomiting, preoccupation with food, as well as post-treatment dissatisfaction with body image, interpersonal distrust and continuing frequent vomiting. It is true to say that the longer a patient suffers from bulimia nervosa, the poorer the outcome of treatment and the worse the prognosis will be. Long-term follow-up of patients with chronic disorders is crucial in order to determine predictors of outcome and refine intervention strategies.

Those at high risk of death from medical complications are those who indulge in purging by multiple methods – including vomiting, laxative and diuretic abuse. Russell (1979) has commented on the great danger of suicide in bulimia nervosa patients. More deaths from the disorder may also go unrecorded for, unlike anorexia nervosa, the patient does not present as underweight and a death of cardiac failure is usually recorded. Frequently neither friends nor family are aware of the condition in the individual.

Methodological issues

Reliable data are not easily obtained since these patients can be very secretive about their eating behaviour and relatives are not usually aware of the extent of the illness and cannot help with information. In looking at the accuracy of data in measuring the outcome of the condition there is often a discrepancy in the reliability of the baseline for the bingeing/purging episodes. This is further complicated by relying on patients' recollection as opposed to a proper assessment period where food intake and bingeing/purging behaviour is measured prior to the commencement of treatments. Methods of assessing the outcome of eating symptoms include self-reporting by the patient. This, in itself, is often subject to error as patients may either underestimate or overestimate their symptoms in an effort to please or frustrate the therapist. More research on the outcome of bulimia nervosa would help improve the definitions used for recovery and relapse, help to standardize the methods of assessment and lengthen the follow-up period. Research in measuring outcome should also examine the patient's social relationships and mood, as well as the other factors relating directly to her eating in order to gain a full picture of the measure of her improvement. Areas that need to be examined include self-perception, depression, anxiety, social skills and self-esteem.

PART 3
A sociocultural perspective on food and eating disorders

Chapter 14
A sociocultural perspective on food

The sociology of food and eating is now becoming an area of research interest. This could be due in part to our increasing awareness of nutritional problems, such as world hunger, which we hear about almost daily in the media. However, it could also be due to our increased awareness of the rising prevalence of eating disorders in our society. These disorders are attracting more and more attention as they are discussed publicly by well-known personalities who confess to suffer from, or have suffered from, either anorexia nervosa or bulimia nervosa.

There are very few sociological studies on the role of food in British households. Research by sociologists into food and eating have, for the most part, focused on a concern with social welfare and the unequal distribution of nutrition with early examples including Seebohum Rowntree's *Poverty : A Study of Town Life* in 1901 and Reeve's *Round About a Pound a Week* in 1913. Warde and Hetherington (1994) collected information about food preparation, the place of food in domestic routines and aspects of food preferences. They argue that, despite extensive debate on the changes that have taken place in the social aspects of food practice, such as men's participation in food preparation, the concept of 'grazing', the distribution of tastes for new foods and the increase in dining out, that any conclusions drawn are for the most part still purely speculative. Much of what we know about British food habits is derived from market research that concerns itself almost exclusively with nutrition and statistics from the food industry. Sociological studies are very limited in their investigations regarding the role of food.

Nowadays, when we overeat, the health experts tell us that too much food is bad for us, while morally we are told it is bad for our souls. By their mid-twenties 31% of men and 27% of women are said to be overweight to the point of incurring a health risk. However, even our most gargantuan dinner today is but a mere snack compared to the huge meals consumed by the upper classes in Edwardian times. Breakfasts alone would consist of porridge (with cream of course), bacon, ham, sausages, kidneys and kedgeree as part of 'the cooked' breakfast, whereas the cold table included pressed beef, ham, tongue, pheasant, grouse, partridge and fruits such as peaches, melon and soft fruits before finishing with bread, scones, honey and jams. Lunch consisted of eight courses and dinner of 12 courses and, during the day, when drinking tea, there was always the accompaniment of scones, sandwiches and cakes. So, really, for the Edwardian upper classes life was one long binge! However, could it be said that they had bulimia nervosa?

There is an assumption that most people eat only as much as they need; however, the literature through the ages from the Bible to the present day highlights that this is not the case as we have always been tempted to eat more than is necessary. What we eat will be determined by social and economic circumstances. Approximately 25% of household expenditure is devoted to food but this can increase with greater economic wealth as the higher social classes spend more on fresh foods such as fruit, meat and fish. People also spend less time cooking, so we are to a certain extent rejecting the abundance and variety of food that is now available to us in the Western world.

The meaning and role of food

Behaviour around food is intimately connected with issues of domestic divisions of labour, gender, and with household relationships. The preparation and eating of food is central to a household's organization. Murcott (1982), while examining the meaning of food, carried out a study that investigated the significance of the cooked dinner. This she found was represented by 'a proper meal' – that is, meat, potatoes, vegetables and gravy. She argues that not only is the cooked dinner of social importance but it is also of symbolic significance. Family and other household members share a cooked dinner, although Murcott found that, among the working class, a dinner only ever included direct family members. The idea of 'a proper meal' is seen as the idea of a 'proper' family life. However the concept of 'a proper meal', when the whole family sits down together, is changing as more children are having school meals or, if the mother goes out to work in the evening, then the father cooks for the children. Murcott argues that the cooked dinner symbolizes the home, the husband's relation to it, his wife's place in it and their relationship to one another.

Charles and Kerr (1988) have studied several aspects of the family food system in England. They found that 'a proper meal' was not only defined by its contents but included other parameters. The way the meal was eaten and who was present were also issues of importance. 'The proper meal' should ideally include all the family and would be cooked by the mother in the household for all its members. However, their study revealed that only 85% of households reported a daily family meal and it would appear that an increasing number of families are moving towards eating more snacks. It could be argued that 'the proper meal' itself is in decline as more people enjoy 'eating out' or 'fast food'. This increase in restaurant eating is significant in that it reduces domestic labour resulting in the work of the household being transferred to the formal market sector of the economy. Restaurants, pubs, cafes and take-away food outlets accounted for 3.9% of total household expenditure in 1988 (Family Expenditure Survey, 1988) and Warde and Hetherington (1994) found that 34% of their study bought 'take-away' meals at least weekly.

Warde and Hetherington (1994) found that those in their survey viewed 'the proper meal' as one taken with all of the family sitting around the table and talking to each other. 'The proper meal' consisted of meat, occasionally fish, potatoes and vegetables and is referred to as the main meal of the day. Women see 'the proper meal' as a healthy meal. Sunday dinner was seen as 'the proper meal' *par excellence*. It is a meal cooked by the woman for the rest of the family. Sunday roast dinner is seen as an important part of family life. It symbolizes a family day at home on Sunday. Often if the husband is absent, the woman will not cook 'a proper meal' for herself but will replace the main meal with a snack meal.

Meals that are cooked for friends are usually different from those cooked for the family. They will be more elaborate, demand more preparation time, and usually include two or three courses or more. This is especially true of the higher social classes and is a display of the family's status and welcome for the guests. The presentation of the food, the plates and dishes used, and the table decorations are seen as important. Of course providing elaborate meals can also be seen as a way of impressing others as well as welcoming them.

Food can be used as a means of communication with others, which is why we eat certain food on particular occasions such as birthdays, celebrations, Christmas and other feast days. These meals are not eaten in response to hunger but are part of long-held traditions and the symbolic representation of special relationships. The Christmas dinner is fundamentally a celebration of the coming together of family members. The food is special and we over-indulge in foods that are rich and are themselves seen as high status foods. Self-indulgence, as opposed to self-denial, is the order of the day. The sharing of such food is held to signify 'togetherness'. However special feasts are also used for many other occasions such as to cement agreements, treaties and alliances as well as to help patch up quarrels and differences.

There are certain foods that enjoy a higher status than others. These include foods such as steak, cream and gateau. Red meat is in fact the most gender-based food in the British diet. It is associated with male aggression and strength whereas white meat is seen as weaker and more feminine. If we look at the Christmas turkey, the dark meat of the drumsticks is usually given to the men, whereas the women and children share the white, tender breast meat. Meat is seen in Western industrialized culture as the most masculine of food, reinforced by the advertising slogan 'feed the man meat'. MacClancy (1992) highlighted the masculinity associated with meat arguing that meat symbolizes strength and power as it is often referred to as the king of foods. It is associated with potency, improved aggression, warming our passion and producing macho men. Men going to war have their meat intake increased in an effort to take advantage of meat's virility and strength-building characteristics. During the Second World War men were given two-and-a-half times more meat than the average civilian. This, argues MacClancy (1992), made them the greatest meat eaters in the world. Vegetables on the other hand are perceived as feminine food and this is particularly so of salads as they provide a fragile, leafy addition to a meal. Fruit is not generally seen as male food. This is in part due to the concept that men's large hands cannot readily peel small fiddly fruits. Interestingly the banana is seen as the only masculine fruit, probably because it can be so easily peeled. Celebration cakes such as those eaten on birthdays and at Christmas are also seen as high status food. Puddings or gateaux that contain cream also receive a higher status position in comparison with a fresh fruit salad or yoghurt for dessert.

Charles and Kerr (1988) argue that food is important to the social reproduction of the family and that food practices help to maintain and reinforce a coherent ideology of the family throughout the social structure. However, meal provision can also be seen as representing the subordination of women within the family and cementing the idea of their position as servers. Meat avoidance is now becoming common among women with Fiddes (1991) reporting that half of all British women state that they are eating less red meat. Food can be charged with emotions. A couple's identity is reinforced by sharing a special meal together, alone and with no children. However it can also be the centre of hurt and conflict as women constantly try to make their partner happy through the food that is prepared for him and consumed by him. In this way food conveys messages and highlights social relations and divisions within the family and in society as a whole. Food reflects social status and value and the way in which it is consumed by men, women and children and between classes signifies the differences in power and status. This arises as the result of the social divisions of gender, age and class.

Women can see food as an enemy or friend. As the enemy it leads to weight gain and a move away from the ideal self but, as a friend, women can turn to it in times of stress for comfort or to relieve boredom. Food has considerable social and emotional significance attached to it, from the mother's expression of nurturance to the adolescent's expression of rebellion. The adoption of vegetarianism by a daughter can be her way of asserting her independence with the family by rejecting her mother's 'proper' meal of meat and two vegetables. Lupton (1994) argued that the parent–child relationship is characterized by a struggle for power in relation to the bodily habits of the child. Rules regarding food serve to mark the boundary between acceptable and unacceptable behaviour within the family context. A child also learns what food is acceptable to eat and what is not. It is part of growing up to learn the differences between 'good' and 'bad' food although this often results in conflict between parents and children. 'Good' food equates with vegetables, meat and milk, while 'bad' food is seen to include 'junk foods' and confectionery. 'Good' food is seen to be appropriate and civilized whereas 'bad' food is not usually associated with family meal times. However James (1990) views confectionery as 'naughty but nice' arguing that although it is nutritionally bad for you, it is conceptualized as good for you in its connotations of pleasure and enjoyable wickedness. Sweets and confectionery are seen as important to children as part of normal childhood but there are attempts by mothers to restrict their consumption to 'treats' only. So while mothers enjoy giving children these 'treats' they are also aware of the harm caused by eating too many sweets. Sweets can also be used as a reward or incentive for good behaviour. Children from social classes I and II tend to have their sweet intake restricted more than other children. Charles and Kerr (1988) found that almost half (44%) of the children received sweets on a daily basis but this was less true of social classes I and II than others (26% compared with 50%). Children were also given sweets for rewards such as producing correct schoolwork or other personal achievements. They can also be given sweets to 'cheer them up' – for example, if they have fallen or if they are distressed about something. Sweets are seen to take the pain away.

Children depend very much on others for the food they eat and are influenced by friends, parents and close relatives. Mothers are usually the main food providers so it is likely that the child will develop a similar taste to hers for food. School, exposure to advertising and children's wish to emulate their peers all have an influence on their eating behaviour.

The taste, smell and texture of food can serve to trigger memories of previous food events and experiences around food. Food is also seen as helping to maintain a couple's relationship and in expressing affection for each other but, above all, it helps to keep the man contented and happy. Food is used by women to show their love and affection. They will often prepare a favourite meal for their partner if they want to 'make-up' to him following an argument. Food prepared over a longer time and done with great care also expresses emotions of love and nurturance. So food is often cooked as a special treat and is seen as an emotional investment. Some argue that the time women spend preparing meals for their partners can be seen as symbolizing affection, whereas others see it as highlighting the unequal division of power within the family. Pride in food preparation can help raise self-esteem, especially when creativity in meal preparation has received favourable comments from others. Food preparation can therefore help meet psychosocial as well as physiological needs. The giving of food as a gift can also be quite common. Chocolates are given as a sign of affection and love, but they can also be given in a plea for forgiveness.

Food and drink are seen as a welcoming gesture to an unexpected visitor and sometimes we communicate our interests or concerns with friends by sharing a meal together. In our society a different connotation is placed on eating a meal at home and eating in a restaurant. Eating alone also has different connotations from eating with others. Food can be eaten outside the home in almost every sphere of life – school, work, sports, while travelling and during other leisure pursuits. It is now possible to eat almost every kind of food outside the home, from a snack to a complete meal. This food comes in many different forms. We now have a greater abundance of food than ever before. Most food items today can be bought cooked, packaged and ready to eat, or require only minimal reheating. This takes the total control of the ingredients and how they are prepared away from us in the food we eat. The time needed nowadays for food preparation at home has been drastically reduced due to the availability of these pre-prepared foods in all supermarkets. The introduction of the microwave oven has also paved the way for individual family members quickly and easily to prepare a meal for themselves. Does this mean, however, that the days of the family cook are numbered? This is unlikely if the family cook is the mother of young children and is also financially dependent on her husband.

There is, in fact, a change in the constitution of the meals we eat. Nowadays we tend to eat smaller meals and perhaps different meals at weekends and weekdays. Few families, for example, eat puddings or desserts on weekdays. However the family dinner is still seen as important, especially for the middle classes, but this is less so for the working classes who increasingly eat 'snack' type food on a tray in front of the television.

It is essential that future studies should examine the question of who has power over the food prepared and eaten in families as well as understanding the food beliefs of subcultures within a broader population. Within the family unit there exists a dominance of men's preferences over those of women, which signifies an expression of power. According to Charles and Kerr (1988) although men may not actually stir the cooking pot, they do control what goes into it. This can very much affect the woman in the meals she wishes to provide for her family.

Gender issues

Behaviour surrounding food is intrinsically related to the issues of domestic divisions of labour and gender and household relationships. The activities associated with food (shopping, cooking and clearing up) take up a large amount of time and are central to household organization. Charles and Kerr (1988) studied food preparation and consumption in households in North Yorkshire. They investigated the divisions of labour between men and women in shopping and cooking, their different tastes, the amount of food they and their family consumed, the use of food in daily life, in family celebrations and in entertaining. Their study highlighted the differences in the amount of labour done by men and women in the kitchen. Women did almost all of the work, although they actually had the least control over the food content of the meals as their partners' tastes dominated the family's food choice. Men were also seen to eat more of the high status food. Central to their study also was an examination of the importance to the British family of 'the proper meal'. Like Murcott (1983) before them, Charles and Kerr (1988) found that 'the proper meal' could only be cooked by a woman, primarily for a man, but had to be eaten by the whole family sitting down together at the table. They argue that men control women's activities in relation to food and drink, like those in relation to other spheres of their life. The notion of 'the proper meal' is the key to understanding the complex set of relationships that food involves for women – that is, relationships to their husbands and children, to themselves, to their own diet and to their ideas of health, fitness and goodness. Thus it could be argued that the existence of 'the proper meal' represents and reinforces the division of labour and power within the family; the wife is seen as the homemaker and the man is seen as the breadwinner. Men expect 'a proper meal' on their return from work and most women think they deserve it.

When men do take part in household tasks, including cooking, they are usually rewarded and praised for their help especially in the kitchen when they have cooked a meal, whereas women accept blame and ridicule when things are not to the family's liking. Studies of the organization of domestic labour and marital role relationships indicate that cooking continues to be dominated more by women than men. However Burgoyne and Clarke (1985), in examining couples who had remarried, noted how much more of an active role a second husband would play in cooking. The authors noted that, in many cases, this could be seen as full equality. Often conflicts and difficulties with previous marriages had been centred around mealtimes. The authors describe how some divorced men with custody of their children had adjusted to and accepted cooking since their wife's departure. For these husbands, the cooked Sunday lunch (with its logistical problems of having everything ready at the same time) was very much seen to symbolize 'normal life' continuing, despite marital separation.

Of course women identify with domestic labour and cooking and will be heard to say – 'my kitchen', 'my cooking' and 'my meals'. It goes back to how we have been brought up. Little girls will often spend time in the kitchen helping mother to cook and accepting that one day it will be her obligation, whereas men assume that their role is purely that of the breadwinner. Cooking provides definite viewpoints. It is the woman's role to see that the family is well fed, but it is often assumed that men just don't cook! Although it may be accepted that men can't cook or won't cook, for women cooking is seen as a natural thing to do and it would never be envisaged that a women would not possess cooking skills. Women see their ability to cook and provide meals for their men and children as vital.

Cooking has long been seen as woman's major task within the home. Charles and Kerr (1988) found that 88.5% of women took full responsibility for the regular day-to-day preparation of meals. When men did cook it was generally confined to the preparation of snack-type meals (which do not normally involve active cooking) or being 'in charge' of the barbecue. Most women saw cooking as their domain and did not expect or receive help from their partner. However most men only cooked if their partners were ill – a view also supported by Close and Collins (1982) who found that men saw the kitchen and home as the woman's domain and that men only cooked for the family in an emergency. If the wife continued to be ill then it is likely that a grandmother would be co-opted in to help. Men will generally only cook if they do not have a female in their household. Leonard (1980) found that men were reported as being good at helping to carry heavy shopping, or to prepare vegetables when told, to switch on the oven when told, and that they will often do the washing-up afterwards. These skills were found to exceed their cooking skills. Men will, however, cook Sunday breakfast, fry food for themselves or make chips. Men who are unemployed with a wife working will often take responsibility for cooking a family meal. However if the husband becomes employed, or the wife becomes unemployed, this stops and he reverts to expecting it to be done for him.

About 85% of all British women between the ages of 16 and 64 years are housewives, so it can be deduced that the housewife's role, which includes a high proportion of cooking, is definitely a female role and that it is probably the woman's major occupational role today. Women have not been great chefs simply because the role has never been open to them. Although women write cookery books and create new dishes, they are excluded from the status-conscious public, which prefer to be served by male subjects. Women do the day-to-day domestic food preparation but this is in contrast to higher-status cooking for the aristocracy or commercial outlets. Women are seen as cooks whereas men are chefs.

Shopping, like cooking at home, has always been seen as women's business. When men participate in shopping it is usually to drive their partners to the supermarket or to look after their children in the shopping centre while the woman does the shopping. It is not therefore surprising that women make most of the decisions on the food the family will eat. Women will also complain that their partners throw foodstuffs that they would not normally buy into the trolley and it only comes to their attention at the 'check out' when they are paying. Women take daily decisions on what food the family will eat. Nutritional education is primarily aimed at women, which increases the burden placed on them for providing foods that adhere to positive nutritional guidelines and health promotion, not just for her partner but children too. The time has now come to target men and children – both boys and girls – in order to share the burden of improving or changing the family's diet.

Cooking can be seen either as drudgery or as an intrinsically enjoyable and rewarding activity. Cooking programmes are now seen daily on the television and as a result of their popularity cooking can now be viewed as a more creative and enjoyable activity that can be undertaken by either sex. Oakley (1974) looked at housewives' ratings of six household tasks – ironing, washing dishes, cleaning, washing, shopping and cooking. She found that cooking was on the top of the list as a 'liked' task by 60% of respondents. They rated cooking as an enjoyable activity, representing a challenge to their creative talents while referring to it as a 'work of art'. Of course this creative aspect of cooking is reinforced by the advertisements and cooking articles in women's magazines in their attempt to convince the housewife that cooking is not work but a creative pleasure. However a lot of the enjoyment of cooking is lost by the fact that the woman is often doing other tasks at the same time – amusing children, washing up, attending to a baby or being restricted by time in having to pick children up from their social activities. Time spent cooking often has to compete with other priorities. The need to complete a task within a given time often produces negative attitudes to the task and this can be so of cooking – having to meet the deadlines of mealtimes. Women also have to plan meals while anticipating family needs, including lunchboxes, visitors coming, and other activities and they feel guilty if family members complain.

Food, including its buying, cooking and serving is often a major element in many violent marital relationships. From a young age girls are expected to cook for and provide a service for men. Violence frequently occurs when women appear to fail in carrying out their woman's duties, such as cooking, when men command. This is often the case even when a mother has been delayed because she is breastfeeding their new baby. Violence can result and they are frequently beaten, as Ellis (1985) reports when commenting on how the buying, cooking and serving of food can become the most tension-ridden of tasks as reported by battered women. This violence often occurs in working-class homes if the meal is not ready on time. This occurs irrespective of how late the husband returns home, even should it be in the middle of the night or three days later; he still has the expectation that a meal should be ready the minute he walks through the door. The gender division of labour therefore defines women as the servers and providers of food within the family and they do this not only for men but also for children.

In choosing food for their family women consider carefully the likes and dislikes of their children and partner while disregarding their own. In fact if the woman's preferences take precedence she feels selfish and guilty. Women deny themselves food not only to help keep a slim physique but also because they want to be sure that the rest of the family and husband eat properly, especially when financial circumstances are tight and food is in short supply. So while men and children eat, the woman does not. Women feel they are responsible for their children's healthy diet and try to provide one well-balanced proper meal a day. However children often reject this proper meal in preference to 'snack-like' meals.

Gender and age relations are also evident in the way that food is distributed between family members. Foods are seen in a hierarchy and ranked accordingly. Low status foods are usually given to children, including fish fingers, chips, baked beans and yoghurt. They are usually marketed for children, by children. High status food, such as steak, is seen as a waste to give to children. Children begin their early days with plenty of milk and milky puddings but as they get older and are able to determine food choices for themselves, they begin to eat more sweets, crisps and snack foods.

So food, as well as reflecting gender status within the family, is also indicative of age status. This is not just apparent between adults and children but also between children of different ages. There is also a gender difference in food consumption in that boys would tend to be given higher status food more than girls and this is particularly so for meat consumption. Charles and Kerr (1988) also found that boys were given larger quantities of food than girls as mothers felt they needed it to help them grow. As children become older and reach puberty it is expected that boys will require more food, whereas girls will be expected to eat less in order to fulfil the demand of the ideal slim figure. So, from an early age, girls' femininity is seen to exist in their need to eat less than boys.

There is now a shift of emphasis in schools today in that young boys are now being taught in school how to cook, alongside their female counterparts. Previously children's cooking often involved the baking of cakes and biscuits and was seen more as a form of play rather than preparation for adulthood.

It is not easy for women to be responsible for feeding children and at the same time for feeding husbands as they face a complex of contradictory obligations. They are required to keep children happy and provide a conflict-free family environment while not undermining their husbands' need for authority and power, to provide him with the foods of his choosing and to refuel him so that he can carry out a good day's work. A meal is seen as part of a proper homecoming. If a husband has been working all day then there are roles husbands and wives play on these occasions. The idea of a 'cooked' dinner to welcome a husband home highlights cultural propriety.

Women choose fresh food as being healthier than frozen food because they feel more in control of the preparation of it. Women see food that is more labour intensive as better than pre-packed or frozen foods. The proliferation of modern industrial food production has resulted in an enormous supply of foodstuffs of which a large part is convenience or fast food. At the same time it has provided the means whereby individual family members can cook and eat for themselves at times suitable to them. However the liberating potential of convenience foods has been surrounded by moral and political anxieties about the condition of the modern family and the mother's role within it. Women see any food that has had work done to it in terms of preparation outside the home as convenience foods. So food is labelled by its production process rather than its taste and nutritional value so that any labour-saving food is viewed by the woman as convenience food.

Class

It could be argued that the main determinant of dietary practices is the social organization of food production. In other words, people eat what is available to them. In the Middle Ages there were great inequalities in the social distribution of nourishment, but in all social ranks there was a fluctuating pattern of eating that was related to the insecurity of life in general but of food supplies in particular. Appetite constraint was determined by the shortage or irregularity of food supplies rather than by a desire not to eat. Upper classes were separated from lower classes by the large quantity of food they consumed. Later, in the seventeenth and eighteenth centuries, social distinction was seen more through the quality and refinement of cooking rather than through sheer quantitative stuffing. Some might argue that higher social classes have often used food as a means of distinguishing themselves from lower classes. However there have been obvious major alterations in the economies of food production, distribution and consumption, all determining what we eat. It has been argued that it is very rare (usually only at times of warfare) when the diet of the working class is of interest to the dominant social classes.

Blaxter and Paterson (1985) examined the meaning of food in two generations of working-class families in Scotland. The older generation listed the following foods as 'good' for children – 'meat, soup, potatoes and other vegetables, porridge, fish and fruit'. They were prepared simply either by baking or boiling and using no tinned or processed foods. The opposite to 'good' food was food that was seen as processed, snacks, sweets, buns or anything that substituted 'a proper meal'. A proper meal consisted of meat, potatoes, vegetables and gravy. This was in contrast to the younger generation who listed their 'good' foods as milk, eggs, fruit and vegetables with only a few naming meat, cheese, fish, soup and cereals. Some admitted to using tinned food but thought it to be not so good as the cooked meals their mothers provided. Some saw tinned foods as making people fat. If the husband did not like vegetables then the rest of the family did not eat vegetables. The younger generation substituted milk for soup as representing basic nourishment. The authors did, however, find that the health records of the younger generation, despite eating 'rubbish' food as they put it and eating more processed food, were better than the records of the older generation.

Although the working class refers to the cooked dinner as being 'a proper meal', Murcott (1985) found that among the wives of senior doctors and lawyers, there were other ranges and styles of meals that could be interpreted as proper homecoming meals. These wives recognized 'the proper meal' of meat, potatoes and vegetables, but it was of less importance to them.

Pill (1985) found that food was often seen as synonymous with fresh food and also cooked food. Working-class families also emphasized the importance of quantity in that there should be 'enough', whereas middle-class women thought more in terms of quality of food. Calnan (1990) reports that working-class households in Britain are more likely to have purchased tinned and frozen rather than fresh vegetables in the previous week, as well as white bread, full-fat milk and more sugar than their middle-class counterparts.

Food and its presentation can also signify the social status of those participating in meals. There is the belief that working-class meals will include a lot of fried foods, especially fish and chips, whereas middle-class diets are seen to be better based in terms of nutrition. Income does greatly limit the nutritional status of the diet and higher socio-economic groups are generally reported to consume a greater range and variety of foodstuffs. Class also plays a large part in determining the food we eat, with social classes I and II being more likely to attach a higher priority to the goodness of the food they eat whereas social classes IV and V are more likely to put the cost of food as their main priority. Cooking methods also show a class difference with lower socio-economic classes frying rather than baking or grilling food.

Social classes I and II eat more fresh fruit, vegetables, meat, milk and cheese; social classes III and IV consume a lot more bread, sugar and potatoes. There is a marked difference between the type of bread consumed with the upper classes using more wholemeal in keeping with the latest healthy eating trends. From medieval times, white bread has held greater prestige for the upper classes with bread getting darker the further down the social scale one progresses. However this situation is now changing as white bread is available to all and wholemeal bread is now becoming popular from the upper classes downward. The concept of the health food movement is moving to a younger, more middle-class young woman (Blaxter and Paterson, 1985). It is usually the more prosperous classes that set the trend in fashions, which usually work their way down the social scale, and this might also be the case with the concept of health food. What the middle classes eat today, the working classes will eat tomorrow. Health foods show 'nature and traditional' concepts intertwined. In advertisements we respond to the crusty 'farmhouse' loaf, 'Farmer Giles'' wholemeal pies and 'farmhouse' cheddar cheese.

Advertisements hark back to old traditional times – hand-made chocolates, the Hovis loaf and Mr Kipling's traditional cakes.

Dietary guidelines first appeared in the 1980s and recommended that we should reduce our intake of salt, sugar and saturated fat accompanied by a proposed increase in our consumption of dietary fibre. This has caused a division of the classes: we see the higher classes consuming more skimmed milk, fresh vegetables, fresh fruit and wholemeal bread (Blaxter, 1990). Social classes I and II also seem to be moving away from eating so much red meat and having more fish or chicken but this is not the case for those from more working-class backgrounds. Food ideologies such as vegetarianism also appear to be confined to middle-class families.

During pregnancy, middle-class women are more concerned with their diet while thinking in terms of a balanced and nutritional diet – more so than working-class women. Middle-class women will obtain diet information from books and independent sources and will have had some previous interest in their diet, whereas working-class women use traditional knowledge gained mostly from their mothers or other women.

Charles and Kerr (1988) found that social class appears to have more impact on men's participation in cooking than either the woman's or the man's employment. In fact men in social classes I and II are much more likely to help out with shopping and cooking than their working-class counterparts. The authors also found that shopping was especially low for men in classes IV and V and, as far as cooking was concerned, it was the skilled manual workers in social classes III who were least likely to prepare meals.

Wenlock (1986) found that children's height, which is in part achieved through a diet of high quality and quantity of food, was discovered by sociologists to be greater in those children from the higher parental social classes.

Cultural influences

'Culture' is understood in sociology and anthropology to mean all that is learned, shared and passed down through groups of human beings from one generation to the next. What we eat is to a large extent determined by cultural, social and psychological pressures. Our culture will determine the availability and limits of the food we eat as well as determining the food that is not appropriate for us to eat. Religious dietary laws will also restrict what can be eaten, how, when and with whom. Some see abstinence and in turn 'leanness' as signifying spiritual greatness, whereas others prefer 'fatness' as it equates with wealth and the ability to acquire food in abundance. Some foods can also be seen as a symbol of national culture. Food is seen as being instrumental in marking differences between cultures as well as distinguishing between self and others.

The strong influence of Western ideals may lead to a process of Westernization that is quite different from that seen in developing countries. It has been accepted that exposure to cultural and social change can, in fact, lead to significant health changes. In parts of the population in post-communist countries, an over-identification with Western ideals is now apparent and this can in fact trigger the development of eating disorders.

The terms 'overeat' and 'undereat' mean different things to different people and are influenced by our cultural background and the society in which we live. DiNicola (1990) cites the Efik of Nigeria who would send pubertal girls to 'fattening houses' in preparation for marriage and motherhood. In such cultures eating disorders in any form are the exception. Women in non-Westernized and non-industrialized societies appear to be bound to traditional social roles, which are characterized by subordination to males and restricted opportunities. These women who are offered little choice in their cultures would also appear to escape from eating disorders. Nasser (1997) argues that there are strong indications showing how cultural change, such as identification with Western ideals of slimness is consistently followed by an increase in weight and shape consciousness bringing with it the risk of developing an eating disorder.

In our capitalist society there are many avenues available to promote a pursuit of thinness. There is the huge commercial success of diet, weight loss and fitness programmes, which are generally targeted more at women than men. It could therefore be argued that selling thinness is a profitable industry. There are in fact social controls imposed on woman's appetite so that while they may recognize their appetite they are not allowed to fully satisfy it otherwise they will no longer be seen as 'attractive'. Coward (1984) argues that women are constantly taunted by mouth-watering representations of food by the media. However our culture does not allow them to partake as it demands that they retain a slender form. Coward has labelled this 'food pornography', drawing a comparison with pornography in that the pleasure is there but the satisfaction in looking is very limited and if they were to partake they would be overwhelmed by guilt and remorse. In food advertising the aim is often different for men and women. For example, an advertisement for margarine often promotes the product for men on the basis of health, but for women it is on the basis of a slender figure.

Gender roles and sociocultural expectations have been strongly linked in the development of eating disorders. This is often attributed to the continued emphasis on physical attractiveness and a thin deal for women. This results in women reporting a greater dissatisfaction with their bodies and appearance while frequently engaging in weight-control efforts. It is, however, important to distinguish between attitudes towards the importance of appearance (concern for appearance) with attitudes towards actual feelings about one's appearance (body dissatisfaction). A slim ideal is continually striven for and maintained whereas the woman knows this is expected of her through public and media images of desirable femininity. Currently the beauty ideal for the female form in Western society is about 20% underweight (Nichter and Nichter, 1991), with girls as young as 10 years wishing to be thinner and 40% reporting as having dieted sometimes or often. The authors attribute some blame for this on the 'Barbie doll' factor, arguing that from the age of three years, girls receive and fanatically play with a fashion doll that has no waist or hips but has pencil-thin legs that go on for ever. So when these girls reach 10 or 11 years old and begin to develop normal female curves they see themselves as almost obese by their fashion doll standard. Some are then forced into dieting behaviour. It is true to say therefore that the Western world has adopted an unnaturally thin female form as its beauty ideal.

The media, as they project images of the anorectic figure as the epitome of female attractiveness, conspire with patriarchal society when promoting such a gaunt and girlish image as the ideal figure. Lester (1997) argues that to be fat is seen as lazy, emotional, vulnerable, over-indulgent, sexual, needy and unmistakably female. People who are fat are seen to have 'let themselves go' and there is societal disapproval for fatness. Women feel that if they do not maintain sexual attractiveness by being thin then they will lose their husbands. Even after childbirth, women still want to have the unachievable – the pre-adolescent sylphlike shape. It is true to say that, in Western culture, the only time when it is acceptable for a woman to have a large body size is when she is pregnant and during this time women will crave for, and have, foods that they normally deny themselves. This is in contrast with other cultures where plumpness and fatness are more readily accepted. Mackensie (1980) studied the attitudes of many cultures toward body size and found that in Western Samoa the women are seen to be very large and heavy. In fact after each pregnancy it is accepted that the woman will gain and retain extra weight so that by her middle age she is rather large and, compared to our standard, would be definitely seen as 'fat'. However in Samoa these large women are admired and even envied by their community. At this stage they are allowed to take part in the dancing for the tourists and they participate devoid of any shame or embarrassment about their size because, in their culture, being fat bears no social stigma. Chen (1990) also found a fear of fatness to be absent among many anorectic patients in Hong Kong, and Khandelwal et al. (1995) also found this to be the case in India. This is in contrast to Japanese anorectics, who apparently all demonstrate a fear of fatness (Suematsu et al., 1985) and this is thought to be due to Japan being highly industrialized and as having adopted the Western cultural emphasis on slimness.

Women who have decided to 'diet' have accepted society's demands for a slimmer body so their original decision to reduce their size now becomes one of a symbolic political act. Culture rewards those who comply with its standard. It may be that when a woman loses weight she feels more attractive and finds she experiences less discrimination in her working life. There is the conflict regarding the cultural role of women today. Our culture demands passivity and dependency on the one hand, but on the other hand encourages assertiveness and dominance. Such conflicting roles can be confusing and lead some females to use their eating disturbance to control their environment. The women's self-denial through food can also have a dual role – to promote a sexually alluring physique and at the same time adopting the maternal role of always putting the family's food needs first.

Orbach (1984) argues that 'fat is a feminist issue' because of the manner in which it exemplifies resistance to the ideal. She proposes an ideal of femininity that takes account of the fact that healthy women come in all shapes and sizes, just as men do. Although men do come in all shapes and sizes, society does generally accept this broader range of physical shapes and sizes for men rather than women.

The media could help to slow down the rise in eating disorders if they adopted a more positive role by advertising products, especially food, in a different way so that what we see portrayed by the media more accurately reflects the variety of bodies – sizes and shapes – that we see in everyday life. Images and fertility figures through time have demonstrated the appropriate association of generous female curves with beauty and fertility. In our society the time has now come for us to redress the culturally acceptable debasement and ridicule of the obese and at the same time to review our feelings about female beauty and what it represents.

Religion

There is a longstanding connection between Christian asceticism and food refusal. For some religions fasting was the prime expression of asceticism. By the middle of the fifth century, dietary restriction including fasting, were common features in Christian practice. In anorexia nervosa 'asceticism' refers to self-denial, a dualistic split between the body and mind or spirit, a sexuality and heightened morality and idealism. Some anorectics come from conservative religious fundamentalist backgrounds and their desire to restrict food is based on religious principles and understandings about food, the body and sexuality provided by their religious tradition. Their self-starvation is not, in the first instance, motivated by their desire to achieve the popular ideals of thinness. The fast of Ramadan is begun and ended traditionally by a rather rich and celebratory meal. In the United Kingdom, when Ramadan occurs during the summer months, the fasting period is lengthy and there is frequently one single large meal during the hours of darkness as opposed to the usual two or more. The breaking of the fast begins with prayer and the meal itself is a ritualized family occasion. This period of Ramadan provides Muslims with a socially accepted and even expected period of fasting followed by pressures to consume rather large quantities of food. Several authors have reported that eating disorders tend to occur or worsen following this period of religious fasting (Lacey and Dolan, 1988; Bhadrinath, 1990).

Sykes et al. (1986) found a significant relationship between eating disorders and religion in 160 cases treated clinically. The aim of their investigation was to elucidate demographic information on anorexia nervosa and bulimia nervosa. The authors thought that religion was among several variables that could be related to eating disorders. The 160 subjects included 71 Protestants, 70 Catholics, 11 Jews, two of other religious beliefs and six with no stated religious preference. When the anorectic patients were considered separately from the bulimic patients, the proportion of anorectic Catholics was significantly higher than the proportion of Catholics in the general population whereas the proportion of anorectic Jews did not differ significantly from the proportion of Jews in the general population. When the bulimic patients were examined separately the results indicated that the proportion of bulimic Catholics was significantly higher than the general population, as was the comparison with the proportion of Jews in the general population. The authors feel that this higher prevalence of eating disorders among patients of Jewish and Catholic religious backgrounds could be due in part to the importance placed on food within these religious groups.

Religion can be a major factor in determining the foods that are acceptable. So whereas some foods are actively encouraged, others are prohibited. Islam and Hinduism recognize the need for regular fasting. Others see their starvation as an attempt to meet the normative ideals about controlling the body as laid down by other religious traditions. On some occasions we may abstain from food or not eat at all, as on religious fast-days.

As culture and religion play an important part in our eating habits, it is important for the occupational therapist to consider these traditions as it will encourage greater compliance from patients. It is necessary to recognize each individual's characteristic cultural patterns and the eating practices of different nationalities and religious groups. Food choices are made against the background of the society in which we live and it is possible for most dietary regimes to be organized to allow for religious beliefs.

Chapter 15
Sociocultural and feminist perspectives on eating disorders

A sociocultural perspective

The role of culture in eating disorders is of interest to psychiatrists, psychologists, feminists, historians, anthropologists and sociologists. Sociologists are interested in eating disorders as extreme symptoms of social pressures on people, especially women. The sociocultural model of eating disorders views anorexia nervosa as a response to the popular emphasis on dieting and by the demands for an aesthetic ideal that stresses youth and androgyny rather than the mature female body.

Extreme forms of self-starvation can be traced across time and place. Forms of eating disorders have existed since ancient time, varying in frequency, in manifestation and possibly in motivation. Bemporad (1996) argues that their occurrence throughout history casts doubt on the view that eating disorders are in fact a product of today's current social pressures.

In the nineteenth century the virtue of moderation and abhorrence for gluttony were emphasized by bourgeois gastronomes. The problem of fear of fatness then began to progress down the social scale so that, by the twentieth century, slimming was becoming ever more prominent. Thinness is seen not only as attractive but it is also associated with success, power and other highly valued attributes, whereas obesity is viewed as lazy, gluttonous and out of control.

Anorexia nervosa and bulimia nervosa are no longer seen simply as eating behaviours but as entrenched and extreme patterns of thinking, feeling and interacting with others. Charles and Kerr (1988) argue that while everyone can see eating as a pleasure, this pleasure is one that women have great difficulty in allowing for themselves. On the contrary, eating often induces guilt and shame in the light of the cultural definitions of what a wife should do and what a woman should look like. There is a psychological connection between a slender body and success, sophistication and self-control. Males and females differ in the importance they place on appearance, however both judge unattractiveness more harshly

It has been suggested that the gay male subculture imposes strong pressures on gay men to be physically attractive. Gay men, like women, experience extreme pressure to be eternally slim and youthful looking and are therefore just as likely to be dissatisfied with their bodies. This results in vulnerability to eating disorders. However there has been little attempt made to explain the reasons for this heightened emphasis on physical appearance in the gay male subculture. One explanation is their wish to attract and please men. Thus both gay men and heterosexual women may strive to be physically appealing in order to attract a desirable male. Siever (1994) investigated the hypothesis that gay men and heterosexual women are dissatisfied with their bodies and vulnerable to eating disorders. This is as a result of a shared emphasis on physical attractiveness and thinness that is based on a desire to attract and please men. The authors found that, whereas men place priority on physical attractiveness in evaluating potential partners, women place greater emphasis on other factors such as personality, status, power and income. Therefore lesbians and heterosexual men are less concerned with their own physical attractiveness and consequently less dissatisfied with their bodies and less vulnerable to eating disorders.

There have been few studies that have investigated lesbians and their attitudes towards physical attractiveness, their body satisfaction or the prevalence of eating disorders. On the contrary, lesbian subculture has been described as downplaying or even actively resisting the dominant cultural value placed on beauty for women. In the Siever study (1994) lesbians were seen as the least concerned about physical attractiveness, Relative to the other groups they saw it as unimportant to them in their evaluation of their partners, as well as being unimportant to their partners.

It could therefore be that there has been a recent trend towards increased pressure on men to be physically attractive as well as an increasing sexual objectification of men as can be seen in popular culture. Siever (1994) found that gay men were even more unhappy with their bodies than heterosexual women. The author argues that this could be due not just to their worry that their bodies are inadequate in terms of strength and athletic prowess, but that they may also doubt their physical attractiveness (a feeling shared by the heterosexual female). This is in contrast with heterosexual men who are more likely to see their bodies as tools with which to compete with others through strength and athletic prowess. Heterosexual women on the other hand are more likely to see their bodies as objects for aesthetic evaluation as they constantly strive to achieve the sylphlike figure of actresses and models seen in the media. However it is now possible to see, through the media, products being sold with images of lean, muscular, scantily clad young men who are now being frequently seen with slender, scantily clad young females. This pressure for the perfect body is increasing for both men and women.

in women than in men (Sprecher, 1989). Moreover, what is considere[d] attractive for women has changed through the decades. The ideal form a[s] seen in fashion magazines has become progressively thinner and les[s] curvaceous, resulting in women attempting to lose more and more weight in an effort to attain the current feminine ideal of thinness. This can, in part, account for the increase in eating disorders.

The relationship between body weight and eating behaviour has always been viewed as a direct one so that obese individuals are often rejected by society as being 'out of control' and as having no 'willpower'. Some feel they gain less respect from others. However, obesity is rare in underdeveloped countries of the world, and when it does exist it is seen as a sign of wealth and in some cases as a sign of beauty. Overweight children are often rated as the least likeable. Wooley and Wooley (1979) examined the stigma and hatred suffered by obese children and found the effect of this carried on into adult life so that the anti-fat attitudes learned in childhood formed the basis for self-hatred in those who become obese in later years, as well as provoking anxiety and self-doubt in others who live with the fear of becoming obese. In Western society, those who are fat face intense and widespread criticism for their excesses.

In childhood we love our bodies – we count on our fingers, we compete with our friends in how big we are growing and the curiosity about our bodies is endless. What happens between our contented childhood body and the anguished body of the adult female that now causes so much displeasure? It is not accepted by women that they might have a large appetite, or a body that they think could be more slender. Instead of this being accepted they put themselves through the agony of trying to reshape their body and appetite to fit what they see as the ideal. Attractive women in the nineteenth century were large women often described as 'soft, sensual and inviting'. Their voluptuousness is now no longer admired by our culture. So as children we grow to be women gradually learning to despise our bodies. Men, in fact, grow up learning increasingly to love their bodies. Think of the weight lifter showing off his body to the public as he stands wearing only a pair of shorts and showing us his ability to grow and expand in front of our very eyes.

The term 'beauty' is itself gendered as we rarely associate it with what is masculine. Mahowald (1992) argues that if thinness is an essential component of feminine beauty it is not typically related to a comparable masculine ideal. The closest parallel for men is an ideal of tallness, musculature, strength and physical fitness. In recent years women have increasingly participated in aerobic and body-building programmes in a pursuit of health and fitness. Such efforts may also be associated with a fear of fatness or a preference for thinness since those with anorexia nervosa can have a tendency to exercise with ritualistic intensity. Fitness also requires atten[t]ion to proper nutrition as well as exercise so the anorectic's practice o[f] refusing to eat is incompatible with the goal of fitness.

Brown (1989) sees the stigmatization of fatness and the glorification of thinness as constituting forms of sexism and misogyny that are used as methods to control women. Cherin (1983), however, argues that when women's role in society was focused on nurturing and mothering, the preferred female body shape was seen as more voluptuous and full. Likewise, when the woman's role became more liberated and less restricted (and more threatening to patriarchal society) as seen in the 1920s and 1960s, then women's preferred body shape became more restricted and boyish. Some suggest that eating disorders represent an acknowledgement of the low status of women's nurturing. The anorectic's goal is to avoid or escape from such a female gender role as wife and mother, which is so devalued by society.

The development of breasts and hips in female adolescents signifies the development of reproductive potential and with it comes the risk of moving from the role of dependent daughter to the independent role of mother. The anorectic sees independence without parental responsibility as an option if fertility is delayed. It is to this end that the anorectic begins her dieting in an effort to assume the body and role of the male adolescent. Elks (1994) also suggests that anorexia nervosa can occur in an effort to avoid the encumbered female adult role of wife and mother. Through weight loss, the anorectic takes on an androgynous form and role, in an assertion of her desire for independence and self-actualization as opposed to reverting to the role of dependent child. Consciously and unconsciously, females recognize that only by taking a masculine role – the role of the adolescent male – do they free themselves from the smothering relationships of being a daughter or wife and mother. Anorexia nervosa is therefore seen as regression to a childlike state. For the anorectic it is a sexless state in the absence of her normal curvaceous female form and with the accompanying absence of the menstrual cycle.

For the anorectic, thinness equates with beauty. She has been socialized to believe this equation but the same can not be applied to men. Attempts to reveal one's degree of femininity or masculinity are influenced by our understanding of societal expectations. It could be argued that the anorectic operates in a contradictory way in relation to gender role. On the one hand her obsessive pursuit of a feminine ideal of thinness highlights the insecurity in her gender identity while wanting to fulfil her perceived gender role. On the other hand her non-curvaceous body is more masculine (boylike) than feminine. The anorectic's amenorrhea provides an escape route for the monthly reminder of her femininity. So it could be strongly contested that she very much wants not to fulfil her perceived gender role. Adjustment to one's gender role is often construed as an essential component of healthy maturation; however, few would argue that eating disorders are caused by gender socialization alone. Research examining the relationship between gender role typing and eating disorders among women has provided inconsistent and often contradictory findings. There is evidence to indicate that women who adopt a superwoman ideal may be more vulnerable to eating disorders compared with those who reject the ideal and opt for prioritizing the roles in which they seek to excel (Steiner-Adair, 1986; Thorton et al., 1991).

Controlling one's weight can be an expression of women's frustrated desire to control other important issues in their lives. Are eating-disordered females more sensitive than other women to the sexism present in our society or do their lives feel under greater control by others? Cherin (1983) views the increase in eating disorders as a serious development crisis for women. This has left some women very confused as to their role in modern society especially when having to adopt the rights and prerogatives of the male in society. Some even argue that the increase in eating disorders has resulted from the rise of the feminist movement. Feminists have under-valued the once acceptable role of motherhood with its accompanying fulfilment. Women were told that they needed to go outside their home and family in order to assert themselves and achieve their potential. Minuchin et al. (1978) blame the patriarchal society while commenting on the irony of the situation that has arisen. As women have gained greater emancipation, this has come alongside a greater increase in the prevalence of eating disorders. However Steiner-Adair (1986) suggest that eating disor-ders result from a self-perception of a lack of traditionally masculine charac-teristics rather than from too many feminine characteristics. The author asserts that current social demands for women to be more 'masculine' are not always compatible with their 'feminine' socialization and this may contribute to the gender discrepancy in the incidence of eating disorders.

Lawrence (1984) argues that, while equal opportunities might exist for girls and boys in education, the same does not hold true for the experi-ence of work success and independence. Girls are socialized into a sexual identity centred on motherhood, irrespective of the opportunity to succeed in education and establish their own career. It could therefore be argued that boys are socialized into careers and girls are socialized into carers. A link has also been drawn between the increase in the prevalence of eating disorders and the increase in women graduating from university. This would support the argument that increased achievement aspirations are linked to eating disorders. However, although both of these occurred at the same time it does not necessarily mean that they are causally linked. It could also be that the pressures and stress brought about by leaving home and starting something new, like a university course, could in itself be etiologically related.

There are now conflicting pressures on today's women to achieve not only academically and professionally but also to continue to be seen as feminine and attractive. The pressures to both achieve and be attractive can be less intense for women who are not highly motivated to achieve. Lawrence (1984) is among those theorists who suggest that eating disor-ders represent attempts by successful women to escape from the negative stigma associated with women's achievements that characterize successful women as ruthless, selfish, lonely, sexually promiscuous and unmarriageable. So the conflicting demands for both success and beauty can often present an apparent dilemma. Gilbert (1993) suggests that achieving the anorectic physique can provide a means of conforming to stereotypical femininity and thereby resolving the dilemma of success versus beauty. The ability to diet and stay thin becomes an outward sign to the rest of the world that the woman is in control, even if this thinness is attained by repeated purging and exercise.

Those with eating disorders are often part of a family environment that is chaotic and conflictual. Wurman (1989) suggests that the parents of bulimics often require 'caretaking'. The author argues that the bulimic sufferer grows to feel appreciated for her caretaking abilities but not, however, for her own self. This results in a failure to develop a firm sense of identity because of her acute focus on the needs and feelings of others. The bulimic, like the anorectic, wishes to be seen as 'perfect'.

Boskind-Lodahl (1976) has noted that anorectics reported a dislike for their mothers whom they described an ineffectual and unhappy women who had rejected careers in preference to raising children. Silverstein and Perdue (1988) on the other hand, found that women who binge frequently are more likely than other women to report that (a) their parents saw a woman's place to be in the home, (b) their mothers were unhappy with their own careers, (c) their fathers thought their wives were not intelligent, (d) their father treated a male as the most intelligent sibling in the family. Such findings would support the view that eating disordered females who rate intellectual and professional achievements highly may also feel impaired in such pursuits simply because they are female.

Many authors have suggested that a fear of intimate relationships is a central dynamic in bulimia. Using the Fear of Intimacy Scale, Pruitt et al. (1992) found that, in their study, the bulimic women had significantly greater fear of intimacy than did control subjects. Feminist and psychodynamic theorists have suggested that difficulties with intimate relationships, especially with men, are a central problem in eating disorders. Jacobson and Robins (1989) tested the hypotheses that bulimic women would be characterized by a high degree of social dependency and low levels of social support and that bulimic and non-bulimic women would differ in their interaction of these two variables. A second hypothesis, based on Boskind-White and White's (1983) feminist account of bulimia was that bulimic women are characterized in particular by social dependency on men and a lack of social support from men. In the authors' study of 23 normal weight bulimics and 38 control subjects, the bulimics differed only in their reported need for greater social dependency. The authors found however that there was no evidence that bulimics were lacking in social support compared with controls. Contrary to Boskind-

White and White's (1983) theory, both groups of women reported more social dependency on men than on women but there was no evidence to suggest that bulimics were particularly socially dependent on men. However bulimics will often report that their disordered eating patterns began following some form of social loss or rejection such as, leaving home, the break-up of a relationship, or the death of a close relative or friend.

Both male domination and women's attitudes towards their bodies seem to influence the prevalence of eating disorders. This is affected by affluence. However affluence alone does not produce eating disorders since wealthy Moslem countries that exert extreme control over their women also fail to produce eating disorders. It could be argued, therefore, that eating disorders in one form or another are the price paid for Western civilization. Palazzoli (1985) argues that the higher frequency of eating disorders in affluent societies is due to the situation whereby it is only possible to display rigid self control through fasting when food is in abundance otherwise when food is scarce everyone is fasting. Others take the view that since anorexia nervosa affects mainly the affluent in our society that its prevalence could be reduced by a more equitable distribution of income.

The social value that we attach to food, health and physical beauty has risen constantly in recent decades. Those in modern industrial societies are now very aware of such things as calories, joules and the composition of foodstuffs. Today's nutritional scientists in Western countries are emphasizing the relationship between food and health and wellbeing. Much time and money has been invested in the promotion of healthy eating. Health problems have now shifted from those related to malnourishment such as rickets to those of obesity and eating disorders.

A feminist perspective

Proponents of the feminist cultural model of eating disorders and supporters of the traditional medical model of illness and treatment have been debating for some time. Feminist approaches have been offered as etiological explanations for the development and maintenance of anorexia nervosa and bulimia nervosa. According to feminist perspectives a multitude of societal pressures on women result in chronic dieting, binge/purge behaviours and hypervigilance about weight and appearance. Feminist scholarship is seen to depart from traditional methods not only in analysing for gender differences but also in recognizing the bias inherent in all scientific research. Some argue that science is biased by scientists' personal values and that scientific research has traditionally been conducted by white, middle-class males.

Feminist theory is of the view that masculine privilege and power have thwarted the strivings of women. These feminists emphasize the thin female body as a particularly powerful medium for communication, while slenderness communicates competence, self-control and intelligence it also indicates an individual with self-restraint, non-impulsive and a will to win over her body. Feminists blame eating disorders on gender socialization and propose socially corrective measures as preventative therapy. However more liberal feminists view sexism as a cause of anorexia and propose that gender stereotyping which imposes such an unequal burden on women be eliminated. If women are to be liberated so that they can develop as individuals then their choices also need to be expanded rather than restricted by an ideal of feminine behaviour or appearance. Brumberg (1988), however, has attributed the rising incidence of eating disorders to the impact of the women's movement.

The most often cited femininity theorist Boskind-Lodahl (1976) defines femininity as passivity, dependence, and a need for approval from others. She maintains that these characteristics play a role in the development of eating disorders. Boskind-Lodahl argues that these patients have an exaggerated need for approval from others, especially men, for their sense of self-worth. She views the relentless pursuit for thinness as one component of an exaggerated embrace of the feminine ideal. She sees the bulimic as having a tremendous desire to please others and bases her sense of self-worth on the approval of others. Bulimics, she proposes, expect to be rewarded by men for their striving to fit the perfect feminine role and thus are very vulnerable to rejection. As the bulimic gains her sense of self-worth through others, her resultant overdependence on others creates a self-perpetuating pattern of rejection. Bulimics also fear men because, although they desire self-validation from men, such dependence gives men the power to reject. The bulimic's eating patterns also distances her from others, both through anxiety about eating with others and also through the secretive nature of her behaviour.

Control is an important dimension that has been identified by feminist scholars who have also commented upon the growing importance of dietary control for women in Western cultures. Orbach's *Fat is a Feminist Issue* (1984) looks at feminism and women, arguing that it is the norm for women to experience distress over food and dissatisfaction with their body size. She argues that bingeing occurs because of women's natural hunger mechanism being subjected to social and psychological distortion and also because of a woman's desire to become 'thin' being undermined by her unconscious desire to be 'fat', thus providing an unconscious defence mechanism. The author sees this as a woman's response to social oppression. The body provides us with physical cues when we should eat, but bulimics eat irrespective of such cues. 'Diets' also encourage women to disregard their internal physical cues. Orbach (1984) argues that 'diets' actually encourage binge eating by forbidding certain foods that the woman feels she is not being allowed to eat. The diet's dos and don'ts, she argues, only reinforce feelings of deprivation and guilt. The author also argues that overeating and being fat is seen as the woman's rejection of being viewed as a sex object by the media and diet industry. 'Fat' can be seen as a social problem for femininity, whereas 'thin' is seen as the ideal. Women are therefore viewed as having 'weight problems' whereas fat is viewed as a 'social disease'.

Emphasis on feminine attractiveness has continued despite the changing social roles, expectations and opportunities for women that have occurred in recent decades. However these social changes have also contributed to increased stress for women as a result of the conflict between many of the competing role demands facing them in both personal and professional aspects of their lives. The expectations that a woman can be physically attractive and function as an effective wife, mother and working woman is an ideal that many women attempt to achieve but often find to be unrealistic, unattainable, undesirable and oppressive (Orbach, 1984). Hilde Bruch (1978) feels that some women view the increased opportunities afforded to them today as providing excessive demands on them. For some, these traditional and feminist ideologies create difficulties for women in that they can not find security no matter which role they adopt. It is therefore suggested that eating disorders are in fact a woman's response to the stress of these multiple pressures and conflicting demands.

Females are expected to be sweet, or as the nursery rhyme goes 'sugar and spice and all things nice'. In our society today that can be seen as compliant, amenable and co-operative. Varney (1996) argues that Strawberry-Shortcake and other food-imaged dolls that have entered the toy market since 1980 could be said to provide us with a backlash against feminism. These toys emerged in the 1980s with the release of Strawberry Shortcake but were also joined by Tonka's Cupcakes and Mattel's Popcorn Pretties. These toys are based on a female-food amalgam and highlight the social expectations that women should be like food – that is, attractive, appetising and consumable. These toys smell of strawberries, raspberries and other sweet flavours as well as being dressed in such a way as to convey the connection with food. This range of dolls promotes an image of women and food and suggests an interchangeability between the two. Varney (1996) suggests there are areas of gender relations on which these toys are founded: (a) a historical gendering of food, (b) contradictions in women's relation to food and (c) a widespread social perception of women as desirable and consumable objects. These dolls are all female with the exception of the token male – 'Huckleberry Pie' (named after Huckleberry Finn) – who was probably added for those girls who feel the need for a male companion.

Toys often present women as commodities and this is also the case with fashion dolls as they too can be linked to foodstuffs, such as Barbie's version of 'Peaches and Cream'. However Barbie does on the other hand indulge in cheesecake, McDonald's fast foods and ice-cream as we can see from her playsets – one is named 'Barbie loves McDonalds', and another is a functioning miniature ice-cream maker called 'Barbie's Ice-Cream Shop'. Since Barbie's waistline would be only 18 inches if she were scaled up to size, it can only be presumed that she keeps her trim shape by exercising at her gym. One can also only surmise that the Strawberry Shortcake dolls do not in fact eat the puddings and desserts that they cook in their kitchen, otherwise they too would be plagued by weight problems.

Some may argue that Barbie and Strawberry Shortcake dolls do not help to promote a positive view of women's role as they give out mixed messages to young children that can stick with them for the rest of their lives. Toys are seen as the tools children use in their socialization. They have a role in shaping attitudes and providing culture awareness. Food, on the other hand, is also viewed by its social connotations relating to class, culture, status and gender. Girls' toys are often linked with nature, in contrast to boy's toys, which are typically linked with machinery and destruction. Of course the question still remains: will all this affect how the women of tomorrow see themselves? Will today's girls with their Strawberry Shortcake toys think of themselves as sweet, keen cooks, who are above all else consumable?

Food used as nurturance is a global and ancient phenomenon. For bulimic women food serves as a means of self-nurturance gone awry. Cherin (1983) argues that we have only recently been trying to find a deeper meaning about woman's concern with food, eating and weight. The fact that women need to control their appetite and urges can stem from the fact that women have always been told of the need to control their emotions and passion. However all women seem to have the secret ambition to develop anorexia nervosa and to be thin; often one hears one woman saying to another 'I wouldn't mind catching anorexia nervosa for a while – I admire people who can stop eating.'

As with the anorectic, the bulimic suffers from strong sociocultural pressures to be thin and this will convince the unhappy and dissatisfied female that her weight and body shape are the problem. The feminist view of bulimia is that bulimics have an impaired sense of self and, as a result of this weakened sense of self, bulimic symptoms occur. Boskind-White and White (1983) propose that bulimics have been socialized to believe that women should strive for perfection in femininity as seen by their popularity with men. Anorexia nervosa, on the other hand, has been viewed by feminists as a consequence of a misogynistic society that demeans women by devaluing female experience, by objectifying their bodies and by discrediting women's achievement. They argue that anorexia nervosa is a protest against patriarchal values, a rigid sexual division of labour and female subordination.

There is a changing awareness of the position of women in our society. There appear to be two avenues of thinking – one is the feminist movement, encouraging greater power for women, and the second is an avoidance of it backed by those who fear women's strength, such as the dieting and fashion business. Feminist approaches to the etiology of eating disorders offer an insight to the condition and could help us in looking at preventative and treatment interventions. However feminist theories have generally excluded non-feminist theories and this has not always been helpful as eating disorders may result from the interaction of biological, familial and societal factors. To consider any of these factors in isolation is to discount the complexity of these conditions. It is also startling to note that most of the high profile writers on anorexia nervosa and bulimia nervosa in the United Kingdom are males. High-profile women are few and tend to be less concerned with quantitative research. This gendered pattern of role distribution could in itself be said to influence the clinical application with eating-disordered patients.

Chapter 16
Eating disorders in other cultures

Eating disorders were previously thought to be isolated to achievement-oriented, upper- and middle-class individuals in Western countries. It now appears that these disorders may be increasing in other sectors of society and in a number of diverse cultural settings. Eating disorders are unique as they appear to be the only form of psychopathology in which culture plays a major part in determining prevalence.

Bruch (1966) was one of the first modern investigators to suggest a relationship between sociocultural factors and the development of eating disorders. In her series of 43 patients with anorexia nervosa, there were 7 Catholics, 11 Protestants and 25 Jewish individuals. Ten of these subjects came from an upper-class background, 23 from a middle-class background and 6 individuals were from a lower-class background. However she noted a complete absence of Negro patients, despite the fact that there was a proportionate number of blacks hospitalized for other problems at the time of her study. She suggested that the main psychological conflicts in eating disorders pivoted around a struggle for control, a sense of identity and a sense of effectiveness with the final step being the 'relentless pursuit of thinness'. These attitudes she saw as stemming from the strong achievement orientations and psychological insensitivity of the upwardly mobile social and cultural backgrounds of the patients' families.

Halmi et al. (1977) found not a single well-documented case in the literature of anorexia nervosa in a black female, whereas Crisp et al in 1976 also found no black subjects in a survey of nine British schoolgirl populations. Hall (1978) found none in a similar study carried out in Australia. In contrast with these earlier findings from the 1970s, later reports from the 1980s show an emergence of both anorexia nervosa and bulimia nervosa in various ethnic groups, suggesting that eating disorders may be becoming more common in non-Western populations. Anorexia nervosa, which was often seen as a culture-bound disorder of Western Europe and North America, can no longer hold onto such an assumption since the condition is now being reported in non-Western societies such as

Hong Kong, Taiwan, China, Malaysia, India, Singapore and Japan (Lee et al., 1996; Tseng et al., 1989; Goh et al. 1993; Khandelwal, 1990; Suematsu et al., 1985). However it could be strongly argued that despite its long history of existence and the interest that it has aroused in Western nations, anorexia nervosa is comparatively understudied in non-Western populations. Those reports of eating disorders from non-Western and less industrialized European countries remains relatively uncommon although this could in part be due to epidemiological focus. When eating disorders are found in non-industrialized societies they are typically seen in the daughters of urban entrepreneurs and the professional elite (Prince, 1985).

Body image – fat phobia

Littlewood (1995) report that both anorexia nervosa and bulimia nervosa have been consistently argued to be patterns highly specific to Western and other industrialized societies where they are seen typically among young women. The major causal factor cited for this is the contemporary social pressure on young women to be both slimmer than women in other societies and slimmer than Western women of an earlier period. Evidence points to a cultural shift in European societies towards a preference for a thinner, slimmer female body form. However there is no agreement as to why this has occurred.

Powell and Kahn (1995) investigated why white women are more prone to develop eating disorders than black women. They explored the effects of race and cultural identification on women's perceived body images, ideal body image and perceived pressures to be thin. Using self-reports the authors found that white women chose a significantly thinner ideal body size than did black women as well as expressing more concern than black women with weight and dieting. White women also felt greater pressure to be thin than did black women. White men, on the other hand, showed less desire than black men to date a woman with a heavier than ideal body size and white men felt they would more likely be ridiculed than did black men if they did date a woman who was larger than the ideal. The authors concluded that black women experience eating disorders less than white women, at least in part, because they experience less pressure to be thin. Black culture is more accepting than white culture of women seen as larger than the extremely thin ideal and places less emphasis on thinness when assessing social desirability. Black culture therefore appears to protect black women from eating disorders by providing an environment where thinness is less valued. Belonging to this subgroup is likely to lead to less concern with weight and fewer eating disordered individuals.

There is now a need for a better understanding of attitudes to body shape and food within different subcultures. Cross-cultural differences in the perception of the female body have been investigated by Furnham and Alibhai (1983) who found that in some countries, where there is a scarcity of food, larger women are seen as representing family fertility and wellbeing and are liked by themselves and their male relatives. This was the case in the Kenyans studied: despite exposure to Western preferences they continued to rate larger figures more favourably and smaller figures less favourably than the British.

In China anorexia nervosa is almost unknown and is also very rare among the Chinese populations of Singapore, Malaysia and Hong Kong. Emaciation, food refusal and amenorrhea are commonly found among Chinese anorectics, but body-image distortion, which is a core diagnostic feature among Western anorectics, is consistently absent among Chinese patients. These patients blame their wilful starvation on indigestion, bloatedness or fullness. Compared to their Western counterparts, Chinese girls are slim, if not underweight. The Chinese have traditionally accepted and even valued some degree of fatness. Lee et al. (1992) confirm that to greet any Chinese individual with 'you have put on weight' would still be accepted as a compliment. The Chinese diet is also low in fat and high in fibre content and they do not generally see food in terms of 'good' or 'bad'.

However more recent findings of Lee and Lee (1996) suggest that fat phobic attitudes, body dissatisfaction and a propensity for weight-control behaviours are now being found in some female adolescents in Hong Kong. They examined the prevalence of disordered eating and its relationship with body dissatisfaction, family dysfunction and depression among 294 Chinese adolescent females in Hong Kong. The results indicated that disordered eating was positively predicted by body dissatisfaction and to a lesser extent, family cohesion and conflict. Body dissatisfaction was, in turn, positively predicted by depression, which was negatively predicted by family cohesion. So, although once thought of as rare in Chinese people, these behaviours do have a real potential for becoming more common as a source of distress in female Chinese adolescents.

In contrast, Japanese anorectics all demonstrate a fear of fatness (Suematsu et al., 1985) and this would be consistent with the view that this results from Japan being highly industrialized and having adopted the cultural emphasis on slimness and this is also true of Arab, Asian, Indian or Pakistani women who develop eating disorders while living in the West and uniformly demonstrate a fear of fatness (Bhadrinath, 1990; Nasser, 1997). It could therefore be presumed that they have come under the same cultural emphasis on slimness that effects their Western counterparts and it could be the case that as Hong Kong, India and other countries become more modernized and adopt Western conventions, then their anorectic patients will also increasingly adopt this fear of fatness.

Boskind-White and White (1983) suggest that female adolescence is vulnerable to the development of an eating disorder because the cultural message to be slim is constantly being transmitted to girls through their family, peers, teachers, books, magazines and television. In an effort to be accepted the adolescent behaves in a way that is consistent with the beliefs and behaviours of people in the groups to which she aspires to belong.

However, the absence of the fear of fatness in some cultures has led to much debate about whether the development and clinical manifestation of anorexia varies in different cultures. Since most research on eating disorders has been conducted on Caucasian women, considerable uncertainty exists as to their presentation in ethnic minorities. Fat phobia does not seem to receive as much emphasis in the less affluent parts of Europe. Faltus (1986) reported that, in Czechoslovakia, aversion to food, refusal to eat, extreme emaciation, amenorrhea and the absence of a primary disease, not fat phobia, were used for the diagnosis of anorexia nervosa.

There can be some possible explanations for these cross-cultural findings. It could be that those who do not demonstrate a definite fear of fatness are in fact suffering from an atypical variety of anorexia nervosa. It could also be that perhaps the fat phobia had been overlooked or concealed in the Western cultural emphasis on female thinness and may not yet have become widely prevalent in these other cultures. It could also be that questions related to body shape and fasting do not have quite the same meaning in different societies. In Hong Kong, for example, purging is typical rather than the self-induced vomiting found in the West.

In the nineteenth century, when detailed reports of anorexia nervosa cases were made by Gull (1868) and Laseque (1873), such cases occurred in a culture where slimness and dieting did not exist. The paintings of the time did in fact equate beauty with large voluptuous bodies as can be seen in the paintings of Reuben and the photographs of Demachy. So the drive for thinness that occurred in the patients of Gull and Laseque in the nineteenth century must have arisen from their own internal conflicts and not from external cultural or media pressures, which are reported today as etiological factors. It could therefore be the case that eating disorders do occur in other countries that do not have a cultural emphasis for thinness but occur due to the individual's internal conflicts. There is also a greater need to understand attitudes towards food and eating within subcultures because some of these attitudes and values are likely to be influential in the treatment of eating disorders.

Le Grange et al. (1997) argue however that the treatments which are seen to be effective with Caucasian subjects may not need to be modified when applied to minority patients with eating disorders since the clinical characteristics of both groups are similar. Their study of 109 Caucasian and 40 minority eating disorder subjects differed on key eating disorder symptomatology and general psychopathology. The authors examined the separate and combined influences of eating disorder diagnosis and ethnicity on eating disorder symptomatology and general psychopathology. The results indicated clear differences in terms of eating disorders and general psychopathology between the eating-disordered groups, with bulimia nervosa subjects scoring consistently higher.

However ethnicity, on the other hand, failed to explain any difference between the groups. Similar findings were reported by Dolan et al. (1990a) who show that attitudes and concerns with weight and shape are not limited to Caucasian British women but are also seen in both Afro-Caribbean and Asian women.

Afro-Caribbean culture

In Britain, Thomas and Szumkler (1985) described the first three patients of Afro-Caribbean extraction with anorexia nervosa or bulimia nervosa to be seen in a specialist eating disorders clinic at the Maudsley Hospital. The authors report that the key clinical features were, in the main, typical for the conditions presented. However, less typically, these three patients came from lower social class backgrounds and had great pressures on them from their mothers to eat more as their anorexia nervosa developed. This only had the effect of the patients developing vomiting as a means of weight control. Similar findings were found by Holden and Robinson (1988) who compared 13 black patients (12 with anorexia nervosa and one with bulimia nervosa) with 13 matched white patients. The authors concluded that blacks had more commonly experienced parental divorce or separation and premorbid obesity and were more likely to be referred by the emergency services. Their lower educational achievements and their tendency to have fathers of lower socio-economic status reflected variation among the general black and white populations in this country, but their educational levels and social statuses were higher than in the general black population.

Dolan et al. (1990a) examined attitudes towards eating, weight and shape in 479 Caucasians, Afro-Caribbean and Asian-British women. The Asian women were found to have significantly more disordered eating attitudes than the Caucasian women but no difference was found between the three groups in their concern with body weight and shape. However the authors found that, whereas in the Caucasian group disordered eating attitudes were significantly positively correlated with feelings of anxiety and depression, this was not the case in the other two groups. The authors argue that although the concerns of British Afro-Caribbean and Asian women are similar to those of the Caucasian women, there could perhaps be ethnic differences in the relationship between feelings about eating, weight, shape and mood.

Warheit et al. (1993) found that adult blacks reported eight of 10 bulimic symptoms as frequently as or more frequently than did whites. In another study Langer et al. (1991) found that blacks were more likely than whites to report bingeing followed by vomiting, eating less in public, followed by heavier eating when alone, perceiving a weight problem and having their lives dominated by conflicts about eating. Soomro et al. (1995) also found there was a lack of differences between the white and non-white populations and this included patterns of family relationships, social class and parental status characteristics. They compared two groups of anorexia nervosa patients – non-white and white – on a variety of clinical and social characteristics. The main findings indicated a clinical similarity between the two groups. The non-whites were shorter in stature and reported earlier menarche. They also were younger at presentation, were less emaciated and practised veganism slightly more than the white group. The authors argue that, in certain instances, such as in Asian families where the shift towards middle class status has often been rapid, then it is likely that the incidence and prevalence of eating disorders are likely to increase to that of the white population. It could be argued that as one moves up the socio-economic ladder, the pressure to conform to social norms (of the thin ideal) increases.

It has now become accepted following the large-scale study of Garn and Clarke (1975), which carried out a 10-state nutrition study involving 40 000 subjects that:

- at all ages, and among both black and whites, females tend to be fatter (as measured by triceps fat fold) than males;
- females tend to gain fat and males to lose fat during adolescence;
- among white females there is an income-related reversal of fatness during adolescence seen by adolescent females in high-income families starting out being fatter but ending up being leaner than those of lower income families;
- there is a reversal of fatness of white and black females during adolescence – that is, the former start out being fatter but end up being leaner than the latter during adolescence.

This could, in part, explain the differential fatness patterns of black and white females and of higher and lower income white females and the conscious decision to diet on the part of the white higher income adolescent females.

It could, however, be that concerns about weight problems with eating might be more common among black women than at once thought. Pumariega et al. (1994) report on a survey study conducted by *Essence* magazine, which indicated that the levels of disturbed eating attitudes and behaviour reported by black women were similar to the levels reported by Caucasian women who participated in a similar survey conducted by *Glamour* magazine. The *Essence* study showed that black females engaged in moderate to extreme weight reduction behaviours as frequently as their white counterparts, while also reporting similar levels of disordered eating. It was interesting to note that those who displayed stronger levels of black identity appeared to be protected against the desire to be thinner. The Holywood movies have, of course, played their part in depicting a certain image for black women as they have frequently been portrayed as large, even obese and are often cast in the roles of black 'mammies'.

It has been suggested that the development of eating problems among 'non-Western' individuals may be the result of a process of acculturation, i.e., the individual absorbs the norms of Western society including its emphasis on the value of thinness. Although anorexia nervosa is classically associated with Western conventions such as body image and size, few studies of non-Western people have directly attempted to study acculturation to such convention.

Silber (1986) studied seven minority adolescents with anorexia nervosa including five Hispanics and two blacks, most being children of professional upper-middle-class parents who were achievement orientated. Silber noted that the eating disorders tended to be more severe in these minority patients than in the other non-minority patients whom they encountered. Their parents saw the patients as somewhat clingy and rather conservative. These black adolescents attended highly competitive, predominately Caucasian schools in which there was no black peer group. These individuals were seen as being physically attractive before the onset of their illness, but they describe a feeling of disappointment about what they considered as their 'big' (athletic) bodies. They reported exhibiting a strong desire to please others. The histories of the Hispanic women were similar to those of the black women except that all of them had recently arrived in the United States and were expressing losses associated with leaving their homeland, including the feelings associated with leaving behind a peer group, grandparents, the extended family and a familiar culture. Silber saw their illnesses as developing as a result of the process of acculturation. However since six of these seven minority patients required hospitalization due to the severity of their illness at the time of presentation, this would at least suggest the possibility that minority status increases the risk of not receiving the proper diagnosis and treatment until the disorder is more serious. It could be that the delay may also occur because minority group members have a high threshold for seeking treatment or have a more limited access to treatment. It could also be the case that the health care system has a higher threshold for diagnosing a minority individual with an eating disorder because of assumed lower risk. However it may be that fewer are exposed to the pressure of higher social status but also thinness may not be viewed so highly by black societies.

Minority groups are also disproportionately underrepresented as socioeconomic status increases. As socioeconomic status increases so does dieting, and as socioeconomic status declines, concerns with being overweight also decline. It has been shown that, in in-patient and non-patient samples, higher income and education are associated with increased rates of the full syndromes of both anorexia nervosa and bulimia nervosa in both Caucasian and non-Caucasian individuals. So it could therefore be argued that lower socio-economic status could in effect be a protection factor against anorexia nervosa and bulimia nervosa. As minority groups make up a disproportionate percentage of the population as socio-economic status declines, they may be at a reduced risk for these disorders.

The apparent lack of eating disorders among minority groups might conceivably arise from the fact that minority groups do not get help for an eating disorder because they do not present complaining of an eating disorder and clinicians do not recognize, or look for, eating disorders in non-white women. Ways of showing distress vary between cultures and some argue that, given distressing circumstances and emotional distur- bances similar to those exhibited by Caucasian women, non-Caucasians will present with other neurotic disorders. It could also be that they are less pressurized to adopt a thin ideal body shape. In fact in several non-Western cultures, fatness and obesity symbolize beauty. Interestingly, being overweight is a risk factor for eating disorders among minority women, whereas perceiving oneself to be overweight when one is not is a more likely significant risk factor among Caucasian women. Black adolescent girls have also been found to have higher self-esteem than Caucasian girls and this, in itself, may also be a protective factor against eating disorders.

Crago et al. (1996) reviewed eating disturbances among American minority groups and found that, compared with Caucasian females, eating disturbances are equally common among Hispanic females, more frequent among Native Americans and less frequent among black and Asian- American females. Risk factors for eating disorders are greater among minority females who are younger, heavier, better educated and more identified with middle class values.

As a group, African-American women tend to be heavier than Euro- American women and also find it difficult to lose weight (Rand and Kuldan 1990). However, despite this, African-American women are more satisfied with their bodies and have less concern about their weight. Women's desire for thinness is, in part, based on their correct perception of men's preferences (Fallon and Rozin, 1985). Greenberg and La Porte (1996) looked at racial differences in body type preferences of men. The results indicated that African-American women have a significantly higher preva- lence of obesity, a markedly lower prevalence of eating disorders and greater satisfaction with their bodies than Euro-American women. The authors suggest that one potential contributing explanation for this differ- ence might be differential body-type preferences between the men in the two communities. Their investigation included 63 African-American and 116 Euro-American men who were asked to rank, in order of attractive- ness, a series of silhouettes of women of varying shapes. The results indicated that Euro-American's chose significantly thinner figures and also reported wishing that their girlfriends would lose weight significantly more often than African-Americans. The authors argue that such prefer- ences may result in greater pressure within the Euro-American than in the African-American community for women to be thin in order to conform to men's preferences.

Parental separation or death have frequently been cited as etiological factors for eating disorders in Caucasians. However Pumariega et al. (1984) also found this to be the case in their study of blacks. Robinson and Andersen (1985) reported similar findings in their study on five cases of anorexia nervosa in black American patients. All had lost parents by either death or divorce. Three had a history of obesity and of a physical illness related to obesity. Two patients were male and both had had a previous history of serious psychiatric disturbance.

Maresh and Willard (1996) describe the presentation and treatment of an African-American female from an impoverished family. Here the authors argue that anorexia nervosa in African-American females presents unique challenges for diagnosis and treatment. The illness, they report, can also be overlooked in a population where weight loss is frequently assumed to result from malnutrition, medical problems, or more common mental illnesses and the fact that African-American females typically do not judge their self-worth by the same standard of thinness and beauty as those in the West.

Most research has concentrated on adolescent and adult women but Wifley et al. (1996) study examined racial differences in eating disorder symptomatology in a community-based sample of 538 middle-aged adult black and white women and investigated predictors of body image dissat-isfaction in these two racial groups. Results indicated that both black and white women reported comparable levels of eating disturbance. However after controlling for degree of overweight, the authors found that white women have significantly greater rates of body dissatisfaction than black women. This could in fact suggest that black women live in an environ-ment that is more accepting of being overweight. However their study would indicate that eating disturbance occurs across a much broader age, race and socioeconomic distribution than was previously thought. They also assessed the degree to which overweight socio-economic status, social pressures about thinness and negative attitudes about overweight were predictors of body dissatisfaction. The results would suggest that, as women age, they may become increasingly dissatisfied with their bodies, which could be due to weight gain or changes in body composition from ageing and/or pregnancy. However, although they may be more dissatis-fied with their body than younger college-aged women, they may be less inclined to pursue thinness to the same degree or in the same manner as their younger counterparts.

Toriola et al. (1996) investigated intergenerational and cross-cultural aspects of body weight satisfaction in 103 female Yoruba students, 48 adult women in Western Nigeria, and 68 Nigerian women living in Britain. The authors found (as was predicted) that the students living in Nigeria had a lower current and desired body weight than the adult Nigerian group. The students also showed a discrepancy between their current and desired body weight, which was greater than the adult sample although, in contrast to Western populations, neither group showed a marked overall dissatisfaction with their current body weight. The 68 Nigerian women living in Britain were matched for age, marital status and parity with the 68 women from the Nigerian sample. The sample living in Britain showed significantly lower desired weight than their matched counterparts in Nigeria and significantly greater discrepancy between their current and desired body weight. These findings would suggest that younger women in Nigeria could be moving towards a Western body image dissatisfaction, which is already evident in their peers in Britain. It would also support the view that culture exposure may cause immigrants from cultures where thinness is not seen as highly desirable to adopt Western positive valuations of thinness. The authors chose Nigeria for their investigation as its indigenous culture has been influenced by Western colonization and by more recent independence. Nigeria is also accepted as the most populated country in Africa. The authors suggest that attitudes regarding body shape and weight vary across the major Nigerian ethnic groups, for the most part being determined by people's cultural, religious or socio-economic backgrounds. However they argue that, in Yoruba society, an endomorphic build is positively regarded as a mark of affluence, health and mother-hood, whereas a Yoruba woman who is plump (but not obese) is viewed as attractive. However Nigerian adolescents associated undesirable physical and psychosocial characteristics with endomorphic build. Toriola et al. (1996) suggest that exposure to Western cultural norms over the past 20 years may have led to a detectable difference between generations of Nigerian women regarding their body image perceptions. There could also be a shift in the younger women in Nigeria towards a Western body image dissatisfaction like that experienced by their peers who are already in Britain. This would support the view that dieting behaviour and other serious eating disturbances are related to the level of acculturation to Western ideals in a multicultural society.

Hooper and Garner (1986) who assessed black, white and mixed-race schoolgirls in Zimbabwe for eating disorders would support such a view. Their study included 399 girls aged 16–18 years. About 20% of them had high eating disorder scores and, of these, 12.5% were black, 17.5% were of mixed race and 70% were white. Following interviews with respondents, the authors found that anorectic and bulimic eating behaviours were most common among the whites and least common among the blacks, with the mixed race group occupying an intermediate position. Buchan and Gregory (1984) also describe a case in Zimbabwe. This was a girl of 20 years who developed anorexia nervosa. The patient came from a family with high aspirations and pursued higher education in Britain. The authors suggest that psychosocial rather than biological factors account for the rarity of the disorder in the Zimbabwean black population, as well as highlighting the absence of slimness as a desirable attribute.

Asian culture

Indian, Pakistanis and Bangladeshis are commonly referred to as Asian for the purpose of research investigations and are in fact the largest immigrant group in the United Kingdom. Eating disorders in immigrant families in Britain have been commonly interpreted as the consequences of 'acculturation' among young women from more traditional families. The Asian population in Britain has been viewed as a culture in transition. Mumford et al (1991) studied a group of young girls in the town of Bradford (England), which has a very high proportion of Asians. They found the prevalence of bulimia nervosa amongst the Asian girls to be almost as high as that of the white girls. It would seem that the effects of removing external controls are even greater when the population is suddenly immersed in a society with new values as opposed to being in a society that gradually acquires new values from outside. Mumford et al. (1991) reported that the Asians with eating disorders, had high scores associated with a more traditional cultural orientation and not with greater Westernization. Others have claimed the opposite to be true (Nasser, 1986).

Using the same methodology as their Bradford study, Mumford et al. (1991) conducted a survey of 369 schoolgirls aged 14–16 years in Lahore, Pakistan, using the eating attitude test (EAT). They chose Lahore because it was relatively easy there to survey English medium schools that serve a healthy population of the upper social class. Girls who scored highly on the EAT were invited for interview. One girl met the criteria for bulimia nervosa and five subjects were found with partial syndrome bulimia nervosa. This prevalence of bulimia nervosa seemed to be similar to that among Caucasian schoolgirls in Bradford. No girls suffered from anorexia nervosa. There was evidence that indicated that the most 'Westernized' girls were at greatest risk of developing an eating disorder. Westernization scores were measured by the consumption of Western food and the speaking of English in the home. It would seem that many Asian countries are presently undergoing a rapid change towards a consumer-orientated economy and its attendant advertising industry. Among this prosperous élite, there is widespread adoption of Western styles, habits and attitudes. The girls in Lahore freely reported dieting as seen in their mothers, siblings and friends indicating that many of them live in a 'dieting' environment. There were also reports of significant roadside advertisements for slimming clinics and keep-fit clubs, which are also on the increase in the wealthier suburbs of Lahore.

In comparing Lahore (Mumford et al., 1992) and Bradford (Mumford et al., 1991) the prevalence of bulimia nervosa among ethnic Asians in Bradford was 3.4% and much higher than the prevalence of the condition in Lahore. Among Asian schoolgirls in Bradford the risk of eating disorders was greater among those girls from the most traditional families and not those from the more Westernized families as seen in Lahore. Mumford (1992) suggest that, in Bradford, Asian parents feel threatened by Western culture and unenthusiastic about its impact on their daughters. These parents therefore tend to be more overprotective, especially since the prevailing Western values are so influential.

The information regarding eating disorders in India is very limited, however. Khandelwal et al. (1995) describe five cases of young women who chiefly presented with refusal to eat, persistent vomiting, marked weight loss, amenorrhea and other somatic symptoms. The women did not exhibit any of the signs of disturbances in body image that are so characteristic of anorexia nervosa. All of the cases came from middle class nuclear families.

Chandra et al. (1995) reported on family pathology and anorexia nervosa within an Indian context by looking at three families of anorexia nervosa patients (one male and two females) where the symptom was a reflection of family pathology and was being maintained by it. In all three cases the anorectic's symptoms served to decrease the marital conflict or individual psychopathology in the parents. The cases also highlight an ambivalence towards autonomy and independence among the three adolescents. Palazzoli (1978) used the term 'three-way matrimony' to indicate how the anorectic female is used as a go-between for her parents and she has therefore no energy left to allow herself to become autonomous and independent. Crisp et al. (1974), on the other hand, found that the anorectic's parents did in fact become more depressed and anxious as the child's illness improved. Chandra et al. (1995) emphasize the need to assess families of anorectics in detail and to view them within the cultural context of eating. There are, in fact, very few studies that look at family issues among Asians in their countries of origin; however, in a culture where there is little emphasis on slimness or dieting, the authors argue that if anorexia nervosa does occur it should prompt clinicians to investigate for associated pathology in the individual or the family.

McCourt and Waller (1996) looked at the factors contributing to the eating psychopathology of Asian women in British society and report that some Asian girls living in the United Kingdom have greater levels of eating pathology than their Caucasian counterparts. This difference is most marked in girls from the most traditional Asian homes and particularly where the girl's personal control is low. These girls seem to be caught in a conflict or culture clash between their home environment and the prevailing social norms. This culture clash differs from the proposal that eating pathology develops in ethnic minorities to the degree that they adopt Western ideals. McCourt and Waller (1996) also point to particular aspects of the Muslim religion in relation to eating pathology, particularly the feast of Ramadan where many aspects of food preparation and consumption have symbolic meanings for Muslims. It could also be that, for many Muslims, the secular decadence of Western societies is seen as threatening. The home is seen as the final bastion of patriarchy where men take charge and women's main role is to manage the house and have children. Women are seen as the symbolic guardians of the family honour. It could therefore be argued that Muslim women experience conflicts over control that others have associated with eating disorders.

Although reports of anorexia nervosa in adolescents of Asian extraction are rare, this is especially so in males. However Bhadrinath (1990) reports on three Asian (Indian subcontinental) adolescents with the disorder, one of whom was male. The author also discussed the impact of the Muslim festival of Ramadan in the two Muslim cases, arguing that there is a need for better understanding of attitudes towards body shape and food within this subculture. The condition of the two Muslim girls worsened over the Muslim feast of Ramadan. During this lunar month all Muslims are required to fast from dawn to dusk but may eat during the hours of darkness. For the two Muslim patients, their condition worsened over Ramadan in terms of weight loss and they both began vomiting after their meal.

Hispanic culture

Story et al. (1995), in a large-scale study of adolescent girls, found significant rates of dieting behaviours, vomiting and laxative abuse were reported across Hispanic, American-Indian, Caucasian, black and Asian groups. Although there were some group differences in the rates of specific pathological eating and weight control behaviour, no group was immune from such problems. As in the case with blacks, surveys of Hispanics indicate that they are heavier, exercise less and are less concerned about weight than Caucasians (Harris and Koehler, 1992). However the studies of the prevalence of eating disturbances among Hispanic women and girls indicate that the frequency of these disturbances is similar to the frequency among Caucasian females (Gross and Rosen, 1988). In a case study of five Hispanic adolescent girls who were diagnosed with anorexia nervosa, Silber (1986) reported that they were all perfectionistic over-achievers who desperately wanted to fit into white middle-class society and were prepared to engage in long periods of restrictive dieting to try to achieve this goal. In the study by Thompson (1992), five Hispanic women with eating disorders were interviewed and found to have eating problems that were seen to be in response to a range of traumas including racism, sexism, poverty and physical and sexual abuse.

Pumariega (1986) also looked at Hispanic adolescent girls in his comparative and correlational study of acculturation and eating attitudes in white and Hispanic adolescent females between the ages of 16 and 18 years. The author noted a significant correlation between acculturation and higher EAT scores in the Hispanic group. There was also a positive but non-significant correlation between socio-economic status, both current and projected. The author notes that the results support the view that cultural factors are related to a higher prevalence of eating disorders but fail to support a hypothesized relationship between higher socio-economic status and vulnerability to eating disorders, suggesting that the greater adherence to the Western culture, the greater the individual's vulnerability towards the development of eating disorders.

Children in different cultures

Striegel-More et al. (1995) examined racial differences in the drive for thinness, which is seen as a motivational variable in the etiology of eating disorders in 613 black and white pre-adolescent girls aged nine and ten years. The authors found that black girls reported significantly greater drive for thinness than white girls. A drive for thinness was significantly associated with adiposity in both groups. However additional predictors also included criticism about weight for black girls and dissatisfaction with physical appearance for white girls. This finding of a greater drive for thinness among young black girls is an interesting one since there is a higher prevalence of obesity and a lower prevalence of anorexia nervosa among black women. It could however be that these nine and 10 year olds become more accepting of their size and shape as they get older and may show a decline in drive for thinness, reflecting an increased acceptance of being overweight as they mature.

Dieting may be a behaviour promoted by cultural perspective but the age at which dieting starts is uncertain. Hill et al. (1992) compared the reported dieting behaviour of nine- and 14-year-old Caucasian girls from a middle-class school environment. Not only were there girls from both age groups in every category of dieting but the highly restrained girls expressed greater body shape dissatisfaction, had a thinner ideal shape and lower body esteem than their non-dieting peers.

The study by Hill et al. (1992) was followed by one by Hill and Bhatti (1995) which investigated the vulnerability to eating disorders of British pre-adolescents of Asian origin. The study included 55 Asian and 42 Caucasian nine year olds who were attending three mixed-sex state middle schools located in the inner city of a northern British city. Two of the schools had a high proportion of ethnic minority pupils. They were assessed on dietary restraint, body esteem, body satisfaction and body figure preferences. The results indicated a high preference for thinness in both the Asian and Caucasian girls. This was the case even though Asian girls had a significantly lower body weight than their Caucasian peers. There was also an association found in the Asian sample between reported dietary restraint and the cultural orientation of their family. These results confirm the findings of Hill et al. (1992) and show that nine year old girls have an awareness of dieting and some appear to put their motivation into practice. Hill and Batti (1995) argue that body shape dissatisfaction and dieting can and do transcend apparent ethnic barriers at this very early age.

Bryant-Waugh and Lask (1991) also reported on young Asian children in the United Kingdom. They describe four cases of anorexia nervosa in Asian children. They identified intrafamilial and cultural conflicts in families of anorectics and believe the disorder to be a manifestation of these conflicts. The authors suggest that the children of immigrants, while sharing their parents' and grandparents' physical and psychological characteristics and heritage, can also be exposed to a different and conflicting set of sociocultural norms and ideals. Conflicts can arise if parents insist that their children participate in activities of the local Asian cultural centre, of which they are a part. These children would frequently prefer to spend their time with new English-speaking school friends who do not participate in a traditional Asian upbringing. The authors report that it seems to be the case that the more 'traditional' the family, then the greater is the sociocultural conflict within the family. The second generation of children from ethnic minority families does not necessarily follow the views and values of its parents, nor indeed that of the host culture in which they are presently living.

A study of similar-aged children was carried out by Lawrence and Thelen (1995) as they investigated third- and sixth-grade African-American and Caucasian children's eating habits, body image concerns and self-concept. In fact few studies have addressed dieting and body image concerns in young children. The authors found that third-grade African-American boys and girls demonstrated no association between physical appearance subscale scores and overweight concerns, whereas all other groups demonstrated a significant negative association between these two concepts. Caucasian girls exhibited a greater negative association between physical appearance subscale scores and dieting behaviour than did Caucasian boys and African-American girls. So the girls, as compared to the boys, were more concerned about issues related to being overweight. They also desired a body figure that was thinner than their own self-perceived figure. Dieting behaviour was associated with lower general self worth for Caucasian boys and girls, but not for African-American boys and girls. Of course different emphasis is placed on physical appearance for African-Americans and Caucasians. However, boys seemed to be more concerned with muscle mass rather than being overweight.

Chinese culture

In 1983 Hsu found it methodologically impossible to specify a single cause of anorexia nervosa, attributing this to the disorder which is probably multifactoral in origin. Predisposing factors such as obesity and the desirability of slimness, pubertal stress and issues regarding dependency versus autonomy are frequently seen to play their part in the development of anorexia nervosa. It is in these areas that cultural differences are frequently seen to arise.

Most Chinese girls in Hong Kong are slim and even underweight by Western standards. There is little stigmatization of obesity. Popular Chinese beliefs are that 'being able to eat is to have Luck' so that gaining weight means good fortune 'and fat people have more luck'. The desirability and pursuit of the thin ideal as seen in the West is therefore much less intense in Hong Kong. As a general trend, puberty occurs later in the Chinese in Hong Kong compared with Western countries, and the physical changes of contour such as breast development are much less marked for Chinese girls. This would naturally cause less embarrassment for girls. In 1993, Chen et al. found only one case of possible anorexia nervosa among 3786 females interviewed so that the prevalence of anorexia nervosa in Hong Kong in the 1980s was seen to very low. However, more recent reports indicate that the rates of anorexia nervosa and bulimia nervosa are increasing in Hong Kong (Lee, 1991; Lee et al., 1992). Of special note is that some anorectics in Hong Kong did not present with the 'weight phobia' currently seen in Western anorectic patients. However since the 'pursuit of thinness' has now penetrated many cultures it could be expected that the rates of anorexia nervosa and bulimia nervosa will increase in these cultures.

Kok and Tian (1994) examined the susceptibility to anorexia nervosa of 656 GCE O level Singapore Chinese schoolgirls who attended schools of good academic standing where the pressure was expected to be high. These girls were found to have high drive for thinness scores.

Bond and Hwang (1986) report that, within the Chinese context, the traditional collectivistic culture places an individual's right at the bottom of the hierarchy, below that of the country, society and family. The individual's needs are frequently sacrificed for the sake of a higher cause, whereas open conflicts are avoided in an effort to preserve social order. Submission and conformity are expected. There is unquestioning acceptance of parental authority and expectations. Moreover, sons are traditionally the preferred sex and have the added responsibility of continuing the family lineage.

Kelly et al. (1995), however, report on the case of early-onset anorexia nervosa in a male patient from Hong Kong and discuss the implications of being the only son in a traditional Chinese family. They suggest that the process of acculturation and cultural conflicts of growing up in a Western-oriented society are put forward as significant key factors in the etiology of the illness. This patient presented with a 31% loss of his original weight after food restriction and excessive exercising. Fear of fatness and body image disturbance were denied. However, despite this lack of body image disturbance and lack of fear of fatness, a diagnosis of restrictive anorexia nervosa was made.

Clinical research in Hong Kong (Lee, 1991) has demonstrated that the Western criteria of DSM IV are inadequate. The typical features of Western cases, which are included in the professional diagnostic criteria, require fear of gaining weight and distorted body image. These were noticeably absent among patients in Hong Kong with symptoms of anorexia nervosa. Social stressors associated with anorexia nervosa in the Lee (1991) group included examination pressure, loss of relationships, overprotective mothers, parental conflicts, sibling rivalry, physical illness and distant fathers.

Hong Kong has not been entirely devoid of the usual list of predisposing factors for anorexia nervosa as it has more recently undergone a great deal of modernization and urbanization, associated with adaptation to Western values and lifestyles. It could be that these changes may account for the increased stress reactions and psychosomatic disorders. The extremely competitive educational system, coupled with the high value that Chinese parents place on educational achievements, are thought to contribute to greater anxiety among secondary school students in Hong Kong.

In contrast to the West, Lee et al. (1992) found bulimia nervosa to be rarer than anorexia nervosa in Hong Kong. The authors report on four female normal-weight bulimic patients with mostly typical clinical features and conspicuous morbidity and they argued that binge eating is used to regulate unpleasant affect. The condition is, however, on the increase in Hong Kong and this could be due to the recent emergence of the relevant risk factors in Hong Kong's culture. Obesity is becoming more widespread among Chinese adolescents and, with the introduction to more Westernized eating habits, particularly 'fast foods', and ideals of female slimness becoming part of the Hong Kong culture, we could in fact be seeing a continued increase in the prevalence of the condition.

Japanese culture

Both anorexia nervosa and bulimia nervosa were seen as rare illnesses in Japan until the recent rapid increase in the reported incidence of these disorders (Susuki et al., 1995). Suematsu et al. (1985) noted that the number of patients seeking treatment for anorexia nervosa in Japan had actually doubled between 1976 and 1981. Kuboki et al. (1996) carried out an epidemiological survey on anorexia nervosa in Japanese hospitals in 1985 and 1992 using a questionnaire. The reported number of patients with anorexia nervosa was higher in 1992 than in 1995. It is now argued that the cultural pressures experienced by young Japanese women to lose weight and to stay thin are in some way responsible for the sudden increase in the conditions. Prevalence of eating-disordered tendencies, such as weight and diet preoccupation and negative body image, is reported by Suematsu (1985) to be comparably high among Japanese adolescent girls. The author found that 85% of those in the normal weight range expressed a desire to be thinner and so did 45% of those who were 10–20% under weight. Forty per cent of the sample reported having attempted to lose weight. There is in fact a traditional standard of beauty for Japanese women that emphasizes a slender body.

Mukai et al. (1994) examined overall eating disorder tendencies in 197 female Japanese high-school students and looked at the influence of family and friends upon Japanese adolescent girls with such tendencies. The authors looked particularly at maternal influences and whether the students had ever been encouraged to diet. The findings show a high prevalence of weight concern and dieting practices in this non-clinical sample of Japanese schoolgirls. It was the perception of being overweight, rather than actually being overweight, which was associated with their eating behaviour. Their strong desire to be thinner, irrespective of their current weight, largely determined the level of disturbance in eating attitudes and behaviour. The authors also found the amount of encouragement to diet that these girls received from others to be significant. Girls who reported talking more frequently with their mothers about food and dieting were more likely to be eating disordered, as were those who felt their mother saw them as being fat and as eating too much. In fact nearly 90% of the girls who had been encouraged to diet to lose weight were within the normal or underweight range.

The thin body ideal for Japanese women may not be the result of recent influences as it is in itself seen as Japanese tradition. There is also the traditional view of femininity in Japan, which accounts for women eating less than men and could have a considerable influence in shaping Japanese women's attitudes about eating and body weight.

Eastern European culture

Only a few studies have described the incidence and treatment of eating disorders in Eastern Europe. The first came from Prague, in the Czech Republic, where the first eating disorder unit in central Eastern Europe was established (Faltus, 1986). From a transcultural viewpoint this is an interesting former communist country. So this region may have something to offer in the evaluation of sociocultural factors in eating disorders.

At present very little is known about the epidemiology of eating disorders in Eastern and Central Europe. Szabo and Tury (1991) provide some data from Hungary and former East Germany that suggest that eating disorders may be at least as prevalent in Eastern Europe as in the West, although public awareness of the disorders is more limited.

The first Hungarian eating-disorder unit was established in Miskolc in 1990 and the first epidemiological study was carried out before the rapid social change in 1989. The prevalence of bulimia nervosa was surprisingly 1.3% among female university students and 0.8% among males. In a secondary school no bulimic or anorectic cases were detected but the authors found a binge frequency of at least twice a month in 7.2% of females and 5.9% of males students.

Ratner et al. (1995) found that, in a multicentre study of 538 university students, the prevalence of bulimia nervosa was 1.0% among women (0% among men) whereas no cases of anorexia nervosa were found. The authors argue that eating disorders are not very well known in Hungary and could probably be hidden due to the suppression of psychological sciences during the communist era.

Taking into account the available data, Central and Eastern Europe are faced with the problem of a rising incidence of eating disorders. Historically the role of cultural traditions can play a part in the development of Western cultural values as, historically, Hungary was a part of the Austro-Hungarian monarchy and belonged much more to Western Europe than Eastern Europe.

Polish culture

Anorexia nervosa has received increasing attention in Poland during recent years, especially in child and adolescent specialities. However no case of bulimia nervosa originating from Poland has been reported. Wlodarczyk-Bisaga and Dolan (1996) looked at eating attitudes and prospective risk factors in 747 Polish school girls aged between fourteen and sixteen years. They found no clinical cases of anorexia nervosa or bulimia nervosa, however there was a point prevalence of 2.34% for sub-clinical eating disorder and 28.6% for dieting. Several family factors distinguished the dieters from non-dieters at the initial stage. The study demonstrates that the prevalence of abnormal eating attitudes and behaviours in adolescent Polish schoolgirls is not markedly different from that reported in America and the United Kingdom. There was an unexpectedly high prevalence of abnormal eating attitudes and behaviours in Polish adolescents. The study also indicated that 'normal' dieting and weight control were as common a phenomenon in Polish schoolgirls as in their Western European counterparts.

Greek and Arab culture

There is now evidence from transcultural research that immigrants from less-developed countries such as Greece and some Arab states are more likely to develop eating disorders while staying in Western Europe than their peers in their homeland. Timimi (1995) looked at the mental health problems encountered in adolescents from immigrant Arab families. The author argued that proper regard should be given to the sociocultural background of the family and the importance of the family in Arabic culture, and to understanding Arab attitudes toward female sexuality.

Arabs do, in fact, place a great deal of importance on food and the digestive tract. Attractiveness in women is equated with a certain degree of plumpness and thinness is considered socially undesirable.

El Sarrag (1968) and Okasha et al. (1977) both found anorexia nervosa to be rare in Arabic cultures. However Nasser (1986) compared two matched groups of female Arab students attending London and Cairo universities and identified six cases of bulimia nervosa in the London group, but none in the Cairo group, giving support to the view that exposure to Western values is a strong pathogenic factor in the developing of these conditions. No cases of either anorexia nervosa or bulima nervosa were found in the Cairo sample. Explanations for the differences between the London and Cairo findings could be that the two groups differed in their level of Westernization. The London Arab students were similar to European students in dress and social behaviour as opposed to the Cairo group who were generally more traditional in their dress, with some of them even wearing the veil. Nasser argued that the London students may also be more achievement orientated and more competitive and this is in itself seen as a predisposing factor for anorexia nervosa (Garner and Garfinkel, 1980).

It could be predicted that the increase in eating disorders in Egypt will continue due to the rapid socioeconomic changes that have occurred in the country. In fact, a significant proportion of Egyptian society has gained considerable wealth in recent years either through employment in the Gulf states or through liberalization of the economy. This has resulted in an increasing display of wealth – shown by the designer clothes market, the owning of expensive cars and the purchase of properties in exclusive resorts. However, it has more importantly seen a notable increase in the consumption of all types of food. Nasser (1986) also cites the influx of Western fashion designs that fit only slim figures into the market as contributing to an increased prevalence of eating disorders. The television is also now portraying new concepts of beauty and femininity, which are for the most part influenced by imported television series and advertisements. These rapid changes towards Westernization, however, run alongside religious fundamentalism. This has been shown by the manner in which some of Cairo's students have adopted the wearing of the veil as a way of their personal rejection of such changes.

Spanish and Portuguese culture

Toro et al. (1995) aimed to ascertain whether patients with anorexia nervosa in Spain are similar to those in other countries. The authors compared the records of 185 Spanish adolescents with anorexia nervosa to a group of 185 psychiatric patients without anorexia nervosa matched for sex and age. The authors found no significant differences with regard to broken homes, order of birth or parent–patient conflict. The parents of the anorectic patients had a higher standard of education and had more affective disorders. When compared with other patients those with anorexia nervosa performed much better academically but were more socially withdrawn. Anorectic males performed worse academically than females and had more anxiety diagnoses. The authors concluded that anorexia nervosa sufferers in Spain are clinically analogous to patients with anorexia nervosa in other countries.

Carmo et al. (1996) looked at the prevalence of anorexia nervosa in a Portuguese population. They argue that in terms of the economy and social and cultural areas Portugal is in a transitional situation. The authors found that the prevalence of anorexia nervosa in the Portuguese population was lower than in any other European study and this actual prevalence is possibly linked with socioeconomic factors.

The use of the Eating Attitudes Test (EAT) in other cultures

The EAT was developed and validated in Canada using standardized criteria for eating disorders in Western society. Despite careful translation into local language it could still be the case that some rather subtle questions may be misunderstood when it is applied not only to Third World countries but also other cultures. Nasser (1986) suggests that the high prevalence of bulimia nervosa found in his study could be due, in part, to cultural misinterpretation of the questions.

King and Bhugra (1989) screened 580 schoolgirls, living in a small north Indian industrial town, for eating disorders and found that although 29% scored above the threshold for the questionnaire, closer examination of the pattern of responses revealed misinterpretations of a large number of questions possibly on a conceptual basis. The authors argue that linguistic and conceptual pitfalls inherent to cross-cultural epidemiological research are of paramount importance. The investigators found that these teenage girls responded positively to several questions that were clearly vulnerable to misinterpretation for social and religious reasons and their responses were clearly different from English populations. In contrast, only a very small number of girls agreed with the most specific questions of the EAT relating to eating behaviours seen in anorexia nervosa and bulimia nervosa. Mumford (1992) also reported unexpectedly high rates of positive responses with Third World samples.

Cross-cultural studies would also indicate that eating disorders may not be represented adequately by the current diagnostic criteria of DSM IV.

Conclusion

Numerous studies have now demonstrated that anorexia nervosa is a Western illness, with predominance in industrialized developed countries. However, more recent reports also indicate an increased incidence in former Eastern Bloc countries, which are now more influenced by Western culture. Studies have shown differences in prevalence depending on geographical distribution whereas studies of incidence have shown a progressive increase in recent years. However an estimation of the true rate of eating disorders in non-White groups within Western societies is impossible without a large epidemiological survey.

There is no single factor that is necessary or sufficient to create eating problems. It is important to consider the interaction of a number of possible causal factors in order to understand the development and maintenance of unhealthy eating attitudes and eating disorders. Food itself can take on special significance for those individuals coming from countries where food is in short supply and variation is small in comparison with those countries where food is abundant an affordable. The abundance of food also serves as a continuous reminder of the fortune of the immigrant relative to the deprivation faced by those left behind. So immediately food becomes a symbol fraught with guilt. It could also be the case that, especially in bulimia nervosa, the amount of shame and guilt associated with wasting food would also lead to an under-reporting of the phenomenon in foreign-born populations.

The examination of risk factors for eating disorders has for the most part concentrated on individuals from the dominant cultures within Western societies. Despite recognizing that sociocultural factors do influence disordered eating the important sociocultural factor of ethnicity has been largely overlooked.

A variety of factors, including socio-economic status, cultural norms, reporting biases and genetic factors all contribute to the risk factors for eating disorders. Future studies would be useful in helping us to establish how the risk of developing an eating disorder varies with ethnicity. Some suggest that the prevalence of eating disorders is low in non-Western countries, but others have found ethnic differences in disordered eating within Western countries. It is important when examining ethnic differences to assess whether migrant groups assimilate to a dominant Western culture and start to show Western body-shape preferences and disordered eating.

The symptom patterns for individuals with eating disorders seems to be consistent across race as seen in the Hiebert et al. (1988) study of treatment outcomes with anorexia nervosa patients. Their results would suggest that ethnicity does not appear to have a major influence on treatment outcome. It is necessary in the future to examine racial identity, cultural assimilation and the affects of acculturalization on eating behaviour and attitudes about eating, weight and body shape. It would also be interesting to investigate how various cultural traditions either protect against or encourage eating disorders.

Anorexia nervosa and bulimia nervosa are serious disorders that will continue to challenge mental health professionals. The question of how culture and Westernization affect the epidemiology and experience of eating disorders still requires further investigation.

Chapter 17
Eating disorders in a culture of exercise and fitness

Exercise

Relentless and excessive exercising has been reported among eating disordered patients throughout the history of the conditions. Some see this behaviour as simply a method of expending unwanted calories, others see it as occupying a more central role in the pathogenesis of the disorder. Most estimates of the incident of exercise addiction in the anorectic population are high and such behaviour is seen in both pre- and post-eating disorder. It is estimated that between one–third (Crisp et al., 1980) to three-quarters (Kron et al., 1978) of anorectics show a substantially increased level of physical activity.

In 1967 Crisp reported on extensive clinical observations and argued that starvation facilitates generalized compulsive behaviour so that exercising, like various other activities can involuntarily become stereotyped, ritualized and excessive, simply as a consequence of the disorder. However Crisp noted that this need for ceaseless exercise tends to diminish when patients are refed. Kron et al. (1978) collected retrospective data from the hospital records of 33 anorectic patients and, in some cases, from follow-up interviews. They found that 21 of these patients were described as extremely physically active well before they ever dieted or lost weight. Kron et al. (1978) also found that, contrary to earlier assumptions, excessive exercise continued for those who had regained their weight.

Many would see the state of starvation in anorexia nervosa to be biologically incompatible with high levels of physical activity. However this co-existence of excessive calorie restriction and hyperactivity in eating-disordered patients has been reported throughout its history (Gull, 1868; Crisp, 1967; Yates, 1991). There is also a great variation in the form of excessive activity that eating disorder patients exhibit. Even at rest, the patient is constantly restless and unable to keep still even for a short period.

In the last few decades we have seen a fitness craze which has swept industrialized nations. This has created an upsurge in physical activities like jogging, and aerobic and strengthening exercises. However, since the 1980s this emphasis on fitness has been promoted through videos, magazine articles and television programmes concerned with fitness as well as the rapid increase in the number of gymnasiums and health clubs. The desire to be physically fit is still continuing. The fitness movement is seen by some as another effort to distract women from social and political areas that might truly empower them. Yates (1991) found that the number of individuals claiming to exercise regularly had doubled in the past 25 years with approximately 50% of Americans exercising daily and it is thought that this number continues to increase.

Dieting behaviour, like exercise, has become part of our contemporary culture. Both of these body-based activities centre on the intake and output of the body in terms of the number of calories consumed in food and the number of calories expended on exercise. Exercise creates a heightened focus on physical appearance and an increased awareness of the relationship between weight and maximal performance. It also encourages a preoccupation with the interdependence of diet and exercise for weight control. In contrast to this view, McDonald and Hodgdon (1991) show how corresponding research has clearly highlighted the benefits of regular exercise in promoting both physical and psychological health. The authors report on the qualities of aerobic exercise as elevating mood, enhancing self-esteem and providing a sense of mastery and control while also helping to combat anxiety and mild depression.

Given that vigorous exercise can elevate mood and produce a euphoric state of wellbeing, it is possible that chronic excessive exercising may be addictive. There are some individuals who have been identified as exercising compulsively and excessively, despite illness, injury or personal commitments and these have come to be referred to as 'obligatory exercisers' (Yates, 1991). Iannos and Tiggeman (1997) investigated personality characteristics of excessive exercisers, in the light of the suggestion that they may share a dysfunctional personality profile with eating-disordered individuals. Their study included 205 men and women who were recreational exercisers recruited from gymnasiums. They found, contrary to their prediction, that excessive exercisers were not found to have lower self-esteem, more external levels of control or to be more obsessive-compulsive than moderate exercisers and neither did they find any relationships between self-esteem, levels of control and obligatory exercise behaviours. Their findings would suggest that exercise is not in fact an expression of a dysfunctional personality but rather the authors propose that the personality of the excessive exerciser seems to be one of a normally functioning individual whose alleged 'addiction' to exercise causes no psychological ill effects.

Frederick and Ryan (1993) examined the motivation of 376 adults engaged in individual activities and fitness activities in relation to the amount of participation and scores on psychological measures. The authors report that those who participated in individual sports were motivated more by interest and enjoyment whereas those involved in fitness activities were driven to participate for motives regarding body appearance, and they reported less competence and satisfaction with their participation.

Biddle and Bailey (1985) looked at those engaged in a fitness class to elucidate their reasons for participation. The reasons for involvement differed for men and women. Men rated health and fitness as the main reasons for participation and women indicated the release of tension and social aspects of exercise as the most appealing. Exercising can give the exerciser an enhanced sense of self; however it can also be that extrinsic motives to conform to an ideal standard of appearance create a situation whereby the number of exercise sessions become increased. Rigid conformity to a training schedule then becomes the norm with increased time being spent per week in physical activity. Feelings of self-worth become dependant on a strict training schedule.

Yates (1991) claims that excessive exercising and eating disorders are 'sister' activities and are strongly related to obsessionality. Rothenberg (1986) has also claimed that anorexia nervosa is a modern variant of obsessive-compulsive syndrome among women in Western cultures. This view the author based on anorectic's obsessional nature of their concern with food, their extreme perfectionism and their preoccupation with matters of control. Davis et al. (1995) argue that the relationships of physical activity, starvation and obsessive compulsiveness tend to become self-perpetuating in their resistance to change and can have a significant influence not only in the development but also in the maintenance of eating disorders.

There has for some time been increasing evidence of a connection between neurotic obsessions and compulsions and eating disorders. Comparisons between obsessive patients and anorectic patients indicate a close resemblance in many aspects of symptomatology in that anorectic patients can have such personality traits as rigidity, restraint in emotional expression and greater impulse control, all of which are highly compatible with obsessive compulsive personality disorder.

Davis et al. (1995) aimed to investigate the relationship between obsessive compulsiveness and behavioural and psychological aspects of exercise in women with anorexia nervosa. The authors compared them to a non-clinical sample of females classified as either moderate- or high-level exercisers. The results showed that obsessive compulsiveness, weight preoccupation and pathological aspects of exercise were significantly related to the level of physical activity among the eating disordered patients.

Strober (1980) found that although there was a significant decrease in the extent and severity of symptom obsessionality after weight restoration, there was no change in the obsessional personality characteristics of anorectic patients. Others (Holden, 1990), however, have found that the progression of the illness does tend to exacerbate obsessional thoughts and compulsive behaviour. Hyperactivity is a salient feature of anorexia nervosa and is significant in its link with obsessive compulsiveness.

Beumont et al. (1994) share the view that activity in some anorectic patients does take the form of an obsessive-compulsive disorder when they adopt a rigid exercise schedule to which they strictly adhere. They become distressed if they cannot carry out the same routine each day, including passing the same landmarks, doing the same or more laps and performing their exercise at the same time on each occasion. If their regime is interrupted they may repeat the whole process again from the beginning and if they fail to achieve their perfect routine they will become anxious and self-recriminatory. Brewerton et al. (1995) carried out a comparative study of eating-disordered patients with and without compulsive exercising. They studied 113 patients with eating disorders and found that 28% reported exercising more than 60 minutes daily and were thus defined as compulsive exercisers. These compulsive exercisers had significantly greater ratings of body dissatisfaction than non-compulsive exercisers. However, non-compulsive exercisers were significantly more likely than compulsive exercisers to vomit and use laxatives and they also had a higher frequency of binge eating. There was in fact a significantly higher frequency of compulsive exercising in the patients with anorexia nervosa (38.5%) than in those with bulimia nervosa (22.5%). In bulimia nervosa excessive exercise is seen as reflecting their chaotic eating behaviour. Like having binges of food, these individuals have binges of activity in between which they are very inactive.

Davis et al. (1994) aimed to establish the pathogenic significance of sport and exercise in the developing of eating disorders. The authors assessed hospitalized eating-disordered patients and an age-matched control group by collecting historical and current physical activity data. The results indicated that patients were more physically active than controls from adolescence onwards as well as prior to the onset of the primary diagnostic criteria for anorexia nervosa. Seventy-eight per cent of patients engaged in excessive exercise, 60% were competitive athletes prior to the onset of their disorder, 60% reported that sport or exercise pre-dated dieting and 75% claimed that physical activity levels steadily increased during the period when food intake and weight loss decreased the most. The authors argue that over-activity should, as a matter of course, be seen as a secondary symptom in anorexia nervosa but that, for a number of anorectic women, sport and exercise is an integral part of the pathogenesis and progression of self-starvation.

Media influence

The media have frequently been implicated as sources of overconcern with body focus, attractiveness and thinness. However, there now appears to be a recent media trend that is focusing on physical health and fitness rather than just appearance. During the last 10 or 15 years there has been a steady increase in the number of articles in popular women's magazines that advocate dieting and exercise for the punitive purpose of weight loss. Wiseman et al. (1992) found that the number of diet articles alone had decreased whereas those promoting dieting in combination with exercise had increased. The media have, in the past decade or so, promoted the idealized female body shape as even more slender than in previous years while at the same time promoting the physiological and indeed psychological benefits of regular physical activity, weight control and low-fat diets. This has resulted in health-related lifestyle changes becoming more of a national obsession. It could be that the health promotion propaganda presented by the media is responsible for its portrayal of physical attractiveness as being synonymous with physical fitness and that both qualities are personified in the young and ultra-slender female form.

Societal norms for attractiveness are becoming more specific and the accepted 'look' now includes an image of fitness as well as thinness. Regular exercise is now advocated as a desirable behaviour in promoting improved body tone as well as a means of losing weight. There may in fact be an assortment of physical ideals represented in the media, which can vary according to the different audiences being targeted. Nemeroff et al. (1994) assessed the content of magazine articles, examining gender differences, time trends and magazine audience type. Four areas of content were examined – health, fitness, beauty and weight loss – in an effort to capture the major aspects of body focus. This study was undertaken over a 12-year period in a sample of magazines oriented to three distinct audiences: traditional, high fashion and modern. The results indicated huge gender differences with female-targeted magazines, not surprisingly, well exceeding those of male-targeted ones for all content categories assessed. There were also clear differences in content between magazine types. There was, in fact, a decrease in emphasis on weight loss in women's magazines over the period studied and with an increase in weight loss focus in men's magazines. Mishkind et al. (1986) propose that males are now receiving more dieting messages than they did in the past so that today's male needs to be (a) not fat, but also (b) not too thin and (c) muscular. However men are very much an understudied group with regard to body image and media influence on it.

For some time now, thinness has been seen as a desirable attribute for women, however this acceptable female shape is becoming thinner. Slimness is associated with self-control, elegance, social attractiveness and youth, whereas obesity promotes feelings of isolation, depression, failure and unattractiveness. It is undoubtedly true that many eating-disorder patients become physically overactive in response to media pressures that link self-worth and happiness to physical activity and fitness. Wichman and Martin (1992) argue that compulsive exercising has now emerged as a clinical problem.

Furnham et al. (1994) investigated the perception of body shapes by females from four different exercising backgrounds but from a similar socio-economic background. The four groups each consisted of fifteen women:

- female bodybuilders;
- rowers;
- netballers;
- a sedentary control group.

The sports were chosen by the authors because of their traditional acceptance or non-acceptance as feminine sports. The authors found that those women who exercise, possess more positive perceptions of their own bodies and an increased acceptance of muscular body shapes, despite their divergence from cultural ideals. Such increased tolerance, the authors argue, appears to be linked to the importance of muscular power in the individual sport. This study would suggest that exercise could play a role in creating a greater tolerance for shapes which deviate from the norm and may have a valuable role in helping a broader range of female shapes to become more culturally acceptable.

Athletes

Research regarding dysfunctional weight maintenance in athletes focuses on two main areas – the actual eating and dieting behaviours and psychological attitudes. There is evidence that athletes engage in pathological food behaviours but the question still exists as to whether the runner who resembles the eating-disordered patient in food and weight-related issues also shares the same psychopathological symptoms found in the clinical population. This research has been made difficult at times as studies have failed to separate subjects by sport and in some cases by gender.

The prevalence of eating disorders in female athletes is reported to be between 15–62% (Nattiva et al., 1994; Rosen, 1986). However Davis et al. (1994) found that 60% of their eating disordered patient sample had been involved in competitive athletics or dance before the onset of their illness. This would indicate that the prevalence rates could in fact be very high. It is often the case that individuals begin to exercise as an initial pursuit of fitness, after which it then becomes a pursuit of thinness. The typical female athlete experiences body-image pressures at a number of levels, from those performance-related pressures reinforced by coaches and trainers, to those seen in the judging criteria where often the physically attractive athletes have the 'winning edge'. There has been an enormous increase in serious athletic participation by women so that what traditionally had been almost exclusively the domain of men has now become an important aspect of living for a substantial number of women in industrialized societies.

Taub and Blinde (1994) carried out a study to determine whether certain groups of adolescent females were more vulnerable to disordered eating patterns or usage of pathogenic weight control techniques. Subjects included 650 high-school females and, of these, 302 were athletes (basketball, track and field, cross country, volleyball, tennis and softball) and 89 students were performance squad members (such as cheerleaders) and 259 students were not engaged in any of these activities. The results indicated that high-school students participating in selected sport teams and those in performance squads were no more at risk than their classmates who did not participate in these activities for disordered eating patterns or pathogenic weight control usage. It could possibly be that, at this level of sport, these students do not receive intense pressures from coaches or squad sponsors to maintain a certain weight.

Athletes have long been seen as models of physical fitness and health. However it has recently been postulated by some researchers (Black et al., 1988) that the sports environment is a critical factor in the etiology of unhealthy eating and weight management behaviours as well as of distorted attitudes concerning body size and shape. Petrie (1996) looked at the relative frequency of behavioural and psychological indices of eating disorders in college athletes and non-athletes. The participants were 230 and 250 female non-athletes and 187 male and 113 female athletes. The male and female athletes were classified separately as being in either a lean sport (that is where weight or appearance are central to success) or a non-lean sport and then compared with their non-athlete counterpart. The authors found a generally low bulimic score and argue that the preoccupation with and pursuit of thinness did not manifest itself through bingeing or purging but it seemed likely that the students engaged in other pathogenic weight-control behaviours such as excessive exercise and strict dieting to help achieve their desired weight and appearance. Their other findings show that female athletes, especially non-lean sport athletes, are more satisfied with their bodies and feel more worthwhile, effective and in control of their lives than non-athletes. This would indicate that sport provides a positive relationship between sport involvement and various aspects of psychological health. The male athletes also possess more positive psychological states, such as increased feelings of worth and security as well as greater satisfaction with body shape. These males, like all males, are socialized to pursue a body shape that is defined by increases in strength and muscle mass as well as improvements in physical conditioning.

Stoutjesdyk and Jevne (1993) argue that athletes in certain sports display a higher tendency towards eating disorders than athletes in other sports. The authors gave 104 female and 87 male athletes the EAT. The athletes were classified according to their type of sport. The results showed that 10.6% of the female athletes and 4.6% of the male athletes scored in the 'anorectic' range. This prevalence for female athletes is comparable to other research on college populations but it is higher for the male athletes than would be expected in the general population. Activities that emphasize leanness, and athletes in weight-matched activities, were found to have higher EAT scores than those in non-weight-restricting activities. The authors therefore suggest that different groups of athletes may be at different risks for developing eating disorders.

Athletes share many anorectic characteristics such as dietary faddism, controlled calorie consumption, specific carbohydrate avoidance and low body weight. There is the argument against eating disorder psychopathology among athletes in terms of their motivation for slimness. Athletes are seen to exercise to lose weight as a means of improving their performance, whereas eating-disordered individuals exercise to burn calories and shed weight. However athletes are often introduced to pathogenic methods of weight control such as purging and self-induced vomiting by well meaning but unknowledgeable teammates. Athletes participating in activities that emphasize leanness for the sake of better performance and appearance, as in gymnastics, long-distance running and diving, are more prone to develop eating disorders than athletes in non-weight restricting sports.

Williamson et al. (1995) studied the risk factors for the development of eating disorder symptoms in female college athletes. They investigated three risk factors – social influence for thinness, athletic performance anxiety and self-appraisal for athletic achievement. They recruited 98 women from eight sport teams at a major university and their results indicated that eating disorder symptoms in college athletes were significantly influenced by sociocultural pressure for thinness, athletic performance, anxiety and negative self-appraisal of athletic achievement. Should these risk factors lead to overconcern with body size and shape, then the authors argue that the occurrence of an eating disorder is more probable.

Bale (1996) found that obsessive dieting and demanding training schedules of some athletes can cause changes in physical body composition and menstrual abnormalities indicating common factors between them and anorectics. Their findings would suggest that a link between disordered eating, dieting and over-participation in exercise can cause a dramatic decrease in body composition and menstrual problems, which can cause health problems. However amenorrhea in athletes may be more a result of being an athlete than being anorectic. Amenorrhea can be associated with sustained and frequent exercise in athletes whose weight and body fat levels are within normal limits (Kaplan and Woodside, 1987).

In such individuals the critical factor seems to be that their low energy intake rather than low weight may be burning too many calories through excessive exercise in order to support their menstrual periods. Therefore it may or may not be related to an eating disorder.

Runners

Yates (1991) reports on the similar attitudes and behaviours of runners, gymnasts and dieters. These include an emphasis on food restriction to help maintain a low body mass, intensive exercise and a concern for a slim physique. It could therefore be that distance runners and gymnasts are at a greater risk of developing an eating disorder similar to that of anorectics.

Ogles et al. (1995) compared the participative motives of male and female runners registered in races of varying lengths, such as, marathons, half-marathons and 5K and 10K races. They found that shorter races were composed of a high proportion of women. Women saw weight concern, affiliation, self-esteem, psychological coping and life meaning as more important motives for running than men. Men, on the other hand, were characterized by an emphasis on achieving recognizable success.

Obligatory runners are those runners who spent large amounts of time on running numerous miles and hours per week despite injury and at the cost of interpersonal relationships. Yates (1991) argues that the obligatory runners run excessively as part of a compulsive process that is similar to the compulsiveness evidenced by individuals with anorexia nervosa. The obligatory runner is seen to be perfectionistic, anxious and they may also have depressive symptoms. Yates (1991) argued that running is an analogue of anorexia nervosa for men and that men are more likely to become obligatory runners. However women are reported to derive greater benefits from running than men in terms of opportunities to meet people, relief from depression and feeling less shy.

Morgan (1979) reported that, in many instances of running, the commitment far exceeds any reasonable effort to achieve physical fitness. Warning signs when this has occurred include the person (a) insisting on exercising daily as if life depended on it (b) experiencing withdrawal symptoms such as irritability, anxiety and depression when restrained from exercising and (c) continuing to exercise even when it is socially and medically contra-indicated.

Dancers and gymnasts

Clearly there are a number of sports like gymnastics and dance where success is not only determined by technical prowess but by grace and physical appeal and therefore an ultra-slender figure provides an important performance advantage. Garner and Garfinkel (1980) indicated that dancers, models and athletes are among those possibly at high risk of developing eating disorders. Factors such as high levels of competition and leanness linked to success have been cited as possible predisposing factors for developing eating disorders.

Ballet dancers are particularly vulnerable individuals in a subculture where extreme pressures of slimness exist. Ballet dancing places considerable emphasis on control over body shape and weight that reflects an aesthetic preference for thinness. Garner and Garfinkel (1980) found that the demand for dieting and slimness is often encountered by dancers to a greater extent than by any other females in a Western cultural environment. The prevalence of anorexia nervosa in ballet dancers is significantly higher than in the normal population. Garner and Garfinkel (1980) found this to be 6.5% in three professional dance schools whereas Szmukler et al. (1985) found it to be 7% of students in a London ballet school.

Le Grange et al. (1994) examined the presence of anorectic-like symptoms in a group of 49 female ballet students and the results indicated a prevalence of 4.1% for anorexia nervosa. Over one-half of the students were underweight and reported deliberate attempts to lose weight during term times. Almost the same number indicated that they saw themselves as fat and controlled their food intake either by dieting, vomiting or laxative and diuretic abuse. The students' commitment to a dancing career, the authors felt, served as a positive reinforcer not to allow weight loss to continue since it would ultimately force them to be asked to leave the ballet school. The authors proposed, therefore, that their commitment to dancing as opposed to dieting seemed to exceed any secondary gains that could be derived from having an eating disorder.

Pressure to succeed

Families can also influence family members' commitment to exercise and this is especially so of parents who are themselves very much involved in sports or physical activity and consciously or subconsciously pass this commitment on to their children. Older children are pressurized to succeed in their sporting or dancing achievements in order to fulfil the psychological needs of their parents. Totler et al. (1996) have referred to this as 'achievement by proxy' – that is, where there is a strong parental encouragement of a potentially dangerous endeavour for the purpose of gaining fame and financial reward.

Comments by coaches or judges that the loss of a few pounds will improve athletes' scores may only exacerbate the symptoms of eating disorders. Beumont et al. (1994) report on some ballet teachers who openly urge their students to maintain a body mass index at a level within the anorexia nervosa range in order to achieve success.

Conclusion

Some may take the view that there are very definite health benefits to regular exercise and our society's preoccupation with thinness and weight loss may not in fact be pathological. Psychologically oriented explanations of the mental health benefits of fitness training have also associated exercise with improvements in mood states and an improved sense of wellbeing. However, although exercise is seen as healthy when done in moderation it can also result in other problems such as injuries, muscle breakdown, fatigue and excessive weight loss if it is carried out excessively (Wichman and Martin, 1992). When exercise reaches a level of compulsive behaviour it can also affect social and work competence.

It could be that women who are particularly anxious about their weight and appearance gravitate toward sport environments that normalize and provide an outlet for their concerns. There is also the possibility that athletes whose natural body builds do not match the ideal characteristics for their sport may also take extra steps to remain thin without considering the negative side effects involved in harmful weight-control techniques. Further action should be taken to reduce pathological dieting in the athletic community. Coaches should educate themselves and their athletes on healthy nutritional practices, the consequences of pathological weight-loss techniques and warning signs of actual eating disorders. In order to appreciate fully the influences of sport environments on disordered eating it will be necessary to conduct longitudinal investigations looking at athletes before, during and after their involvement in organized sport. There is, in fact, a great absence of studies describing the treatment of compulsive exercising in eating disordered patients and this could be indicative of the difficulty in treating such patients who compulsively over-exercise.

A serious commitment to sport or exercise has significance not only for its potential to create a psychological predisposition to an eating disorder but also as a contributing factor in its progression and maintenance.

PART 4
Occupational therapy in eating disorders

Chapter 18
Occupational therapy in the treatment of eating disorders

Eating disorders now affect a large number of individuals. In our culture, thinness provides a means whereby people of all shapes and sizes express their feelings of loneliness, anger, fear and hurt by harming their bodies with food or self-starvation. A single mode of treatment is no longer seen as appropriate and it would appear that the treatment for eating disorders is moving towards eclecticism. Martin (1990) suggests that since the causes and cures of eating disorders are multifaceted and involve patients, their families and their social values, then successful treatment may require the concurrent use of various therapeutic techniques. Yager (1994) has shown that a variety of treatment approaches for anorexia nervosa and bulimia nervosa including cognitive-behavioural therapy (CBT) and interpersonal therapy are useful as well as psychodynamic approaches, particularly in long-term treatment. Herzog et al. (1992b) confirmed that most therapists do, in fact, routinely use a combination of CBT and psychodynamic therapy in their work with this patient population. All anorexia nervosa and bulimia nervosa patients need a psychotherapeutic intervention in order to reverse their entrenched ideas and distorted body images as well as to help them achieve other life goals. The model of human occupation (Kielhofner, 1985) would suggest that eating-disordered individuals are dysfunctional not only in their attitudes and habits regarding eating and weight control but also in pursuing and engaging in meaningful activity (occupation).

The primary focus of occupational therapy is therefore to normalize weight and eating behaviours, modifying unhelpful thought processes that maintain the disorder, while dealing with the emotional issues in the individual's life that create a need for the eating disorder. The use of activity that is carefully planned so as to facilitate change in the patient is a unique characteristic of occupational therapy. Occupational therapy closely resembles the actual living situation more than any other treatment setting and therefore provides a realistic environment in which the patient can test her developing skills in living. The occupational therapist enables the patient to achieve maximum function at all levels of psychological, physical and social competence.

Activities are central to the practice of occupational therapy. Hinojosa et al. (1983) argue that activities are seen as tasks or experiences in which the person participates actively. Crafts are seen as creative activities and they are differentiated from other occupational therapy activities in that they result in a tangible end product. This end product is indicative of success or failure by the patient. Of course creativity need not only be oriented towards achieving specific end products; it can also be associated with the capacity to think in new and different ways. Eating-disordered patients are dysfunctional not only in their attitudes and habits related to eating and weight control, but also in their pursuit of engagement in meaningful occupation. Anorectic patients can be perfectionists who set themselves high standards of performance but Boskind-Lodahl (1976) reports that their occupational goals are frequently unclear. The occupational therapist can contribute to the multidisciplinary care of the eating-disordered patient by focusing on dysfunction in occupational behaviour. It should not be assumed that the individual participates in activities just to achieve. It should be highlighted that the goal of participation in activities can also be fun and enjoyment. Play is an essential part of everyday life and it should also occur in occupational therapy. However the occupational therapy environment should also encourage a degree of risk taking without the fear of feeling rebuked for it. What is essential is that the choice of activity will help to bring about change in the individual.

Strober and Yager (1985) provided a long list of attributes that they saw as vital for a therapist working with eating-disordered patients. They felt the therapist should be knowledgeable about the illness and the therapeutic principles, open and non-evasive, intuitive, patient, non-critical and should be able to instil trust and confidence. The therapist should also be able to relate to the patient in a manner that conveys empathy for, and tolerance of painful emotions and challenges to treatment. Above all they felt that the therapist should show a genuine spontaneity, humour and flare for the dramatic. Almost all of the research would suggest that an emotionally healthy therapist is more likely to elicit a good outcome than an emotionally disturbed one.

Therapists such as Boskind-Lodahl (1976) and Palazzoli (1978) have always held the view that female therapists work better with eating disordered patients than male therapists. The therapist's personal attitude towards our society's current emphasis on slimness is also relevant to the treatment of eating disorders and it makes good clinical sense that an occupational therapist who has her own preoccupation with weight is probably not best suited to working with eating disordered patients. Hsu (1990) suggests that therapists who are perceived as warm, accepting and credible tend to produce better outcomes.

It is essential for occupational therapists to remember that the individual they are dealing with often reports feeling devalued, ashamed and 'out of control'. Patience is the key to treatment with these patients. It is essential not to put them into an aggressive treatment programme before they are ready, otherwise these individuals will be lost – at best to self-discharge or at worst to suicide. At all times the occupational therapist needs to place great emphasis on her conviction that the patient will get better. The occupational therapist's sense of empathy with the patient's struggles will greatly help her on the road to recovery. Yager (1994) has described empathy as having an insightful awareness, including the meaning and significance of the feelings, emotions and behaviour of another person. Empathy is generally seen to be a desirable element in treatment. However, great importance is also placed on developing rapport and a solid therapeutic relationship with patients if treatment is to be productive.

The complexity of these patients makes it helpful to integrate various theoretical approaches. It would appear that occupational therapists use the occupational dysfunction and cognitive-behavioural frames of reference most in their work with eating-disordered patients. However Peloquin (1989) argues that, as more theoretical models are developed, there is a need for occupational therapists to apply both the art and science of their profession to the treatment and care of their patients. The occupational therapist's role is to evaluate, treat and assist with discharge planning and follow-up care in order to return the patient to as normal a lifestyle as possible. Although working with this patient population can be extremely frustrating and challenging, this author would have to say that being a part of the recovery process can be extremely rewarding.

How the anorexia nervosa patient presents

The typical anorectic patient is a girl in her teens or early twenties who appears depressed, tearful, perhaps hostile and frequently agitated. She will appear emaciated, often having lost between 10–40% of her pre-illness body weight. Some patients present as walking skeletons but, despite this appearance, they will be full of energy, becoming restless and overactive. Despite the withered and emaciated face, often their eyes are conspicuously vivid and bright. In anorexia nervosa, the patient's hands and feet may become mottled red and purple, even in a warm atmosphere. Some patients may complain of discomfort when the weather is mild, though this may change to pain when it is cold. Other physical effects of this condition may include a dark and dirty appearance of the skin despite the fact that personal cleanliness is rarely, if ever, a problem with this patient group. Skin texture is often rough and desquamation is also common. Thinning of head hair and the growth of fine downy hair over the normally hairless parts of the body, especially the trunk and face, are also common. Some patients may also show signs of minor self-mutilation.

If the patient's illness is of long duration then her muscles may waste, shrink and ultimately become weak. Their growth may cease and this may result in the young adolescent never reaching her full height potential. It also helps to explain why a lot of these patients look so much younger than their age.

The psychological manifestations that are frequently found in anorectic patients include pressured defiant speech, explosive anger, a low frustration tolerance and a short attention span, although they can also have the appearance of being alert and aloof.

Even after admission to hospital, patients may still present an active refusal to take any food and every effort must be made by the occupational therapist to encourage the patient to eat. However it may be that a small number of patients may swing from severe starvation to acute bulimia, when they will stuff themselves with an excessive amount of any type of food that they can find. During such a phase all efforts by the therapist should be made to impose control on the patient and prevent access to food, other than the prescribed diet. The patient will welcome such control as bouts of over-eating are usually followed by grave feelings of guilt. Such guilt is likely to lead to depressive reactions or even suicide attempts.

In hospital the patient will be keen to continue her daily ritual of exercises and it is often difficult to persuade the anorectic to settle into a pattern of bed rest. Such reserves of energy alongside her continued dedication to her schoolwork go hand-in-hand in providing a safe diversion from her other premorbid occupations. Initially irritability is a frequent component of the clinical picture and anorectic patients will avoid discussing the significance of their starvation and try to behave as if the problem did not exist or concern them.

Manipulative behaviour on the part of the patient toward occupational therapy and other staff is likely to present during the early stages of treatment while the patient tests to determine the limits set for her. At this stage it is also likely that the patient's mood will be variable and she will often deny that she or her family have any problems.

The patient may recall how her general behaviour changed as her weight dropped and she will describe the bizarre means she adopted to avoid carbohydrate foods, at the same time taking an active interest in the family cooking. Some patients find that by spending time on cooking it helps make them feel somewhat less depressed and anxious. The patient does not complain of her loss of appetite but explains how her steady loss of weight is a triumph in self-discipline. This gives her a sense of achievement, usually over other members of the family. The anorectic patient is proud of her lean appearance and will often complain endlessly about her feelings of being fat and being overfed. She particularly remarks on areas such as her waist, tummy, hips and thighs as being particularly huge. She will talk about this more after she has seen herself naked in the shower or after having a meal.

The patient may describe herself as a perfectionist and a 'doer' who carefully plans and organizes all her activities. She will describe a life chronically concerned with body functions, hypochondriasis, food – above all a lonely and withdrawn existence. The anorectic may also recall her dreams, which can provide further details about her attitude to food. Such dreams are frequently bizarre in nature and frightening to the patients.

A large number of patients, both male and female, display an essential fear of sexuality. They will talk about their fear of growing up and maturation and will recall their difficulty in accepting their sexual identity. In the male patient, this author has found that anorexia nervosa occurs mostly in preadolescent or conspicuously immature adolescent boys who present with an inadequate sexual identity and those boys who have not yet accepted themselves as males.

The patient's initial account of idealized intrafamilial relationships often proves fallacious at a later stage of treatment, when the patient feels more secure in her environment and more confident in relating the family problems. The anorectic may talk about her life as having been an ordeal when she was constantly trying to live up to the expectations of her family, always fearing she has not achieved enough in comparison with others and therefore being a disappointing failure. The patient's recall of her childhood is often in complete contrast to her parents as she remembers it as a constant state of misery and frustration. She could never do what she wanted, but it always had to be as her parents wished. The weight loss accomplishes much as far as the patient is concerned as her parents often withdraw into being protective and non-demanding toward the child who will, for the first time, experience power and control over them.

Despite the fact that anorexia nervosa patients seem to wish to dominate all around them, they do in reality feel quite helpless. It is necessary for them, in the early stages of treatment at least, to feel that the staff are in control. Until they regain their ability to take decisions, all decisions are made by the staff. Bed rest is advocated as a step in implementing control. Bed rest will also help to decrease the patient's physical activity, which will reduce caloric expenditure and allow for weight gain. Control is a central feature of anorexia nervosa. The anorectic patient experiences herself as not being in control of her behaviour. The methods employed by her to gain control over her body include not just dieting but also vomiting, purging and excessive exercise, practised singly or in combination.

As treatment progresses, it is common for the patient to become more depressed. If menstruation returns while she is still in hospital it can be a very distressing time and she is likely to become more anxious and depressed.

'Obstinate', 'manipulative', 'deceitful' and 'stubborn' are words that are often used to describe manifest behaviour of the anorectic. However such descriptions convey nothing of the despair and helplessness that these individuals experience. The increasing isolation that anorexia nervosa brings into these patients' lives is probably one of the most devastating effects of this disorder as the patient becomes completely self-absorbed, ruminating only about weight and food. Thoughts of food crowd out her ability to think about anything else.

The anorectic patient is a person who, on the one hand, clings in a desperate attempt to control, while making strenuous efforts to be a separate being with her own individuality. She is a perfectionist who works hard at achieving her goals. However, what the occupational therapist sees is an adolescent who presents with a self-imposed, smothered, stunted and threatened lifestyle.

Occupational therapy in anorexia nervosa

The anorexia nervosa patient is, for the most part, treated in an in-patient unit due to the severity of her illness and to bring some control and stability back into her eating. However a proportion of these anorectic patients do well as out-patients provided their emaciation is not severe (this will usually be about 70% of target weight), provided they have no serious medical complications, are motivated for change and have supportive friends and relatives. If successful, out-patient treatment has many advantages including costing less, avoiding the stigma of admission and the danger of being influenced by the behaviours of other patients. It may also cause less disruption to the patient's life. Treasure and Ward (1997) argue that there is now a greater need to consider out-patient treatment for anorexia nervosa. This view is supported by the Royal College of Psychiatrists (1992) and is reflective of the general move to provide psychiatric care within the community. However it does also highlight the reluctance of many anorectic patients to accept in-patient status. A few small-scale studies also suggest that out-patient treatment alone can be effective (Hall and Crisp, 1987; Treasure et al., 1995). It is the case, however, that out-patient or day-patient treatment does not provide as strong a sense of containment as might be found in an in-patient unit.

The management of the anorectic patient's treatment can be divided into three stages:

1. weight restoration, followed by
2. weight maintenance once target weight has been reached. The patient is then expected to be stable at this weight for at least four weeks during which time she moves into the
3. preparing for discharge and after care stage.

For this treatment to work it is essential that all staff work in close liaison.

The main points of the regime include:

- The patient being given a target weight that is assessed on the patient's present height and age of onset of illness – not the patient's present age as studies show that biological growth actually stops at the point of onset of illness.
- The patient is not allowed to eat anything in excess of the given diet, which consists of 3,000 calories daily.
- The patient is put on bed rest until target weight is achieved.
- The patient is weighed twice per week and is expected to gain 1–2 kg per week.
- Ongoing psychotherapy, family therapy and occupational therapy form an important part of the treatment programme.

Most patients achieve their target weight with this treatment.

Occupational therapy objectives

- To establish and retain a rapport with patients.
- To engage the patients willingness to collaborate in treatment. The patient is more likely to participate collaboratively if the patient and therapist can agree on treatment goals.
- To begin the process of weight restoration by replacing dietary restrictions with normal eating.
- To stimulate social, intellectual and emotional progress.
- To provide activities that encourage self-expression.
- To provide an opportunity to experiment with food shopping, cooking and eating with others.
- To encourage patients to accept their new shape and size.
- To help the patient experiment with fashion and make-up appropriate to her age.
- To encourage continuity of schoolwork.
- To provide social skills training.

Motivation to participate honestly in treatment is almost always difficult for patients with anorexia nervosa. Asking these patients to stop their anorectic behaviour is like asking them to give up their prized coping mechanism. Anorectic patients are afraid to change, which automatically limits their motivation to change. Even the smallest change in behaviour should be encouraged and praised. The occupational therapist should also be mindful of these patients' vulnerability to shame, criticism and judgement. The fears and tensions that are relieved by anorectic behaviour reflect deficient coping abilities in a number of areas. These include developmental transitions, fears of maturation, helplessness, poor self-esteem and disturbed relationships with family members or friends.

exia nervosa patients are often portrayed as competent, accom- and even academic overachievers. However, the anorectic patient lacks an awareness of her resources and confidence in her achievements. Bers and Quinlan (1992) in their study of perceived competence deficit in anorexia nervosa found that in areas not related to weight, anorectics indicated a high level of interests in a similar range of activities comparable to that of normal females. However, in contrast to normal participants, the anorexia nervosa patients felt unable to perform well in activities that did interest them. This disparity between interests and perceived abilities supports the view that anorectics, on the whole, feel incompetent and unable to perform well even though they participate in many activities and can claim many successes. Interestingly, dieting was one area in which the anorectic indicated a high level of ability, comparable to their level of interest and therefore experienced no deficit in competence there.

Stage I activities

The patient will be on bed rest for most of the time during this stage.

Creative activities

Occupational therapists use purposeful activity (occupation) as a medium to help patients achieve their desired goals. Crafts have been used as clinical tools since the profession of occupational therapy was established. For many patients craft activities are very meaningful. However the end product needs to be pleasing and skilfully executed if the patient is to regard it with respect. Sometimes teaching new skills is a good way to develop skills. Crafts help eating-disordered patients to develop a feeling of mastery and increased self-confidence if they can complete a challenging project. Many anorectics will say that they won't be able to do anything but it is difficult to maintain this stance when positive feedback and compliments are coming from others after their success in completing the task.

The choice of crafts and other creative activities have changed over the years, mostly due to trends in fashion but also due to the length of hospital stays being reduced. Breines (1995) supports the view that crafts do demand problem solving, physical ability, orientation and perceptual constancy in order to achieve a finished object. The patient gains from the feedback received in seeing the tangible end product as well as gaining feelings of personal and social satisfaction.

The choice of such activities is left to the patient, who has as wide a variety as possible offered to her. Trends in fashion and crafts will vary and influence her choice. However the following can be useful and popular.

Beadwork can be carried out in virtually any material (wooden, copper, pottery, wire, cardboard and glass etc.). Making bead articles is a precise activity. Designing the article, such as a necklace, encourages creativity in the patient and in order to carry out this activity the patient needs to acquire endless patience and concentration, as well as fine motor and sequencing skills. There is always great pleasure in wearing a pleasing finished product and being complimented on its worth helps to improve self-esteem.

Enamelling is going through a popular phase, especially with adolescents, as it can be used to produce various articles including jewellery and pictures. This activity, however, demands great care since the objects are very hot coming out of the kiln. It also demands great patience and fine motor skills.

Other popular creative activities that are used are macramé, appliqué work and decoupage work as these can be easily accomplished while in bed. They also lend themselves to a wide choice of finished articles and can be carried out at all skill levels. Of course the anorectic's striving for minute detail and her perfectionistic attitudes have a major contribution to play when it comes to creative activities. The basic principles and values of occupational therapy are seen in the use of crafts. However in recent years there has been a decline in their use. This departure from the use of crafts as therapeutic activities can in fact be seen as a departure from occupational therapy itself.

Beauty and make-up care

It has been claimed that the problems concerning adolescent maturation, which are basic but not specific to the disorder, are rooted in such matters as gender identity, individualization and adolescent challenges (Crisp, 1974; Bruch, 1974; Kalucy et al., 1977). The aim of this activity is to build up the patient's self-confidence in the area of personal appearance and to provide her with the opportunity to experiment with make-up so as to establish a self-image appropriate to her age. The anorectic, as a child, may have been under great pressure to fulfil her mother's image of how she should look. Unfortunately such attitudes are not easily acceptable to an adolescent girl who is trying to establish her own identity. To imitate her mother, in terms of make-up techniques, is usually much too ageing and outdated for adolescent girls. The latest trends in adolescent make-up are usually much brighter, more eye-catching and less subtle than make-up worn by adults.

The occupational therapist and patient spend a lot of time looking through fashion magazines, while paying special attention to make-up and hair styles. If the patient is hesitant about using a lot of make-up it may be necessary to progress in stages, starting with polishing fingernails, then using lipstick, eye make-up, foundation and so on. Of course once their enthusiasm grows patients may spend the full day just experimenting with putting on and taking off make-up and painting designs on their fingernails. The fingernail designs can often be 'works of art' showing minute fine line details executed with the anorectics' usual obsessional craving for perfection.

Feedback is important to the patient and it is often not necessary for this to come from the occupational therapist as other patients and members of staff will spontaneously comment on their attractive appearance. Often the anorectic patient will hold in higher esteem those comments from other patients as they see them as individuals who are removed from the treatment programme.

It is important to allow the patient freedom of choice in finding their identity but often it is necessary to discourage parents from sabotaging such a venture. Sessions should be as relaxed and enjoyable as possible and may bring together two or three other anorectic patients who are also on bed rest so that all four of them may work and learn from each other. This activity also has a great morale boasting aspect, which any patient on bed rest will fully appreciate.

Schoolwork

As a group these patients have been referred to as academic over-achievers (Bruch, 1974). They will usually excel in their school performance and this has often been interpreted as indicating great giftedness and intelligence. However those achievements are often the result of great effort, which becomes even greater after they have become ill as it provides them with a safe-diversion from their other more disturbing preoccupations of food and eating (Halmi et al., 1977; Crisp, 1995). The role of the occupational therapist is to encourage the patient to continue with her schoolwork only on a modified scale. The patient is encouraged to keep in contact with school-friends and liaise with her schoolteacher in an effort to keep her work up to date. Certain hours are negotiated with the patient to be used for school-work in an effort to establish a more acceptable work routine for her.

If this plan is to work then it is important that the patient is able to use her spare time constructively. The patient would be encouraged to develop a hobby that she might be able to continue after discharge from hospital. She will also be encouraged to invite other patients to share a game of scrabble, a jig-saw or a game of cards, in fact almost anything that would encourage socialization and prevent her from withdrawing into her school studies.

Projective art

Projective techniques are based on assumptions regarding how an individual responds to a situation. It is assumed that the responses are based on past experiences and contain information on how inner feelings and relationships with objects and persons are organized into one's life experience.

The success of the occupational therapist in using projective techniques will depend on her knowledge of psychodynamic and psycho-analytic theory and practice and the quality of her emotional maturity and self-knowledge. This discussion is focused on the use of projective art, but clay modelling, music, poetry, puppetry, dance and drama can be used successfully as projective techniques.

The use of projective materials alone, however, does not provide a comprehensive treatment programme for the purposes of occupational therapy. Validation of information gained in a projective technique should be sought in other treatment areas and by other evaluation methods. A projective treatment approach provides the patient with the opportunity to show how she thinks and feels and to externalize her experiences and communicate these, either individually to the therapist or group members if in a group situation. Projective art encourages insight and self-awareness in the patient and it gives many of the anorexia nervosa patients the courage to be themselves as well as providing the staff with the opportunity to draw from them their conflicts, fears and emotions. This art material rests heavily on imaginal processes or fantasy and it provides a permanent record to the treatment team, to see, to interpret, or discuss as appropriate.

The power of art media to evoke emotional rather than intellectual responses is at the core of the basis of the usefulness of art as a therapeutic medium (Howard, 1990; Peacock, 1991). The use of art helps the occupational therapist to gain access often to the unexpected thoughts and feelings of the patient while also relieving the patient of the pressure of verbalizing some of these feelings.

Art is used with eating-disordered patients to help increase the patient's awareness of unrecognized and unacknowledged feelings. It is seen as an outlet for expression, to help increase self-control and to encourage mastery over impulses and fears (Wolf et al., 1986). Art gives form to chaos and provides a means of productive functioning. It also helps the patient to 'work through' her problems. Art can provide visual evidence not only of the patient's struggle but also of her progress.

Art begins as soon as the patient is admitted to hospital and on bed rest. She is given a box of paints and a thick paintbrush and asked not to spend more than half an hour on the given subject. The patient is asked to express her feelings about the set subject rather than being concerned about producing a pretty painting with lots of detail. Alternatively clay may be substituted for paint when the patient may be asked to model specific subjects such as 'the animal I think I am' or 'the animal I think I'd like to be'.

The quality of the artwork is much less important than the act of producing a painting that patients feel they can discuss. The emphasis is on the patient's own interpretation and self-understanding of her work. Some of her concerns expressed in her art can provide a focus for treatment in individual or group therapy.

During the early stage of treatment, the subject titles given to the patients may be less threatening and might include 'my family', 'friendship' or 'myself after a meal'. These are good subjects as a starting point in helping the occupational therapist establish a rapport with the patient.

Paintings 1 and 2

These two painting were carried out by two sisters who were both admitted to hospital suffering from anorexia nervosa. In the first painting the patient described how fragmented she sees her family, while painting herself to the left as having no boundaries and no control.

The family were never together for meals, as their father ate business lunches so that when he came home in the evening he would refuse to eat with the family and instead would eat just bread and honey on his own.

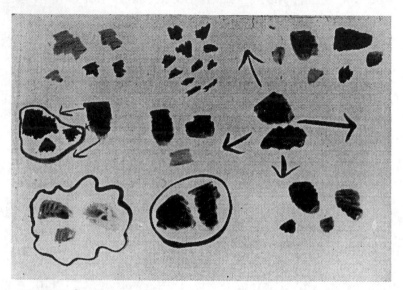

Painting 1 – My family

Painting 2 – My family

Painting 1 – My family

This painting is carried out by the elder sister. This patient was 21 years old and had three previous admissions to the unit. Her illness was of eight years standing. Her history goes back to when she was at school and weighed 27.3 kg at a height of 1.3 metres and was told she was overweight and should diet. The patient was admitted at a low weight of 22.2 kg. During her dieting the patient talked of a 'new-found freedom'.

Painting 10 - The animal I think I am

After her third hospital admission, the patient began to overeat and at a height of 1.3 m reached a maximum weight of 88.9 kilos, which is very overweight. During her bouts of overeating it was virtually impossible to control her behaviour. She would steal food from the ward kitchen and devour a loaf of bread in a matter of minutes while hiding in the kitchen. So great were her fits of eating that she would munch eggs whole from the fridge without removing their outer shell. It took some time to bring this patient's weight down, but she did become stable and continued to function well just slightly above her target weight.

Painting 2 – My family

This is the same family painted by the younger sister. She has not included herself. Her father is in the centre playing the dominant role and her mother, who is depicted as an incomplete person, stands in the wings. Although the patient has painted details such as the father's clothes and hair, she has omitted to give anyone in the family a mouth with which to eat. The patient has depicted her elder sister as just a little child, when in fact she was 21 years old at the time.

Painting 3 – My family

Painting 4 – My family

Painting 3 – My family

This reflects the patient's family as she saw it. She has described it as a church with sound foundations, when in fact there is little warmth coming from it and we can see in the foreground the coldness of the cemetery. This patient felt that both her family and social life were centred around the Church.

This patient's father was himself very underweight as a teenager and weighed under 54 kg at a height of 1.83 m. He was described as liking a quiet routine in the house and did not like the patient to bring friends home. He was seen to run his family as a 'tight ship' with very high moral beliefs.

In this family there was a complete absence of any physical contact or cuddling and the patient recalls how she cried with joy on receiving her outstanding A-level results only to be sent away to dry her eyes before her mother saw her crying. The patient also recalls the difficulty her father had when she reached puberty at 14 years and stopped coming down after a bath to get dried in front of the fire. Puberty was also seen as a difficulty with her mother, whom the patient recalls as having made her a very small bikini top in order to flatten her bust.

Painting 4 – My family

This patient, although married, painted her family as consisting of her parents, sibling and herself. They are represented as chairs situated in a warm and cosy room in front of the fire, but still, however, no warmth within the family itself. This girl married a quiet, independent and self-willed husband and their relationship was poor. She was a patient who often vomited and who resorted to purging as well in an effort to control her weight. She had many previous admissions to various hospitals but her admission this time lasted only four weeks when she discharged herself. Unfortunately this patient died of starvation less than a year later.

Painting 5 – Friendship

Painting 6 – Myself after a meal

Painting 5 – Friendship

This painting of friendship is simplicity itself and is very typical of the work of the anorexia nervosa patient. It shows the hand of friendship being extended in offering an apple but no one has been given a mouth with which to eat it. You can see how young and childlike these figures are, with the children playing with toy blocks in the foreground.

This patient described a series of friendships, but only one friend at a time. She had strong feelings for each girl and developed different interests and a different personality with each new friend. The patient felt she had to go along with what others enjoyed and the idea that she had something of her own individuality to contribute to a friendship never occurred to her.

Patients' paintings will often contain the same gross distortions as those revealed in body image assessments. Useful titles that expose this distortion include, 'myself after a meal', 'myself at target weight' or 'how I see myself'. These paintings will often show greater distortions in the early stages of treatment when the patient is of a very low body weight. However as she nears target weight and maintains this weight, often her paintings will show less exaggerations and distortions.

The next two paintings are the work of the same girl aged 17 years.

Painting 6 – Myself after a meal

It is possible to see clearly just how enormously fat and shapeless this patient sees herself and the conspicuous absence of any hands by which to feed herself. This patient always expressed the feeling that she was being overfed by others on whom she could exercise no control. This painting is explicit of the sadness that this girl continually expressed. Her parents were divorced and she lived with her stepfather. On the ward she would totally isolate herself and curl up on her bed and pretend to sleep in an effort to ward off any staff and patients who might wish to engage in friendly interactions. However she became involved in a social skills programme, which, although extremely threatening for her, she did attend with great enthusiasm.

Following her discharge this patient became very depressed but she somehow managed to control her eating habits. She progressed well as an out-patient and completely changed her image – she had her long hair cut and re-styled. This was the long hair that she used to cover her face to hide away from everyone. She also began to wear very fashionable clothes and new make-up and was last heard to be doing well and studying medicine.

Painting 7 – Myself at target weight

Painting 7 – Myself at target weight

This next painting shows the patient's gross exaggeration of body image. She always compared her 'fat' with whale's blubber. Her body distortion would dictate everything she was involved in and was clearly visible in the drama group where she had great difficulty joining in activities that demanded close physical contact with other members. The patient felt that they would not only see her as fat, but also feel her 'blubber' if anyone was to touch her.

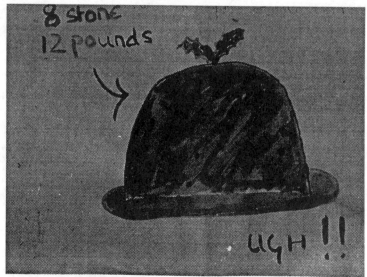

Painting 8 – Myself at target weight

Painting 8 – Myself at target weight

Here we have a large Christmas pudding weighing 8 stones, 12 pounds (56.2 kg). Although this is heavy for a Christmas pudding, it is an average weight for a young girl, but to this patient it seemed too 'revolting' to have to accept.

Painting 9 – Myself at target weight

This patient imagines how at target weight she feels only half a person. This she depicts in her painting by showing only half a house, explaining that the new part of her has yet to be revealed before she can get to 'grips' with her feelings.

Painting 9 – Myself at target weight

Painting 10 – The animal I think I am

This reflects the sadness of this patient who continually remarked on how enormous and shapeless she felt. The 21 little faces that she has painted just reiterate these feelings.

Painting 10 – The animal I think I am

Stage II activities

The patient will have reached target weight.

Regulated exercise

The physical effects of excessive exercising depend not only on the extent
and nature of the exercise, but also on the health and lifestyle of the
person doing the exercise. In anorexia nervosa patients overactivity will
exacerbate the state of under-nutrition and can also lead to physical
complications. Some patients even feel that excessive exercise brings a
certain respectability to weight-losing behaviours. However, their preoccupation with exercise can isolate the patient from her family and friends
and thus increase her social isolation.

The management of exercise in anorexia nervosa remains difficult and
controversial and little consideration has been given to containing the
patient's hyperactive behaviours. Exercise is viewed as being bad for the
anorectic patient because of its high energy requirements and also the
manner in which it encourages obsessional thinking and behaviour
patterns. However there are positive benefits to permitting regulated
exercise since exercise allows for behavioural reinforcement and cognitive
restructuring and has obvious metabolic effects. Most behavioural
programmes severely restrict activity whereas others deliberately use the
patient's drive to exercise as a motivational factor, permitting increased
activity as a reward for weight gain.

It is usual to severely restrict activity in the early stages of treatment
when target weight has still to be reached. As the aim of therapy is to
return these patients to as normal and healthy a lifestyle as possible, it is
important to provide a model of healthy exercising that is not excessive,
while the patients are still hospitalized. This would also be the view of

Beumont et al. (1994). Regulated, supervised exercise provides the patient with an acceptable model of exercising that she can apply to life outside the hospital. A supervised exercise programme helps to moderate the uncontrollable physical activity that is so characteristic of anorexia nervosa. It will also help to relieve the abdominal discomfort associated with rapid weight gain. Patients also seem to accept weight gain more easily if they are allowed to exercise.

Treatment studies in anorexia nervosa are plentiful but there is a marked absence of studies describing the treatment of compulsive exercising in the disorder. Mavisskalian (1982) included one hour of bed rest after meals with a view to overcoming compulsive overexercising. However the author found that his patients adapted to this only after an enormous number of sessions.

The one hour of supervised bed rest after a main meal is not only to prevent compulsive exercising but also to prevent self-induced vomiting. It is unrealistic to expect eating-disordered patients to be completely inactive when moderate exercise is generally accepted as necessary for a healthy lifestyle. Total prohibition of all exercise is both difficult and time consuming to control. Exercise sessions should be seen as enjoyable, social, anxiety-reducing and mood elevating as well as relieving the discomfort felt from eating.

Stretching and posture improvement exercises are actively encouraged. Impact activities such as jogging are very much discouraged due to the danger of stress fractures (resulting from osteopenia often found in anorexia nervosa). Other forms of exercise such as swimming, walking, low-impact aerobics, aqua-aerobics or cycling are encouraged particularly since these can be easily continued following discharge. All activity should be structured within healthy limits and be as social as possible. Patients are not encouraged to chose exercise activities that are performed in isolation.

A structured exercise programme is planned with the patient. This helps set realistic exercise goals once target weight has been reached. However if the patient's weight drops from their target weight, all exercise is stopped and they may have to return to bed rest for certain periods of the day. A structured programme of exercise provides a safe physical outlet for their energy, thus protecting them from the excessive, vigorous exercise in which they had previously engaged.

The occupational therapist plays an important role in assisting patients to change potentially dangerous exercise patterns. Hornyak Baker (1989) argue that this intervention can teach the patient to engage in acceptable moderate levels of exercise while at the same time increasing social, recreational and leisure activities in a non-compulsive manner.

Relaxation

Having achieved target weight and faced with all that it implies some anorexia nervosa patients become very tense and anxious but do respond well to, and benefit from, a relaxation programme. Most patients with eating disorders have problems relaxing, and in their attempt to control their eating they may have lost some of the sensitivity to their musculature. They will often fail to recognize varying degrees of tension in their bodies. The anorectic needs to create and feel tension in her body by contracting muscle groups and releasing them so that she can experience the feeling. Yoga, deep breathing and stretching sequences can all be effective, as well as the deep muscle relaxation technique first described by Jacobson (1938) but adapted widely since its inception, often incorporating guided imagery as part of the programme.

Connors et al. (1984) have reported on the successful use of progressive relaxation as a component in several treatment programmes. Relaxation techniques are important in that they help to reduce anxiety levels and help to reduce the effects of stress. Since patients are particularly anxious at meal times, it can be useful to have relaxation sessions scheduled just before or just after meal times.

Social skills training

The anorexia nervosa patient is selected for social skills training if it appears that her inadequacies in this area are likely to hinder her prognosis. This she may begin during stage two of her treatment and may continue it through to discharge and as an out-patient. There have been many well-designed studies that show that skills training can improve social inadequacies (Becker et al., 1985; Goldmith and McFall, 1975).

Social skills training is based on the idea that skills are learned and therefore can be taught to those that lack them. The aim is to learn through demonstration, practice and feedback and those patients who are deficient in skills can be taught new and more socially accepted skills. It is said that some of the problems that anorectic patients have can be due to, or aggravated by, their general lack of social skills. This training helps them to use their skills better or to learn new ones.

Social skills imply reciprocity, interaction and mutual reinforcement. Those anorexia nervosa patients who lack these functional skills are less able to socialize and reap rewarding experiences in relationships with others. Assertiveness is itself another set of skills that teach us how to approach, interact, support, deny or otherwise cope with the person or situation in which we are interacting. Social skills are extremely numerous and cover almost every facet of one's life. One of the main points in producing constructive social skills is to be able to set a target of desired behaviour change for the individual that is specific and appropriate enough to allow for success.

Areas that would be covered with the anorexia nervosa patients would include basic conversation skills including listening, asking questions and talking, expressive skills and the use of body language, social techniques for special situations and assertiveness training. Demonstration plays an important part in social skills training. This can be achieved through either verbal instruction, videotapes or films or by using group members to initiate or roleplay the skill being studied. Demonstration forms the basis for imitation and through demonstration it is possible to magnify important components in the task being examined and thereby provide a standard for the patient to work towards.

Clothes shopping

As the patient will now be at target weight it is unlikely that any of her former clothes will fit her. Therapeutically it is important for the occupational therapist to help the anorectic patient to come to a more realistic awareness of her body image and new size. The patient will often interpret any curve and extra weight as grotesquely fat. Patients will often recall their experiences of any bodily changes during puberty with extreme discomfort and they wish to deny that they have developed breasts or rounded buttocks. However their fears are often reinforced by their mothers who buy them bras that aim to flatten their breasts.

Anorexia nervosa patients will often express their body awareness through their clothing and whether it is fashionable or not they will often hold their dresses in with tightly buckled belts. The belt seems to serve as a control, as long as it can be closed at the same hole every time then they feel reassured that they have gained no weight. On the other hand, there is the group of anorectics who continually wear the same heavy sweaters and trousers or long flowing skirts, which are intended not only to mask their gaunt frame but also to help keep themselves warm. Despite their denial of their figures many do seem to dislike the skeleton-like appearance of their arms and will wear long-sleeved sweaters and dresses, summer or winter in an effort to cover up their unsightly arms.

The patient is encouraged to use the shopping experience to find new clothes for her 'new' size. Initially patients do find this a very tense and anxious experience when they are confronted by their body image in shop windows and in changing room mirrors. They constantly remark how everyone seems to be looking at their shape and large size. The anorectic patient is encouraged to dress in a stylish fashion appropriate to her age and in clothes that flatter her, since dressing in an unappealing way reduces the probability of social reinforcement and only confirms the patient's already low opinion of herself.

Shopping is usually carried out in large shopping areas that have a sense of anonymity about them. The patient is encouraged to buy well-fitting clothing rather than the loose, formless garments that many of these patients prefer. Many anorectic patients will not have shopped outside the children's department before so encouragement to buy in the adult's department helps them address their womanliness and sexuality.

Stage III activities – The patient is still maintaining her weight and planning for discharge

Food-related activities

Meal planning

Since the anorexia nervosa patient's illness is centred around food and eating, it is essential that the occupational therapist should incorporate menu planning and meal cooking into the patient's treatment plan. Treatment strategies should emphasize the acceptance of foods that vary in nutrient and caloric content. The patient should be encouraged to adjust her diet to include this variety of foodstuffs as these are key factors in regaining and maintaining good health. Stoner et al. (1996) support this viewpoint, suggesting that therapeutic interventions need to focus on instilling in patients an acceptance of a variety of foods, rather than of food in general, because good nutrition necessitates eating a variety of foods, including fats. The challenge for the occupational therapist, of course, is getting patients to consume these foods in the appropriate proportions that are required for good health and long-term recovery.

Calorie counting has been part of the anorectic's life since the onset of her illness and this behaviour is very difficult to break when encouraging her to think of a 'normal' balanced meal. Cookery books and recipes are available to the patient but they can often be more of a hindrance as the patient becomes overwhelmed by the choice and is unable to make a decision.

Meal planning and cooking are usually carried out with four patients. It is important, therefore, at this planning stage, that individual nutritional needs and food preferences need to be co-ordinated into one single menu since the emphasis is on a joint effect. This session also emphasizes the need for realistic eating after discharge and to take account of the individual's needs and lifestyles. Patients are permitted to use convenience items and short cuts (such as buying pastry instead of making it) in order not to unnecessarily prolong the activity by becoming snowed under with the logistics of cooking. It is also necessary to look at suitable alternatives to home-prepared meals, especially if the patient uses school lunches or packed lunches for school and work.

The results of the study of Weltzin et al. (1991) need to be borne in mind by the occupational therapist when planning meals that are expected to maintain the patient's target weight. The authors found that in order to maintain a stable weight following weight restoration, restricting anorectic patients require a significantly higher caloric intake than do purging anorexia nervosa patients. Both groups also require more than that of healthy control subjects. Their findings suggest that this abnormally high calorie requirement for weight maintenance also plays a significant role in rapid weight loss and relapse following discharge from in-patient treatment. It is therefore essential that the occupational therapist provides the opportunity for these patients to practise cooking and eating the necessary diet if they are to reduce their chance of relapse.

Cooking and eating

The occupational therapist helps to prepare the patient for daily living experiences and works with her in the choosing and purchasing of food and the cooking of meals. The occupational therapist will confront the patient regarding her distorted perception and behaviours that surround food preparation and eating. The primary aim of cooking with the eating disordered patient is of course to provide her with the opportunity to cook a well-balanced 'normal' meal, serve it in acceptable portions and eat it in the presence of others. Patients are also encouraged to develop a normal rate of eating. Even though target weight had been reached, the majority of the anorexia nervosa patients still experience difficulties in accepting normal meals. Although they feel guilty and full of remorse when caught, some patients continue to cheat with regard to their food intake. During cooking preparation this could take the form of under-weighing the ingredients, leaving some food on the scales pan, spilling some food during preparation, giving larger portions to the therapist or over-peeling vegetables and potatoes.

Eating in the company of staff or their friends provides the anorectic patient with useful role models. Confrontation during meal times should be avoided and the patient should be encouraged to interact socially in an appropriate way.

Eating-disordered patients need to develop a spontaneous, relaxed eating pattern and to learn to cope with eating in restaurants, school, work, or with friends. This 'eating out' in different surroundings forms part of the patient's final treatment challenge. To this end, we encourage the patient to go into a coffee shop just for a snack, visit a restaurant for a meal and experience casual self-service and a more formal served meal. It is this author's experience that those patients who progressed well with cooking had a lower relapse rate. Unfortunately this is purely anecdotal and there is no empirical data to support such a claim. However the importance of this activity in relation to prognosis is an area of research worth investigating.

Psychodrama

Psychodrama was used by Moreno (1946), mostly in a group context. However, within the group individuals act out feelings or themes common to the group as a whole or to an individual member in particular. Memories, feelings and concerns emerge and are discussed through the group. Members of the group enact past situations, present dilemmas, future expectations, emotions and ideas. It is the role of the occupational therapist to help create an atmosphere conducive to such experiences.

Each psychodrama session is usually organized in three stages: the 'warm-up', the acting of the scene and the final sharing of feelings.

Psychodrama's success very much depends on the clinical sensitivity and experience of the therapist as well as the relationship between the therapist and the patients. Psychodrama is not suitable for all eating-disordered patients. However, these techniques can be applied to both the cognitive-behavioural and psychoanalytic approaches to treatment.

Chapter 19
Occupational therapy in bulimia nervosa

How the bulimia nervosa patient presents

The patient may present at normal weight, however some can be overweight and others underweight. She may report frequent weight fluctuations due to alternating gorging and fasting. The patient may appear nervous and tense and there may be swelling around her ankles or puffiness around her eyes. There may be calluses on her dominant index finger as a result of its constant use to induce vomiting.

The patient may describe her feelings of being misunderstood in terms of her illness and unlike anorexia nervosa patients, she will show no tendency to deny or minimize her symptoms, although she will share similar features to the anorectics in her feelings of helplessness, distorted body image and extreme fear of fatness. In comparison to anorectic patients, bulimic patients tend to be more extroverted, admit more frequently to having a strong appetite as well as tending to be older than the anorexia nervosa patient.

The patient does not always speak directly of shame but will instead speak of feeling foolish, ridiculous, pathetic, damaged or worthless. It is important for the occupational therapist to recognize this language of pain so that she can help the patient to explore underlying feelings and experiences of shame.

The patient may recall how she struggled for years to keep her weight under control and was relieved of this struggle with food control when she discovered purging. However, much later, sometimes years later, she realized that she had become enmeshed in a pattern of chaotic eating that was out of control. Because of her realization that her eating was 'out of control' the patient would begin to dread the feelings of hunger or the occurrence of meal times. She might admit to thinking about food all day long and have little concentration for her work or studies.

Eating patterns of bulimic patients become reduced to episodes of binge-eating interspersed between periods of minimal or little food intake so that 'normal' meals are uncommon. The patient might describe an almost clockwork daily cycle in which the urge to binge rises to a peak at the same time of the day – every day. Evenings are the most common times for binges and there is a strikingly compulsive automatic quality to the binges. Once under way, they are unstoppable. The binge continues unchecked until it is terminated by some external force such as abdominal pain, sleep, social interruption or self-induced vomiting. The patient may have discovered that the consumption of carbohydrates in sweets or ice-cream and the activities associated with the eating process, such as biting, chewing and swallowing have an emotionally soothing effect as she seizes on this mechanism for relief of distressing thoughts and emotions. Not only hunger but other feelings such as frustration, emptiness, tension and boredom induce a craving for food and normal eating does not dispel this tension, whereas binge eating does. The food is consumed so fast that the patient can hardly chew it or taste it properly. The patient tries to restrict her overeating to a time and place when discovery is unlikely. Her binge eating is accompanied by a constant fear that she will not be able to stop and bouts become more frequent when the patient is emotionally stressed by interpersonal conflicts. Some bulimics use food in excess, as a sedative to calm the sense of loss they feel in and around their lives, whereas others use it to cheapen and degrade themselves. The eating itself can serve to relieve the patient's anxiety as they describe an almost euphoric feeling experienced through the eating process. When the binge is over, the patient will describe feeling gross, fat, ugly, dirty, guilty and sick.

The bulimic woman may describe her mother as having been manipulative, domineering and suffocating, while her father is seen to be emotionally distant, rigid and pre-occupied with self-discipline. Mothers, especially, seem to intrude unduly into their daughter's life when it would seem more natural to encourage separation. This can result in a higher than normal mother–daughter conflict.

The personality of the bulimia nervosa patient is seen to be perfectionistic and ritualistic, often being accompanied by a high level of anxiety and disorders of impulse control. She may be methodical, meticulous and obsessed with personal hygiene. The patient is characterized by fears of rejection and low self-esteem. Her accompanying psychological problems may include depression, anxiety, alienation and isolation, poor self-concept, sex-role confusion and compulsive behaviour related to food and eating. The bulimic patient sets unrealistic goals for herself and failure to attain these goals results in frustration. The consequent depression and loss of self-esteem leads to binge eating in order to alleviate these negative states. Social maladjustment is also an important symptom constellation associated with bulimia.

The patient may discuss her abuse of food, drugs and alcohol. She may even describe having stolen food from supermarkets because her need to binge outstripped her income. She may report physical side effects such as tooth decay, sore throats and abdominal pain from excessive use of laxatives.

The bulimia nervosa will have created difficulty in the patient's interpersonal relationships since her low self-esteem and the shame associated with her problems results in an avoidance of relationships with men. What comes across very clearly is the patient's sense of hopelessness.

Occupational therapy in bulimia nervosa

The natural course of bulimia nervosa is not very clear as it may persist for many years unabated, ending up as a lifetime problem. Given the long clinical course of the disorder, hospitalization does not represent a cure, although short-term hospitalization may be necessary for severe nutritional and metabolic disturbances. Long-term care may help to stabilize the bulimic patient through cognitive behaviour therapy (CBT), group therapy, nutritional education groups, or family and individual therapy. Bulimic patients are not easy to treat since the pattern of binge eating, vomiting and purging proves very difficult to break. It could be argued that bulimia is not an illness in itself but a manifestation of underlying psychosocial problems. From its relatively innocent beginning as a simple method of controlling weight, the condition has progressed to a compulsive, uncontrollable habit that can eventually progress to a life-threatening condition.

The focus of occupational therapy is primarily on the modification of eating habits as well as considering the personality deficits that can co-exist with the disorder. The bulimic patient is self-critical and she suffers from inadequacy. She may compulsively overexercise and tend to be hyperactive, hypercritical and masochistic. She may also be seen as an overachiever who is pursuing the goal of self-perfection. The bulimia nervosa patient is susceptible to dichotomous thinking in that she is very much the 'all or nothing' type that is 'if I'm not perfectly thin then I'll be a fat pig'.

Bulimia nervosa patients are more socially anxious, have a greater fear of intimacy and perceive more conflict in their relationships so it could be expected that their ability to seek support may be reduced. Most bulimic patients are treated as out-patients where they will be seen usually weekly in the early stages and then less frequently as they gradually resume control over their eating. Those patients who are referred for in-patient treatment usually have some associated problems in addition to their uncontrollable binge-purge cycles. These problems can include either a very low weight, or obesity, depression or other impulse disorders such as alcoholism or compulsive stealing. Providing in-patient care for a patient with bulimia is often critical in breaking the long-standing and life threatening patterns of behaviour associated with the condition.

Bulimia nervosa affects every area of the patient's psychosocial functioning. The occupational therapist needs to be aware of how this condition affects the patient's physical and psychological health as well as her family and social relationships. It is essential that the patient is helped to recognize the need for structure and purposeful activity in her daily life.

Occupational therapy objectives are:

- to interrupt the binge-purge cycle;
- to improve the patient's ability to monitor their own eating behaviour;
- to decrease impulsivity;
- to increase self control;
- to encourage the patient to keep a diary of her food intake;
- to provide the opportunity whereby the patient may be helped in refuting irrational beliefs;
- to encourage alternative coping skills;
- to help the patient identify situations which lead to binge eating and help her to find acceptable alternatives;
- to promote a more accurate/more acceptable body image;
- to increase self esteem;
- to encourage new interests and leisure pursuits;
- to reduce excessive exercising;
- to provide educational advice on a well-balanced diet;
- to provide information on the complications and course of the illness;
- to promote a 'healthier' outlook on life.

As distorted ideas regarding food, weight and body image are character-istic of bulimia, as well as the bulimic patient's belief that the achievement of thinness will lead to a general well-being, have prompted CBT princi-ples to tackle the misconception. Cognitive-behavioural therapy is based on the assumption that if the individual learns appropriate methods of weight regulation, then the starvation–binge cycles and accompanying purging will be eliminated. The goals of most cognitive-behavioural. thera-pies for bulimia are to restructure cognitive distortions pertaining to the need to be thin, and to re-establish healthy eating patterns. Cognitive interventions target cognitive distortions, over-generalization and miscon-ceptions that contribute to the maintenance of pathogenic weight-control behaviours. Cognitive-behavioural therapy is seen not only to change overt behaviour such as binge-eating and purging, but it also modifies attitudes about body shape and weight, even if the patient's body weight remains stable. Wilson et al. (1997) thought that this was due to an increased self-acceptance. Fairburn (1991) also reported less dissatisfac-tion with shape and weight in the bulimic patients following CBT. This reported improvement in body image occurred even without any actual change in the patient's body shape or weight.

The occupational therapist operates within the CBT model of treat-ment in providing dietary management, cognitive restructuring, interper-sonal problem solving related to poor assertive skills and relaxation training. The treatment programme is provided in three stages.

Stage I

It is important to establish a therapeutic relationship that fosters an environment of mutual trust and active participation by the patient, both inside and outside the session. Self-monitoring of binge eating and purging forms the foundation upon which treatment sessions are built. Individuals are typically asked to record all daily food and liquid intake, as well as to indicate episodes of overeating and episodes during which they felt out of control. Self-monitoring increases the patient's awareness of her eating pattern in general and her bulimic behaviour in particular. The emphasis is on increasing self-control. The patient records the food she eats as well as where and when it is eaten. This helps the patient and occupational therapist to examine the bulimic's eating habits and their context. The patient is encouraged to restrict her eating to recognized meal times, and if she feels that things are getting out of control she is encouraged to undertake activities that are incompatible with overeating, such as exercising or socializing with friends. Each week the patient and therapist set limited, but clearly defined, goals that can be achieved before the next meeting.

Stage II

This stage of treatment begins when the frequency of bingeing is reduced. Each session begins with a review of the previous week's eating. Binge and purge antecedents are identified usually by examining self-monitoring records, in order to establish patterns of loss of control, overeating and episodes of compensatory behaviour. The focus of such identification includes eating habits that precede binge episodes, emotional states, cognitions and situations that give rise to binge eating and purging. It is expected that by now bingeing and vomiting will be intermittent.

Psychoeducation is provided in order for the patient to learn more about her eating disorder, nutrition and weight regulation. The patient is encouraged to develop regular eating habits of three planned meals per day and planned snacks to include her previously 'forbidden foods' into her diet.

Problem-solving techniques are introduced and encouraged at this stage. Problem-solving skills are used to enhance the generation and implementation of coping strategies in response to external situations that may be related to binge eating. These will often revolve around interpersonal difficulties. Precipitants of binge episodes are identified and alternative solutions to the problems are examined. The patient is encouraged to anticipate problems so that problem solving strategies can be implemented before problems become serious.

The patient's irrational concerns about her body weight and shape may also become clear at this stage. Cognitive change methods can be used, with the patient being trained to challenge and replace these maladaptive thoughts.

Going out for a meal may also be planned as part of the therapy session as it provides the opportunity to try out new behaviours in the context of the supportive group environment.

Stage III

Patients are now seen less frequently, usually at two- to-four-week intervals. Relapse prevention techniques are used to identify high-risk situations anticipated by the patient and to help plan coping strategies for these situations. They could include reducing the availability of food, seeking help from friends, keeping herself occupied and not taking more money than is reasonably required when out shopping. The patient should be instructed to practice the self-instructions she has learned to counter the urges to binge or starve, to solve problems and to modify her dysfunctional cognitions. Consideration is also given to introducing new leisure pursuits and interests, which can provide a safe diversion from her previous preoccupation with bingeing and purging.

Stage I activities

Self-monitoring

Patients are asked to keep a record of their food and drink intake, including how they felt at the time when it was consumed. The patient is advised that her symptoms may get worse and she may feel more depressed, especially during the early phases of the group. Patients are expected to disclose their secretive eating and purging behaviour while being advised as to the dangers of continuing to binge and vomit. Any major or ongoing difficulties in monitoring should be explored and solutions sought. As discussed by Fairburn et al. (1993a) the quality of a patient's monitoring is directly related to the degree of attention the therapist pays to it. It is therefore essential for the occupational therapist to spend time going through the monitoring record with the patient while showing interest and providing encouragement for the efforts she had made. This self-monitoring by the patient will not only contain symptoms but also her thoughts and feelings related to food intake, purging symptoms, weighing activity and events leading to the urge to binge-eat. The purpose of this is to help identify food and symptom patterns as well as to facilitate careful monitoring of her nutritional status and weight. The occupational therapist uses this cognitive-behavioural tool to help the patient view her own world of thoughts and feelings, particularly as they relate to her eating disorder. In this way the patient is encouraged to take control of her eating disorder by developing her capacity to realistically observe herself.

Some may argue that this 'food diary' only reinforces the obsession with food but chronic bulimia nervosa patients who are already bingeing and purging 20–30 times daily are already fully preoccupied with food. What the diary does is to structure this preoccupation.

Group therapy

Group therapy is a form of treatment in which people are seen to grow and change through various mechanisms (Martin, 1990). Groups are seen as a cost-effective and useful means of offering treatment to eating-disordered patients. The selection of group members will depend on the patient's suitability including their capacity and motivation for change, interpersonal skills, prior therapy experience and the type of group therapy being considered. Patients who are not motivated to change can be very disruptive in the group. Screening patients and preparing them for group therapy seems to reduce dropout rates and improve the overall quality of the group.

Group therapy in the treatment of eating disorders is increasingly being recognized as an important, effective and economical psychotherapeutic tool. The group can influence the perceptions of its members and encourage them to assist one another's recovery through self-disclosure and confrontation of symptomatic behaviour, ideas and attitudes. Within the group setting, people are seen to grow and change through a variety of mechanisms. The process used to bring about these changes includes confrontation, clarification, interpretation and 'working through'.

In order to meet goals and increased individual growth, cohesiveness needs to be developed within the group. Cohesion is enhanced by the occupational therapist showing support and a caring attitude. Sykes et al. (1987) discusses the steps in helping to develop a productive cohesive group for bulimic patients and these include

- clearly defining group norms and boundaries;
- encouraging members to discover how the group can assist in managing their lives;
- preventing 'scapegoating' while still providing a safe environment;
- providing consistency in time and location, and
- planning for gradual discharge.

Bulimic patients are accustomed to hiding life's crises in the same manner as they hide their eating behaviour. By providing a safe environment to examine internal conflicts, bulimic patients have a place to discuss feelings, especially those connected with their binge/purging cycle.

Often improvements are slow to come about with group therapy, but it is a particularly useful treatment for bulimic patients because of the secrecy and isolation that surrounds their condition. Shisslak et al. (1986) suggest that group therapy is an ideal format for tackling the four distortions common to the beliefs of bulimic patients, namely:

- appearance is the sole criterion by which others evaluate them;
- they will be abandoned if they do not devote themselves to fulfilling the desires of others;

- the expression of emotions is unacceptable; and
- they are unlovable unless they achieve perfection.

Boskind-Lodahl (1976) reported on the use of group therapy for the treatment of bulimia and found that there was a reduction in bingeing and purging by the end of the treatment. The group members also reported improvements in social competence, self-esteem and emotional stability. It could therefore be argued that group therapy provides a unique therapeutic experience for bulimic patients to explore their difficult social and interpersonal fears.

The main emphasis in group therapy is to raise self-esteem; however, it is the author's experience that a number of bulimic patients are reluctant to enter groups and many refuse the offer of such treatment even when no other therapy is available. It could be that these patients may have more severe levels of problems in some areas and are unwilling to contemplate discussing these problems in the relatively open forum of group therapy.

Creative activities

Bulimic patients are generally hesitant to undertake tasks where they cannot control the outcome. In carrying out creative activities they learn how to accept imperfections in, for example, pottery or other activities new to them where they have to acquire a skill in mastering new tools and skills. Their short-term goals in mastering new skills often need to be reviewed and this can be transferred to other areas of their lives, such as self-control and self-esteem issues.

Clay has properties that are especially tactile and encourage sensory interaction and playfulness. Amari (1986) suggests that clay modelling provides the bulimic patient with the opportunity to experiment with her feelings and conflicts regarding merging and separating, fullness and emptiness, bingeing and purging. The bulimic patient can also use the clay to form a family sculpture. This is particularly helpful in seeing relationships and conflicts as well as providing the opportunity to discuss her feelings of struggling for an identity. With clay, the patient can touch and mould her body representatively using the clay in a three-dimensional form as opposed to the two-dimensional form of painting. The clay can be used by the patient to reshape her own identity and also that of her family.

Creative writing

The view that writing is only for the gifted, the educated, or the highly literate person should be dispelled. Writing can be a centre for the client and a bridge for the therapist (Leavitt and Pill, 1995). Creative writing is an aid to self-expression and self-discovery. It is used to encourage new ways to soothe and to support the patient in exploring her feelings about the past and the future. Creative writing is seen as part of a self-healing experience as patients write for themselves and express their innermost thoughts and feelings. Often these can be disguised in metaphorical form.

Writing is seen as a powerful creative experience. Talerico (1995) describes the significant link that writing can provide between the creative process and therapy by helping clients to take risks, express feelings, communicate with their unconscious, develop new insights, resolve conflicts and release energy for problem-solving. Writing is used by some patients to provide a refuge, to reveal their anguish and to search for themselves. The pen is used like a key to unlock doors. The power of expressive writing needs to be recognized, valued and promoted within the therapeutic setting, as it can provide a clear picture of material that might otherwise remain unspoken and it is something that the patient can turn to during periods of emptiness and loneliness.

Stage II activities

Psychoeducational group

Specific dietary counselling can be helpful as a component of occupational therapy for bulimia nervosa patients. The emphasis, in a CBT programme, is on the regularity of eating rather than the composition of the meals and snacks. Many patients also benefit from more detailed assistance in meal planning. It is also important to provide reassurance with planning and estimating portion sizes and modifying abnormal food and weight cognitions and beliefs.

Story (1986) described components of a nutritional approach to include education, weight issues, the food diary and a dietary plan while the educational components involve providing basic information about the physiological and psychological effects of starvation, energy, balance and nutritional requirement and misconceptions about dieting and weight control. However, any desired weight loss cannot be examined until symptoms are under control and a regular eating pattern has been established. Patients are discouraged from regularly weighing themselves and are asked to continue to keep a record of their dietary intake, purging and exercise behaviour.

The rational for nutritional management is to normalize the chaotic eating habits of bulimic individuals. Regular well-balanced meals and snacks are established by prescribing a meal plan based on the patient's history, dietary guidelines and lifestyle. Patients are encouraged to eat their meals sitting down and to include adequate amounts of fat and fibre in the diet. Those patients being weaned off excessive amounts of laxatives will need added dietary fibre (from grains rather than vegetables or fruit). Patients should also be advised to expect dramatic weight fluctuations caused by fluid retention following a reduction in vomiting, laxative and diuretic abuse.

In this educational group the patient also receives information about the symptoms, risks, course and complications of bulimia nervosa. Eating-disordered patients often suffer from misconceptions about the factors that cause and maintain their symptoms. However psychoeducational management is not a replacement for psychotherapy but is part of a multi-modalities treatment programme as well as being a standard component of cognitive-behavioural therapy. Davis et al. (1992) found that after participation in a group psychoeducational programme, which consisted of five 90-minute meetings, that 21% of the patients were symptom free. There were also clinically significant changes in dysfunctional attitudes and psychological distress. Laessle et al. (1991) also produced interesting results when they compared nutritional management and stress management, finding that both treatments led to significant reductions in bingeing and vomiting as well as lower scores on measures of psychopathology at the end of treatment and at 12-month follow-up. However nutritional management produced a significantly more rapid reduction in binge eating, higher abstinence rates and greater improvements on some measures of psychopathology.

Problem-solving and stress management

Stressful life events or difficulties precede the onset of eating disorders in a large number of cases and many of these events and difficulties fall within the normal range of experiences for young women. These patients do not possess the skills that help them to deal with stress or channel tension and often their eating behaviours are the result of poor coping skills in this area.

In this group, the patient is told about the theory of interpersonal stress causing binge eating. The patients are taught to identify and keep records of stressful situations that are likely to cause binge episodes and also to keep their nutritional diary up to date. Patients are taught to recognize situational and internal cues that indicate that a situation may become stressful and trigger a binge episode. Short- and long-term coping strategies are discussed. Short-term strategies include progressive muscle relaxation, self-encouragement and self-distraction. Long-term strategies are training in systematic planning and problem solving and the improvement of communication skills and expression of feelings. These strategies are demonstrated in role-playing situations. Part of stress management can also involve going out for a group meal to a restaurant.

The principles of interpersonal problem solving training emerged with the work of Spivack et al. (1974) and D'Zurilla and Nezu (1982). These authors conceptualized interpersonal problem-solving training in the context of behaviour therapy. Problem solving refers to one's skill in determining the means by which to achieve a specific end or overcome a specific problem. It teaches patients to deal more effectively with problem situations that typically lead to negative moods and pathogenic weight control behaviour. Problem solving has five general steps including problem definition, instigation of alternative coping behaviour, evaluation of outcomes, decision making and verification.

In problem solving, a specific problem is identified in detail with the aim of generating as many solutions to the problem as possible and then the patient devises alternative methods of coping with the problem. The greater the number of potential solutions revealed, the greater the chance that a suitable solution will be found. Patients aim to identify their day-to-day problems accurately, set reasonable goals and instigate decision-making methods in order to resolve the problem. Often problems discussed will include job interviews, moving residence and socializing.

Patients also identify their most difficult situations or time periods with respect to bingeing and purging. They need to recognize the cues that serve to trigger their unwanted behaviour of bingeing and purging. It may be walking past a cake shop or returning home to be alone in the house. These situations are broken down into identifiable components and alternative behavioural solutions are discussed.

While problem solving approaches are a routine component of CBT for bulimia nervosa, their usefulness also extends to relapse prevention.

Cooking and eating

The reported caloric intake during binges has been reported to range from 1200 (Mitchell et al., 1981) to 55 000 (Johnson et al., 1982) so it is therefore essential that a structured programme of eating is designed in order to restore a sense of control over food. Small improvements are expected in the short term whereas a true pattern of normal eating would be considered as a long-term goal. The recommended pattern for acquiring normal eating would include three planned meals each day, plus two or three planned snacks. These meals or snacks should not be followed by vomiting or any other compensatory behaviour. Counting calories is actively discouraged and patients are advised to avoid all 'dietary' products aimed at weight reduction as these foods are counterproductive for weight gain and unnecessary for weight maintenance.

Bulimic patients are generally at an apparently normal weight and do not usually need to go on a weight gain programme. However they do need to resume normal and relaxed eating, avoid restrictive practices and learn to adapt to being a weight that might be somewhat higher than they would ideally choose.

Between binge-eating episodes bulimic patients may completely avoid foods that they consider unhealthy or frightening – often referred to as 'forbidden' foods. Once a more stable pattern of eating has been achieved then the introduction of these 'forbidden' foods takes place.

Long-term normalization of disturbed eating behaviour depends on motivational and ability factors. Even if motivation is there it may not be sufficient to maintain a nutritionally adequate diet, if the knowledge and ability to make a meal plan are missing.

The group meal provides a number of important functions for bulimic patients. In a supportive atmosphere patients share a meal together and eat in front of each other – something that they find difficult. The group meal allows the patient to try out, in a safe environment, some of the techniques that are generally recommended by CBT protocols such as monitoring their feeling of fullness and sampling 'forbidden' foods. The aim of this group is to help patients re-establish control over their eating and provide a therapeutic link between the theoretical and practical aspects of treatment. Some patients enter the sessions filled with anxiety but, with practice, in a structured and supportive environment, they emerge more confident in their cooking and eating abilities. It is often necessary for the occupational therapist to maintain her sense of humour throughout the completion of this task, especially at the final presentation.

The ideal size of the group is four. More than that and it becomes difficult to give attention to everyone. Patients are strongly discouraged from having a meal like salad, fruit and a low calorie drink but instead they must plan a well-balanced meal to include protein, carbohydrates and fats as well as some of their 'forbidden' foods such as doughnuts or chocolate. The meal includes a dessert. The meal is eaten together with the therapist and the patients are encouraged to discuss their thoughts and feelings during the meal.

Those who need to take packed lunches to school or work will be given the opportunity to put sample ones together. Those who will be eating alone on their return home will receive help and practice in food shopping 'for one' so that there is no temptation to binge from the cupboard or fridge. The patient will also be advised to plan a shopping list carefully so that she does not impulsively buy binge foods.

Stage III activities

Physical exercise

The exercise history of the bulimic patient is important. One way to determine whether exercise is pathological or excessive is to find out the purpose of the exercise to the individual. If she exercises in order to compensate for a binge then it may represent a purge method for the patient. However if the patient says she is exercising to promote health but continues to exercise even when injured or sick, then this needs to be further explored. Bulimia nervosa patients will often binge on excessive exercise as a self-punitive compensatory activity used to offset the effects of recent binge eating. It is possible to introduce self-targeting for reducing the activity level by using weekly self-monitoring sheets that have the eventual aim of exercise-free days. However the use of regular moderate exercise and social sport which is done purely for enjoyment helps to establish a healthy routine in the lives of the bulimic patients. It also helps to build up their confidence in their own ability at maintaining a healthy weight without dieting and purging. Appropriate exercise can have anxiety-reducing and antidepressant effects as well as promoting a more positive body image. Patients are therefore encouraged to exchange bingeing and purging behaviours for healthy exercise.

Leisure pursuits

A constructive use of leisure time is a focus of occupational therapy with bulimia nervosa patients. It is important to examine previous leisure pursuits and explore new avenues and support groups. These patients may, previous to their illness, have displayed high levels of creativity and they should be encouraged to develop this side of their talents. Interests should be chosen that are not carried out in isolation as this only encourages bingeing when the patient finds herself alone for long periods. Patients are encouraged to identify leisure pursuits and to allocate time in their schedules for leisure.

Physical exercise should be encouraged to an acceptable level as an alternative means to purging and vomiting for controlling weight. Dance and aerobics also help to develop body awareness and improve body image.

Johnson and Berndt (1983) investigated bulimia nervosa patients in terms of social and leisure adjustment. The authors found that these patients were so significantly impaired that their scoring levels were similar to those of a group of women suffering from alcohol abuse. So an active pursuit of leisure interests needs to be encouraged by the occupational therapist for these patients. Restructuring their weekly routine so that they do different things on different days will help the patient to become less rigid and will also help her to see that she can still be in control of her life. As an out-patient she will be encouraged to do a new activity each week, which will involve other social groups.

Relapse prevention

The bulimic patient needs to be educated about the idea that her eating disorder is an ongoing vulnerability and can be activated at times of stress. Patients should be encouraged to predict future stresses that may provoke bulimic reactions while also applying newly acquired coping skills. Patients need to accept that because they binged in the morning, the rest of the day is not lost. They will be advised that recovery follows an irregular pattern and they must stop applying their 'all or nothing' philosophy to their recovery. Skipping a meal to make up for a binge needs to be discouraged.

The patient needs to identify high-risk situations that may lead to problem behaviours and to make plans and strategies to cope with these situations in order to minimize the chance of a relapse. The patient is encouraged to choose activities instead of turning to her eating disorder. These may include: contacting a friend who can give support, or engage in quickly accessible activities when bulimic urges are present, such as listening to music, reading a book or relaxing in the bath. They are encouraged to only eat pre-planned meals at all times and, as far as it is practical, not to eat or drink except when in the company of others.

Chapter 20
Body image and occupational therapy

Body image distortion was first identified as a feature of eating disorders by Bruch (1962) who described anorexia nervosa patients as consistently overestimating their body size. Bruch also highlighted a connection of body image misperception to be an essential precondition for recovery. Body image distortion includes both body size overestimation and dissatisfaction with the body and serves the function of encouraging restrictive behaviour (dieting) and abnormal bodily control (purging). Abnormality of body image is now one of the essential diagnostic criteria for both anorexia nervosa and bulimia nervosa. Most patients who seek treatment for either of these disorders exhibit an excessive concern with weight or body shape (Garfinkel, 1992).

Multiple factors contribute to the development of body image, including cultural attitudes toward size and shape, family attitudes towards appearance, and neuro-developmental factors. It is commonplace for the patients to complain about being or feeling fat. An unusual clinical feature of body-image disturbance in anorexia nervosa is that it may worsen with weight loss. It can often be worse when the patient is at her lowest weight and can decrease in intensity when the patient is closer to normal weight. Body dissatisfaction is a common characteristic of many women (Cooper et al., 1987). While this is expressed behaviourally by women's attempts to restrain food intake, or adopt purging methods for control, it can also be seen in their discrepancies between perceived and desired body size and in feeling fat.

Crisp (1974) found that pubertal females become sensitive to their fatness, and this is especially so of their breast development and the fatness of their thighs, but also their waist and hips, and less often their lower legs. Crisp believes that dieting in these females is not just a response to the cultural emphasis of thinness but is part of their search for confidence and self-esteem. Garfinkel and Garner (1982) found the disturbance of body image to be twofold. It can result in the anorectic's perceived size being larger than the actual size or it may be such that the perception of size is fairly accurate but there is a belief that one or more parts are larger than they should be or are unattractive so that overall weight reduction is desired as a way of making the particular feature less prominent.

A variety of methods have been used to measure body image. The two major types of body-image assessment procedures are (1) the measurement of attitudes and affect related to body characteristics and (2) those that ask the individual to estimate their actual body size by identifying with a silhouette (Cash and Brown 1987).

Body image parameters measuring a pursuit for thinness and satisfaction with body shape and weight are measured with the drive for thinness (DT) and body dissatisfaction (BD) subscales of the Eating Disorder Inventory (EDI) (Garner and Olmsted, 1984). The DT subscale consists of seven items that measure excessive concerns about dieting, an ardent desire to lose weight, as well as a fear of weight gain, whereas the BD subscale consists of nine items that measure dissatisfaction with body shape and a concern that certain body regions, especially the hips, abdomen and thighs, are too fat. To facilitate the investigation of children's attitudes and behaviour associated with eating and weight control Maloney et al. (1988) developed a children's version of the Eating Attitudes Test (Garner and Garfinkel, 1979). This is a 26-item self-report inventory that includes concerns about being overweight. Gender specific scales were introduced by Collins (1991) consisting of seven preadolescent body figures ranging from very thin to obese and individuals are asked to state which body figure best represents their current size and which represents the way they would prefer to look. Body-size overestimation and body-size distortion have been shown by using a visual size estimation apparatus (Slade and Russell, 1973) and a body image marking technique (Bowden et al., 1989) or a distorting photography technique (Garfinkel and Garner, 1982). In contrast to those with body image distortions a patient with body image dissatisfaction accurately assesses body size but experiences extreme dislike for her body either as a whole or certain body parts.

Body image disturbance and body disparagement can be largely understood as resulting from the pervasive pressure to conform to negative and unrealistic female role models. Garner et al. (1980) and Morris et al. (1989) suggest that media stereotypes create and perpetuate the association between ideals of thinness and positive attitudes such as success and attractiveness. Brodie et al. (1996) carried out an interesting study that investigated the influence of preconception on body image. The authors used 59 healthy females. Each was shown the body shape of the same person dressed differently to appear like a model, a student, and a cook. The results indicated a significant difference between the representations of the types of occupation, with the model being viewed consistently as the slimmest and the cook as the fattest. This would strongly imply that there is a preconceived notion that a model should be slim, that a student should be neutral, and that a cook should be fat. This has implications for the occupational therapist in treating these patients in that people do retain preconceived perceptions developed on the basis of experience so, unless they look like a model they will not view themselves as thin. This stereotypical bias is therefore likely to influence not only patients' perceptions of others but also of themselves.

Orbach (1993) argues that there is good evidence to support the view that women in Western society are stigmatized for not being slim and that women, in particular, internalize this stigma and become dissatisfied with their body shape and weight. The mass media are probably the most powerful conveyors of sociocultural ideals and therefore play an important causal role in the development of eating disorders. Of the psychological factors that are believed to cause eating disorders, body image dissatisfaction is probably the most relevant and immediate antecedent. However what is not clear is whether body image disturbance is a predisposing, precipitating or perpetuating factor in the development of the eating disorder.

Over-estimation of body size has been found in both anorectic and bulimic patients. However Slade and Russell (1973) found that, as anorectic patients gained weight, they became more accurate in their estimation of body size and the degree of overestimation was also predictive of outcome in that the patients who over-estimated the most, lost the most weight following discharge from hospital. Longitudinal studies of at-risk populations found that fluctuations in eating disorder symptoms over time are best predicted by body image. It can be the patient's distorted body image that has precipitated her eating disorder and, in many cases, which still remains with her even after all other symptoms have been controlled. The occupational therapist needs to offer these patients the hope of changing their body image without the need to necessarily change their physical appearance. Recovery from either anorexia nervosa or bulimia nervosa in terms of weight restoration and eating behaviours does not guarantee that the patient has accepted her physical appearance. There is evidence to suggest that about one-third to two-thirds of eating-disorder patients who are seen to be recovered in terms of restored body weight and controlled eating behaviours still worry excessively about their physical appearance (Goldbloom and Olmsted, 1993; Ratnasuriya et al., 1991; Windauer et al., 1993). Rorty et al. (1993) found that bulimic patients expressed their difficulty in wishing to be thin as the hardest part of their recovery, and this was felt even more than their resistance to stop bingeing.

Addressing the body image problem

Attempts have been made to objectively assess body image in eating disordered patients but most of these studies have concentrated on the relationships of body image to body size estimation and have neglected the affective and cognitive component of the individual's body image. Despite an extensive literature search on body image it has not been possible to find a single study that states the amount of time spent on body image improvement. Most psychotherapies address body image problems in some form; however, CBT programmes have produced more clinically significant changes (Butters et al., 1987; Rosen, 1997). A comprehensive treatment approach to eating disorders should include some help in changing body image alongside eating behaviour.

There is little available information on how to change distortion in body image. Rosen (1997) suggests that one suitable technique is to turn the size estimation test into a corrective feedback exercise. Here the therapist confronts the patients with the discrepancy between their estimated and their actual size by getting the patient to repeatedly correct her estimation of the body part being examined until she is accurate. However, although these corrective exercises can help to improve patients' distortion of appearance, they do not directly address patients' satisfaction with their appearance.

The body image group

Body image focuses on body image problems – misperceptions of a dissatisfaction with one's body, irrational cognitive beliefs about the body, and effective ways of coping with difficult situations that cause these problems. Awareness is promoted by identifying problematic thoughts and feelings, and then providing feedback from self-report measures of body image and videotapes. The aim is to substitute distorted, unrealistic views with more constructive perceptions and interpretation. Great efforts are also made to decrease the importance of personal appearance and physical attractiveness.

The body perception group helps patients to come to terms with their distorted body image. Initially discussion focuses on how these distortions affect their lives and sustain eating disorders. Following from this, patients are encouraged to think of ways of adopting a healthier perspective of their body. Treatment is designed to play down the role of shape and weight concerns in everyday life and they are encouraged to find fulfilment in interests and activities other than shape and weight management. The occupational therapist needs to stress to the patient that therapy is designed to change body image by examining the problem – that is, how the person views herself from the inside and not how she thinks others view her from the outside. It can often be the case that the characteristic cognitions of eating-disordered patients may manifest themselves in the 'I hate my body' and therefore 'I hate myself' scenario. It is essential for the occupational therapist to emphasize to the patient that their self-image has in fact been manipulated by our culture, which is providing them with unrealistic ideals of beauty.

Striegel-Moore et al. (1990) found a positive correlation between body image and self-esteem. Fairburn, (1985), however, argues that low self-esteem or negative self-evaluation leads to an undue emphasis on body shape and weight. It is therefore reasonable to assume that improving overall self-esteem may facilitate a greater acceptance of body shape and weight.

Patients are encouraged to keep a self-monitoring diary of the situations that provoke self-consciousness about appearance and bring it to the group session each week. Therapy is aimed at encouraging the patient's acceptance that she may not be as perfect, or as thin, as she would like to be. However some patients see this acceptance as 'letting themselves go' and thus losing control.

Experimental techniques that are found to be useful in the treatment of body image have been described by Wooley and Wooley (1985). These authors used imagery, art and movement to enhance the patient's awareness of her body image distortion and its development. Experimental techniques are then employed to promote a sense of control over her perception and feelings about her body with the final aim being to create a more positive body image.

Dance, movement, exercise and relaxation

Bruch (1982) has reported that the anorectic patient, in dance and art therapy assessments, has many deficits including body image distortions and painful self-consciousness. Therefore it is essential for these eating-disordered patients to develop a realistic body image by being able to touch and know their own bodies. Exercises can help to focus attention directly on to the body. Breathing exercises or relaxation exercises can be used. Sometimes a type of massage can be done when patients work in pairs and one of them massages the other. Deep breathing exercises improve circulation and lung capacity during relaxation and also help the client to gain awareness of the body's interior. Breathing exercises provide a favourable introduction to relaxation. The use of relaxation techniques immediately prior to some of the body image sessions can be beneficial. Anything that draws the patient's attention to the functioning and existence of her body helps to increase her body awareness.

Patients also need to see their bodies as something that can provide pleasure to them and it is to this end that they will be encouraged to do free expression in dance and movement sessions. Anorectic patients have a preference for movements that are small, rigid and within a confined space. They are encouraged to develop their 'personal' space and to express themselves more freely and with a less restricted form. They may be given a theme to explore such as 'open' and 'closed'. Several authors have recommended movement groups such as yoga, Tai Chi, dance and mirror feedback to help patients become happier with their bodies. Eklund and Crawford (1994) found body image to be an important aspect of a person's exercise pattern with subjects demonstrating a more positive attitude toward exercising in an environment that de-emphasized the physical form, such as cycling, walking or jogging as opposed to swimming, aerobics or any sport that demands the wearing of tight-fitting work-out clothes. This is important for the occupational therapist to consider when encouraging the patient in her new leisure pursuits as this attitude by the patient can very much restrict the choice of activities.

Self-confrontation and self-awareness

Patients who are dissatisfied with their shape and weight often engage in a variety of avoidance behaviours designed to conceal their bodies. These include avoidance of certain clothes, activities or situations that might provide feedback on their shape and weight. Patients will often resort to wearing loose-fitting shapeless clothes in an effort to hide their bodies. The patient is encouraged to confront her true shape and size by spending time in front of a full-length mirror and examining the parts of her body that she likes as well as learning to accept the parts that she does not like. This exercise would also be extended into the drama group. The patient may be helped to change her baggy clothes for those that are closer fitting. She will be encouraged to use the shop's fitting room and to perhaps ask the shop assistant for her opinion on her potential purchase. She may have a long-term goal of going to the leisure centre for swimming or aerobics and to be able to undress there in the communal changing rooms. The patient should be discouraged from continually comparing herself with models in fashion magazines.

Videotapes are used in the social skills training group and although the primary aim is to give the patient insight into her social skills behaviour, they also provide a means of directly confronting the patient with her true size in relation to other members of the group. This use of videotape recordings is an area that could be usefully developed for use in the body-image group.

Summary

It is important for the occupational therapist to help the eating-disordered patient come to a more realistic awareness of her body and to integrate various activities to help the patient change. Many of the activities discussed earlier in this book can usefully be employed in the quest for a more accurate and accepting body image by the patient – for example, art, beauty and make-up care, drama, activities which improve self-esteem and leisure pursuits. While working with these patients it is possible to see how they develop and how they gradually become free when discussing their feelings and acceptance of their body.

Body image is a complicated phenomenon. Body image disturbance forms a distressing and disabling component of eating disorders and for patients to change this distortion is a continuous struggle for them. Bruch (1962) was definite in her view that, unless patients with anorexia nervosa changed their attitudes concerning their body image, their immediate outcome would be unfavourable. More extensive body image therapy may not only help eating-disordered patients to conquer their distressing symptoms, but may also provide for changes in eating. Rosen (1997) suggests that body image work should be included and emphasized in the treatment of both anorexia nervosa and bulimia nervosa.

Some authors have reported a better prognosis in those patients who achieve a more accurate body image so there is now a need for a more systematic approach to body image work for this patient population. It is necessary to examine all facets of body image disturbances including situational cues and specific attitudes and behaviour. It is the role of the occupational therapist to introduce activities which will help the patient to do this.

Chapter 21
Conclusion

Anorexia nervosa and bulimia nervosa are disorders that are devastating medically, socially and psychologically. This has prompted researchers to try to find an effective treatment that could be widely disseminated. There are now multiple treatments for these complex disorders, and the occupational therapist plays an important role. If occupational therapists adhered only to the medical model they would be limiting their role in developing prevention programmes for eating disordered patients. In an effort to promote better preventative care the occupational therapist would find the holistic and occupational performance models more useful.

It is recommended that the occupational therapist will help these females resist societal pressure to conform to unrealistic standards of appearance and provide guidance on nutrition, realistic body ideals and achievement of self-esteem, self-efficacy, together with help with personal relationships and coping skills. The occupational therapist also tries to alter their misconceived perfectionism regarding their bodies. The more effective women become in managing their interpersonal relationships, the greater their self-esteem and the less importance body shape and weight have in determining self-identity. However, the effectiveness of expressive and experiential therapies for treating eating disorders need to be assessed empirically in order to measure their success. It may also be beneficial if future research in eating disorders could include greater involvement in social science research as this can help to test the concepts of human occupation scientifically. The model of occupational science could readily be applied to such investigations since this model considers the sociocultural environment as an important sub-system (Clarke et al., 1991) and it could be argued that the sociocultural environment is central to the etiology and maintenance of eating disorders.

Another area of research neglect has been the attitude and feelings of the therapists who work with eating-disordered patients. Zunino et al. (1991) reviewed the impact of therapist gender on the treatment of bulimia nervosa and found that male and female therapists can differ in transference and countertransference interactions with the patient. This is especially so in the areas of body image, dependency issues, gender identity and role modelling. In the Burket et al. (1995) study they also found countertransference feelings. These were commonly reported as frustration, anger, helplessness and anxiety as well as satisfaction and empathy.

The Burkett et al. (1995) study aimed to look at therapists' attitudes about treating patients with eating disorders. The study included 90 therapists who were asked about topics that included the therapists' treatment desires, countertransference, treatment approaches and prognosis. The results indicated that 31% did not wish to treat these patients. In terms of the preferred treatment method, overall therapists considered CBT to be the preferred treatment method but those therapists who wanted to treat these patients tended to use more diverse approaches (dynamic, supportive, interpersonal, etc.). Twenty-nine per cent thought that female therapists were the preferred choice. Therapists reported frustration, treatment resistance and co-morbid conditions as being problematic.

The occupational therapist needs to adopt a flexible style, a caring attitude and a genuine concern for the patient. If the patient is to develop a sense of trust in the therapist then the occupational therapist needs to be very truthful about everything involved in the treatment programme. However, eating-disordered patients do make occupational therapists feel hopeless, powerless and manipulated at times.

Shisslak et al. (1989) also carried out a survey of 71 healthcare professionals involved in working with eating-disordered patients and found that 28% of the participants perceived themselves as moderately to greatly affected by their work with this patient population. They reported personal changes, which they attributed to their work, such as an increased awareness of food, their own physical condition and their appearance and feelings about their bodies. The therapists also reported a positive change in body image and an increased ingestion of healthier foods. However, what we do not know is whether being affected by one's patients is associated with a better or poorer treatment outcome.

As an occupational therapist working with eating-disordered patients, this author would support the view that this work can, at times, be very difficult and frequently frustrating. However it can also be very rewarding and it brought the author great job satisfaction. To help these patients to rediscover their creativity and achieve their human potential is often a long road of torment and struggle, but to see them emerge as more independent individuals is a great achievement for the patient and therapist alike.

References

Abraham S, Beumont P (1982) How patients describe bulimia or binge eating. Psychological Medicine 12: 625–35.

Abraham E, Lucido G (1991) Childhood sexual experience and bulimia. Addictive Behaviour 16: 529–32.

Abrams K, Allen L, Gray J (1993) Disordered eating attitudes and behaviours, psychological adjustment and ethnic identity. A comparison of black and white female college students. International Journal of Eating Disorders 14: 49–57.

Agras W, Rossiter E, Arnow E, Telch C (1994) One year follow-up of psychosocial and pharmacological treatments for bulimia nervosa. Journal of Clinical Psychiatry 55: 179–83.

Amari D (1986) The use of clay to form potential space with a bulimic patient. Creative Arts Therapy Review 7: 13–22.

Anderson A (1990) Males with Eating Disorders. New York: Brunner Mazel.

Attie I, Brooks-Gunn J (1989) Development of eating problems in adolescent girls. A longitudinal study. Developmental Psychology 25: 70–9.

Bakan R, Birmingham C, Aeberhardt L, Goldner E (1993) Dietary zinc intake of vegetarian and non-vegetarian patients with anorexia nervosa. International Journal of Eating Disorders 13: 229–33.

Bale P, Doust J, Dawson D (1996) Gymnasts, distance runners and anorexics body composition and menstrual status. Journal of Sports Medicine and Physical Fitness 36: 49–53.

Bastiani A, Rao, R, Weltzin T, Kaye W (1995) Perfectionism in anorexia nervosa. International Journal of Eating Disorders 17: 147–52.

Beck D, Casper R, Andersen A (1996) Truly late onset of eating disorders – a study of 11 cases averaging 60 years of age at presentation. International Journal of Eating Disorders 20: 389–95.

Becker R Heimberg R (1985) Social skills training approaches. In Hersen M, Bellack A (eds) (1985) Handbook of Clinical Behaviour Therapy With Adults. New York: Plenum.

Bell R (1985) Holy Anorexia. Chicago: University of Chicago Press.

Bemporad J (1996) Self-starvation through the ages: reflections on the pre-history of anorexia nervosa. International Journal of Eating Disorders 19: 217–37.

Beresin E, Gordon C, Herzog D (1989) The process of recovering from anorexia nervosa. In Bemporad J, Herzog D (eds) (1989) Psychoanalysis and Eating Disorders. New York: The Guildford Press.

Bers S, Quinlan D (1992) Perceived competence deficit in anorexia nervosa. Journal of Abnormal Psychology 101: 423–31.

Beumont P, Arthur B, Russell G, Touyz S (1994) Excessive physical activity in dieting disorder patients: purposes for a supervised exercise program. International Journal of Eating Disorders 151: 21–36.

Beumont P, Beardwood C, Russell G (1972) The occurrence of the syndrome of anorexia nervosa in male subjects. Psychological Medicine 2: 216–31.

Beumont P, Russell G, Touyz S (1993) Treatment of anorexia nervosa. Lancet 341: 1635–40.

Bhadrinath B (1990) Anorexia nervosa in adolescents of Asian extraction. British Journal of Psychiatry 156: 565–8.

Bhanji S, Thompson J (1974) Operant conditioning in the treatment of anorexia nervosa: a review and retrospective study of 11 cases. British Journal of Psychiatry 124: 166–72.

Biddle S, Bailey C (1985) Motives toward participation and attitudes toward physical activity of adult participants in fitness programs. Perceptual and Motor Skills 61: 831–4.

Birmingham C, Goldner E, Bakan R (1994) Controlled trial of zinc supplementation in anorexia nervosa. International Journal of Eating Disorders 15: 251–5.

Black D, Burckes-Miller M (1988) Male and female college students: Use of anorexia nervosa and bulimia nervosa weight loss methods. Research Quarterly for Exercise and Sport 59: 252–6.

Blaxter M (1990) Health and Lifestyles. London: Tavistock/Routledge.

Blaxter M, Paterson E (1985) The goodness is out of it: the meaning of food to two generations. In Murcott A (1985) The Sociology of Food and Eating. Gower.

Bliss E, Bruch C (1960) Anorexia Nervosa. Hoeber.

Blouin A, Blouin J, Aubin P, Carter J (1992) Seasonal patterns of bulimia nervosa. American Journal of Psychiatry 149: 73–81.

Blouin J, Carter J, Blouin A, Tener L (1994) Prognostic indicators in bulimia nervosa treated with cognitive-behavioural group therapy. International Journal of Eating Disorders 15: 113–23.

Blouin J, Schnarre K, Carter J, Blouin A (1995) Factors affecting dropout rate from cognitive-behavioural group treatment for bulimia nervosa. International Journal of Eating Disorders 17: 323–9.

Bond M, Hwang K (1986) The social psychology of Chinese people. In Bond M (ed.) (1986) The Psychology of the Chinese People. New York: Oxford University Press.

Boskind-Lodahl M (1976) Cinderella's stepsister: A feminist perspective on anorexia nervosa and bulimia. Journal of Women in Culture and Society 2: 342–56.

Boskind-Lodahl M, White W (1983) Bulimarexia: the binge purge cycle. New York: W Norton.

Boskind-White M, White W (1986) Bulimarexia: A historical – socio-cultural perspective. In Bownell K, Foreyt J (eds) (1986) Handbook of eating disorders, physiology, psychology and treatment of obesity, anorexia and bulimia. New York: Basic Books.

Boumann C, Yates W (1994) Risk factors for bulimia nervosa: A controlled study of parental psychiatric illness and divorce. Addictive Behaviours 19: 667–75.

Bowden P, Touyz S, Rodriguez P, Hensley P (1989) Distorting patient or distorting instrument? Body shape disturbance in patients with anorexia nervosa and bulimia. British Journal of Psychology 155: 196–201.

Bowers W, Andersen A (1994) Inpatient treatment of anorexia nervosa – review and recommendations. Harvard Review of Psychiatry 2: 193–203.

Bramilla F, Draisci A, Peirone A, Brunetta M (1995) Combined cognitive-behavioural psychopharmacological and nutritional therapy in bulimia nervosa. Neuropsychobiology 32: 68–71.

Breines E (1995) Occupational Therapy Activities from Clay to Computers. Theory and Practice. Philadelphia: FA Davis.

Brewerton T, Stellefson E, Hibbs B, Hodges E (1995) Comparison of eating disorder patients with and without compulsive exercising. International Journal of Eating Disorders 17: 413–6.

Bridgeman J, Slade P (1996) Shoplifting and eating disorders: a psychological-medical-legal perspective. European Eating Disorders Review 4: 133–48.

Brinch M, Isager T, Tolstrup K (1988) Anorexia nervosa and motherhood: reproductional pattern and mothering behaviour of 50 women. Acta Psychiatrica. Scandinavia 77: 98–104.

Brodie D, Drew S, Jackman C (1996) Influence of preconception on body image. Perceptual and motor skills 83: 571–7.

Brown L (1989) Fat oppressive attitudes and the feminist therapist. Directions for change. Women and Therapy 8: 19–30.

Bruch H (1957) The Importance of Overweight. New York: Norton.

Bruch H (1962) Perceptual and conceptual disturbances in anorexia nervosa. Psychosomatic Medicine 24: 187–94.

Bruch H (1966) Anorexia nervosa and its differential diagnosis. Journal of Nervous and Mental Disorders 141: 555–66.

Bruch H (1969) The insignificant difference: discordant incidence of anorexia nervosa in monozygotic twins. American Journal of Psychiatry 126: 123–8.

Bruch H (1974) Eating disorders, obesity, anorexia nervosa and the person within. London: Routledge & Kegan Paul.

Bruch H (1977) Psychological antecedents of anorexia nervosa. In Vigersky RA (1977) Anorexia Nervosa. New York: Raven Press.

Bruch H (1978) The Golden Cage: The Enigma of Anorexia Nervosa and the Person Within. London: Routledge & Kegan Paul.

Bruch H (1982) Anorexia nervosa: therapy and theory. American Journal of Psychiatry 139: 1531–8.

Brumberg J (1988) Fasting Girls: The History of Anorexia Nervosa. New York: Penguin Books.

Bryant-Waugh R, Hawkins M, Shafran R, Lask B (1996) A prospective follow-up of children with anorexia nervosa. Journal of Youth and Adolescence 25: 431–7.

Bryant-Waugh R, Lask B (1991) Anorexia nervosa in a group of Asian children living in Britain. British Journal of Psychiatry 158: 229–33.

Bryant-Waugh R, Lask B (1995) Eating disorders – An overview. Journal of Family Therapy 17: 13–30.

Buchan T, Gregory L (1984) Anorexia nervosa in a black Zimbabwean. British Journal of Psychiatry 145: 326–30.

Buckley P, Walsh N (1991) Anorexia nervosa in males. Irish Journal of Psychiatry 8: 15–18.

Burcoyne J. Clarke D (1985) You are what you eat: food and family reconstitution. In Murott A (1985) The Sociology of Food and Eating. Aldershot: Gower.

Burket R, Schramm L (1995) Therapists attitudes about treating patients with eating disorders. Southern Medical Journal 88: 813–8.

Burns T, Crisp A (1984) Outcome of anorexia nervosa in males. British Journal of Psychiatry 145: 319–25.

Bushnell J, Wells J. Hornblow A, Oakley-Browne M (1990) Prevalence of three bulimia syndromes in the general population. Psychological Medicine 20: 671–80.

Butters J, Cash T (1987) Cognitive-behavioural treatment of women's body-image dissatisfaction. Journal of Consulting and Clinical Psychology 55: 889–97.

Button W, Sonuga-Barke E, Davies J, Thompson M (1996) A prospective study of self-esteem in the prediction of eating problems in adolescent schoolgirls. British Journal of Clinical Psychology 35: 193–203.

Calnan M (1990) Food and Health: a comparison of beliefs and practices in middle class and working class households. In Cunningham-Burley S, McKeganey N(Eds) (1990) Readings in Medical Sociology. London: Tavistock/Routledge.

Carmo I, Reis D, Varandas P, Baica P, Santo D (1996) Prevalence of anorexia nervosa: a Portuguese population study. European Eating Disorders Review 4: 157–70.

Cash T, Brown T (1987) Body image in anorexia nervosa and bulimia nervosa. Behaviour Modification 11: 487–521.

Casper R (1983) On the emergence of bulimia nervosa as a syndrome – a historical review. International Journal of Eating Disorders 2: 3–16.

Cauffman E, Steinberg L (1996) Interactive effects of menarcheal status and dating and dieting and disordered eating among adolescent girls. Developmental Psychology 32: 633–5.

Chandra P, Shah A, Shenory J, Kumar U (1995) Family pathology and anorexia in the Indian context. International Journal of Social Psychiatry 41: 292–8.

Charles N, Kerr M (1988) Women, Food and Families. Manchester: Manchester University Press.

Chen J (1990) Behavioural therapy of seven cases of childhood anorexia nervosa. Chinese Mental Health 4: 26–30.

Chen H, Wong J, Lee N (1993) The Shatin Community Mental Health Survey in Hong Kong – major findings. Archives General Psychiatry 50: 125–33.

Cherin K (1983) Womansize. The Tyranny of Slenderness. London: Women's Press.

Clark F, Parham D, Carlson M, Frank G, Jackson J (1991) Occupational science: academic innovation in the service of occupational therapy's future. American Journal of Occupational Therapy 43: 300–10.

Clinton D (1996) Why do eating disorder patients drop out. Psychotherapy and Psychosomatics 65: 29–35.

Close P, Collins R (1982) Domestic labour and patriarchy. The implications of a study in the N.E. England. International Journal of Sociology 2: 31–47.

Collings S, King M (1994) Ten-year follow up of fifty patients with bulimia nervosa. British Journal of Psychiatry 164: 80–7.

Collins G, Katz M, Janasz J, Messina M (1985) Alcoholism in the families of bulimic anorectics. Cleveland Clinical Quarterly 52: 65–7.

Collins M (1991) Body figure perceptions and preferences among pre-adolescent children. International Journal of Eating Disorders 10: 199–208.

Connors M, Johnson C, Stucky M (1984) Treatment of bulimia with brief psychoeducational treatment group. American Journal of Psychiatry 141: 1512–6.

Connors M, Morse W (1993) Sexual abuse and eating disorders: a review. International Journal of Eating Disorders 13: 1–11.

Cooper P (1993) Bulimia Nervosa: A Guide to Recovery. London: Robinson Publishing.

Cooper P, Coker S, Fleming C (1994) Self-help for bulimia nervosa – a preliminary report. International Journal of Eating Disorders 16: 401–4.

Cooper P, Coker S, Fleming C (1996) An evaluation of the efficacy of supervised cognitive-behavioural self-help for bulimia nervosa. Journal of Psychosomatic Research 40: 281–7.

Cooper P, Fairburn C (1993) Confusion over the core psychopathology of bulimia nervosa. International Journal of Eating Disorders 13: 385–9.

Cooper P, Taylor M Cooper Z, Fairburn C (1987) The development and validation of the body shape questionnaire. International Journal of Eating Disorders 6: 485–94.

Courtois C (1988) Healing the Incest Wound: Adult Survivors in Therapy. New York: Norton.

Coward R (1984) Female Desire. London: Granada.

Cox G, Merkel W (1989) A qualitative review of psychosocial treatments for bulimia. Journal of Nervous and Mental Disease 177: 77–84.

Crago M, Shisslak C, Estes L (1996) Eating disturbances among American minority group: a review. International Journal of Eating Disorders 19: 239–48.

Crisp A (1967) The possible significance of some behavioural correlates of weight and carbohydrate intake. Journal of Psychosomatic Research 11: 117–31.

Crisp A (1974) Primary anorexia nervosa or adolescent weight phobia. Practitioner 212: 525–31.

Crisp A (1981) Anorexia nervosa at a normal weight! The abnormal weight control syndrome. International Journal of Psychiatric Medicine 11: 203–34.

Crisp A (1995) Anorexia Nervosa. Let Me Be. Lawrence Erlbaum Associates.

Crisp A, Burns T (1983) The clinical presentation of anorexia nervosa in males. International Journal of Eating Disorders 2: 5–10.

Crisp A, Callender J, Halek C, Hsu G (1992) Long-term mortality in anorexia nervosa. A 20-year follow-up of the St George's and Aberdeen Cohorts. British Journal of Psychiatry 161: 104–7.

Crisp A, Harding B, McGuinness B (1974) Anorexia nervosa. Psychoneurotic characteristics of parents: relationships to prognosis. Journal of Psychosomatic Research 18: 167–73.

Crisp A, Hsu G, Harding B, Hartshorn J (1980) Clinical features of anorexia nervosa. A study of a consecutive series of 102 female patients. Journal of Psychosomatic Research 24: 179–91.

Crisp A, Norton K, Gower S, Halek C, Bowyer C (1991) A controlled study of the effect of therapies aimed at adolescent and family psychopathology in anorexia nervosa. British Journal of Psychiatry 159: 325–33.

Crisp A, Palmer R, Kalucy R (1976) How common is anorexia nervosa? A prevalence study. British Journal of Psychiatry 128: 549–54.

Crisp A, Stonehill E, Fenton G (1971) The relationship between sleep, nutrition and mood. A study of patients with anorexia nervosa. Post Graduate Medicine 47: 207–13.

Dally P, Gomez J (1980) Obesity and Anorexia Nervosa. A Question of Shape. London: Faber.

Dansky B, Brewerton T, Kilpatrick D, O'Neil P (1997) The National Women's Study: relationship of victimisation and post-traumatic stress disorders to bulimia nervosa. International Journal of Eating Disorders 21: 213–28.

Davis C, Kennedy S, Ravelski E, Dionne M (1994) The role of physical activity in the development and maintenance of eating disorders. Psychological Medicine 24: 957–67.

Davis C, Kennedy S, Ralevski E, Dionne M (1995) Obsessive compulsiveness and physical activity in anorexia nervosa and high-level exercising. Journal of Psychosomatic Research 39:967–76.

Davis R, Olmsted M, Rockert W (1992) Brief group psychoeducation for bulimia nervosa. Prediction of clinical outcome. International Journal of Eating Disorders 11: 205–11.

Debow S (1975) Identical Twins. Concordant for anorexia nervosa. Canadian Psychiatric Association 20: 215–7.

De Groot J, Kennedy S, Rodin G, McVey G (1992) Correlates of sexual abuse in women with anorexia nervosa and bulimia nervosa. Canadian Journal of Psychiatry 37: 516–9.

Del Medico V, Qamar A, Dilsaver S (1991) Seasonal worsening of bulimia nervosa. Americal Journal of Psychiatry 148: 1753–61.

Diagnostic and Statistical Manual of Eating Disorders. Edition III 1980 Edition III R 1987 Edition IV 1994. Washington DC: American Psychiatric Association.

Di Nicola V (1990) Anorexia multiforms: self-starvation in historical and cultural context. Transcultural Psychiatric Research Review 27: 165–96.

Dittmar H, Blayney M (1996) Women's self-reported eating behaviours and their response to food and non-food television advertisements. European Eating Disorders Review 4: 217–31.

Dodge E, Hodes M, Eisler I, Dare C (1995) Family therapy for bulimia nervosa in adolescents, an exploratory study. Journal of Family Therapy 17: 79–96.

Dolan B (1991) Cross-cultural aspects of anorexia nervosa and bulimia – a review. International Journal of Eating Disorders 10: 67–78.

Dolan B, Lacey H, Evans C (1990a) Eating behaviour and attitudes to weight and shape in British women from three ethnic groups. British Journal of Psychiatry 157: 523–8.

Dolan B, Liberman S, Evans C, Lacey H (1990b) Family features associated with normal weight bulimia. International Journal of Eating Disorders 9: 639–47.

D'Zurilla T, Nezu A (1982) Social Problem Solving in Adults. In Kennedy P (ed.) (1982) Advances in Cognitive – Behavioural Research and Therapy. New York: Academic Press.

Eckert E, Mitchell J (1989) An overview of the treatment of anorexia nervosa. Psychiatric Medicine 7: 293–315.

Elks M (1994) On the genesis of anorexia nervosa – a feminist perspective. Medical Hypotheses 42: 180–2.

Eklund R, Crawford S (1994) Active woman, social physique, anxiety and exercise. Journal of Sport and Exercise Psychology 16: 431–48.

Ellis R (1985) The Way To A Man's Heart: Food In The Violent Home. In Murcott A (1985) The Sociology of Food and Eating. Gower.

El Sarrag M (1968) Psychiatry in the Northern Sudan: A study in comparative psychiatry. British Journal of Psychiatry 114: 946–8.

Everill J, Waller G (1995) Reported sexual abuse and eating psychopathology: a review of the evidence for a causal link. International Journal of Eating Disorders 18: 1–11.

Fahy T, Eisler I (1993) Impulsivity and eating disorders. British Journal of Psychiatry 162: 193–7.

Fahy T, O'Donoghue G (1991) Eating disorders and pregnancy. Psychological Medicine 21: 577–80.

Fahy T, Russell G (1993) Outcome and prognostic variables in bulimia nervosa. International Journal of Eating Disorders 14: 135–45.

Fairburn C (1981) A cognitive-behavioural approach to the treatment of bulimia. Psychological Medicine 11: 707–11.

Fairburn C (1985) Cognitive-behavioural treatment for bulimia. In Garner D, Garfinkel P (eds) (1985) Handbook for Psychotherapy for Anorexia Nervosa and Bulimia. New York: Guildford Press.

Fairburn C (1991) The heterogeneity of bulimia nervosa and its implications for treatment. Journal of Psychosomatic Research 35: 3–9.

Fairburn G, Beglin S (1990) Studies of the epidemiology of bulimia nervosa. American Journal of Psychiatry 147: 401–8.

Fairburn C, Cooper P (1984) Binge-eating, self-induced vomiting and laxative abuse: a community study. Psychological Medicine 14: 401–10.

Fairburn C, Jones R, Peveler R, Hope R, O'Connor M (1993a) Psychotherapy and bulimia nervosa. Archives of General Psychiatry 30: 419–28.

Fairburn C, Marcus M, Wilson G (1993b) Cognitive Behaviour Therapy for Binge Eating and Bulimia Nervosa. A Comprehensive Treatment Manual. In Fairburn C, Wilson G (eds) (1993) Binge Eating: Nature, Assessment and Treatment. New York: Guildford Press.

Fairburn C, Norman P, Welch S, O'Connor M, Doll H (1995) A prospective study of outcome in bulimia nervosa and the long-term effects of three psychological treatments. Archives of General Psychiatry 52: 304–12.

Fairburn G, Welch S, Doll H, Davies B, O'Connor M (1997) Risk factors for bulimia nervosa. Archives of General Psychiatry 54: 509–17.

Fallon A, Rozin P (1985) Sex differences in perceptions of desirable body shape. Journal of Abnormal Psychology 94: 102–5.

Fallon B, Sadik C, Saoud J, Garfinkel R (1994) Childhood abuse, family environment and outcome in bulimia nervosa. Journal of Clinical Psychiatry 55: 424–8.

Faltus F (1986) Anorexia nervosa in Czechoslavakia. International Journal of Eating Disorders 5: 581–4.

Feldman W, Feldman E, Goodman J (1988) Cultural versus biology: children's attitudes toward thinness and fatness. Paediatrics 81: 190–4.

Ferguson J (1993) The use of electroconvulsive therapy (ECT) in patients with intractable anorexia nervosa. International Journal of Eating Disorders 13: 195–201.

Fettes P, Peters J (1992) A meta-analysis of group treatments for bulimia nervosa. International Journal of Eating Disorders 11: 97–110.

Fichter M, Elton M, Sourdi L, Weyerer S (1988) Anorexia nervosa in Greek and Turkish adolescents. European Archives of Psychiatry and Neurological Sciences 237: 200–8.

Fichter M, Noegel R (1990) Concordance of bulimia nervosa in twins. International Journal of Eating Disorders 9: 255–63.

Fichter M, Quadflieg N, Rief W (1994) Course of multi-impulsive bulimia. Psychological Medicine 24: 591–604.

Fiddes N (1991) Meat: A Natural Symbol. London: Routledge.

Fisher M, Pastor D, Schneider M, Pegler C, Napolitiano B (1994) Eating attitudes in urban and suburban adolescents. International Journal of Eating Disorders 16: 67–74.

Fohlin L (1978) Exercise, performance and body dimensions in anorexia nervosa before and after rehabilitation. Acta. Medica Scandinavia 204: 61–5.

Folsom V, Krah D, Nairn K, Gold L (1993) The impact of sexual and physical abuse on eating disorders and psychiatric symptoms: a comparison of eating disordered and psychiatric inpatients. International Journal of Eating Disorders 13: 249–57.

Fombonne E (1995) Anorexia nervosa. No evidence of an increase. British Journal of Psychiatry 166: 462–71.

Fonari V, Sandberg D, Lachenmayer J, Cohen D (1989) Seasonal variations in bulimia nervosa. Annals New York Academy Science 575: 509–11.

Fosson A, Knibbs J, Bryant-Waugh R, Lask B (1987) Early onset anorexia nervosa. Archives of Disease in Childhood 62: 114–8.

Frederick C, Ryan R (1993) Difference in motivation for sport and exercise and their relations with participation and mental health. Journal of Sport Behaviour 16: 124–45.

Furnham A, Alibhai N (1983) Cross-cultural difference in the perception of female body shape. Psychological Medicine 13: 829–37.

Furnham A, Titman P, Sleeman E (1994) Perception of female body shapes as a function of exercise. Journal of Social Behaviour and Personality 9: 335–52.

Garfinkel P (1992) Evidence in support of attitudes of shape and weight as a diagnostic criterion of bulimia nervosa. International Journal of Eating Disorders 11: 321–5.

Garfinkel P, Garner D (1982) A Multidimensional Perspective. New York: Brunner Mazel.

Garfinkel P, Lin E, Goering P, Spegg C, Goldbloom D (1995) Bulimia nervosa in a Canadian community sample: prevalence and a comparison of subgroups. American Journal of Psychiatry 152: 1052–8.

Garn S, Clark D (1975) Nutrition growth, development and maturation. Findings from the Ten-State Nutrition Survey of 1968–1970. Paediatrics 56: 306–21.

Garner D (1985) Individual psychotherapy for anorexia nervosa. Journal of Psychiatric Research 19: 423–33.

Garner D (1987) Psychotherapy outcome research with bulimia nervosa. Psychotherapy and Psychosomatics 48: 129–40.

Garner D (1993) Pathogenesis of anorexia nervosa. Lancet 341: 1631–4.

Garner D, Bemis K (1982) A cognitive-behavioural approach to anorexia nervosa. Cognitive Therapy and Research 6: 123–50.

Garner D, Garfinkel P (1979) The Eating Attitudes Test: an index of the symptoms of anorexia nervosa. Psychological Medicine 10: 647–56.

Garner D, Garfinkel P (1980) Social-cultural factors in the development of anorexia nervosa. Psychological Medicine 10: 647–65.

Garner D, Garfinkel P, Rockert W, Olmsted M (1987) A prospective study of eating disturbances in the ballet. Psychotherapy Psychosomatic 48: 170–5.

Garner D, Garfinkel P, Schwartz D, Thompson M (1980) Cultural expectations of thinness in women. Psychological Reports 47: 483–91.

Garner D, Garfinkel P, Stancer H, Moldofsky H (1976) Body image disturbances in anorexia nervosa and obesity. Psychosomatic Medicine 38: 327–35.

Garner D, Olmsted M (1984) Eating Disorder Inventory Manual. Lutz H: Psychological Assessment Resources Inc.

Garner D, Rockert W, Davis R, Garner M, Olmsted M (1993) Comparison of cognitive-behavioural and supportive-expressive therapy for bulimia nervosa. American Journal of Psychiatry 150: 37–46.

Gilbert S (1993) Fear of success in anorectic young women. Journal of Adolescent Health 14: 380–3.

Gleaves D, Williamson D, Barker S (1993) Addictive effects of mood and eating forbidden foods upon the perception of overeating and bingeing in bulimia nervosa. Addictive Behaviours 18: 299–309.

Goh S, Ong B, Subramanian M (1993) Eating disorders in Hong Kong. British Journal of Psychiatry 162: 276–9.

Goldbloom D, Olmsted M (1993) Pharmacotherapy of bulimia nervosa with fluoxetine: assessment of clinically significant attitudinal change. American Journal of Psychiatry 150: 770–4.

Goldsmith J, McFall R (1975) Development and evaluation of an interpersonal skill training programme for psychiatric in-patients. Journal of Abnormal Psychology 84: 51–8.

Green M, Rogers P (1995) Impaired cognitive functioning in dieters during dieting. Psychological Medicine 25: 1003–10.

Greenberg D, La Porte D (1996) Racial differences in body type preferences of men for women. International Journal of Eating Disorders 19: 275–8.

Gross J , Rosen J (1988) Bulimia in adolescents: prevalence and psychosocial correlates. International Journal of Eating Disorders 7: 51–61.

Gull W (1868) The address on medicine. Lancet 11: 171.

Gwirtsman H, Roy-Byrne P, Lerner L, Yager J (1984) Bulimia in men: report of three cases with neuro-endocrine findings. Journal of Clinical Psychiatry 45: 78–81.

Hall A (1978) Family structure and relationship of 50 female anorexia nervosa patients. Australian and New Zealand Journal of Psychiatry 12: 263–8.

Hall A, Crisp A (1987) Brief psychotherapy in the treatment of anorexia nervosa. British Journal of Psychiatry 151: 185–91.

Hall P, Driscoll R (1993) Anorexia in the elderly. An annotation. International Journal of Eating Disorders 14: 497–9.

Halmi K (1974) Anorexia nervosa: demographic and clinical features in 94 cases. Psychosomatic Medicine 36: 19–26.

Halmi K (1996) The psychobiology of eating behaviour in anorexia nervosa. Psychiatry Research 62: 23–9.

Halmi K, Folk H, Schwartz E (1981) Binge-eating and vomiting: A survey of a college population. Psychological Medicine 11: 697–705.

Halmi K, Goldberg J, Eckert E (1977) Pre-treatment Revaluation in Anorexia Nervosa. In Vigersky R, Robinson P (ed.) (1977) Anorexia Nervosa. New York: Raven Press.

Harris M, Koehler K (1992) Eating and exercise behaviours and attitudes of South-Western Anglos and Hispanics. Psychology and Health 7: 165–74.

Harwood P, Newton T (1995) Dental aspects of bulimia nervosa: Implications for the health care team. European Eating Disorders Review 3: 93–102.

Hastings T, Kern J (1994) Relationships between bulimia, childhood sexual abuse and family environment. International Journal of Eating Disorders 15: 103–11.

Heatherton T, Baumeister R (1991) Binge-eating as an escape from self-awareness. Psychological Bulletin 110: 86–108.

Herpertz-Dahlmann P, Wewetzer C, Hennighausen K, Remschmidt T (1996) Outcome, psychosocial functioning and prognostic factors in adolescent anorexia nervosa as determined by prospective follow-up assessment. Journal of Youth and Adolescence 25: 455–71.

Herzog D, Keller M, Lavori P (1988) Outcome in anorexia nervosa and bulimia nervosa. A review of the literature. Journal of Nervous and Mental Diseases 176: 131–8.

Herzog D, Keller M, Lavori P, Gray H (1992a) A bulimia family survey. Journal American Academy of Child Adolescent Psychiatry 2: 31–6.

Herzog D, Keller M, Strober M (1992b) Current status of treatment for anorexia nervosa and bulimia nervosa. International Journal of Eating Disorders 12: 215–20.

Herzog D, Norman D, Gordon C, Pepose M (1984) Sexual conflict and eating disorders in 27 males. American Journal of Psychiatry 141: 989–90.

Herzog W, Schellberg D, Deter H (1997) First recovery in anorexia nervosa patients in the long-term course. A discrete-time survival analysis. Journal of Consulting and Clinical Psychology 65: 169–77.

Hiebert K, Felice M, Wingard D, Munoz R (1988) Comparison of outcome in Hispanic and Caucasian patients with anorexia nervosa. International Journal of Eating Disorders 7: 693–6.

Hill A, Bhatti R (1995) Body shape perception and dieting in preadolescent British Asian girls: Links with eating disorders. International Journal of Eating Disorders 17: 175–83.

Hill A, Oliver S, Rogers P (1992) Eating in the adult world. The rise of dieting in childhood and adolescence. British Journal of Clinical Psychology 31: 95–105.

Hindler C, Crisp A, McGuigan S, Joughin N (1994) Anorexia nervosa: changes over time in age of onset, presentation and duration of illness. Psychological Medicine 24: 719–29.

Hinojosa J, Sabari A, Rosenfield M (1983) Position paper: purposeful activity. American Journal of Occupational Therapy 37: 805–6.

Hodes M, Timimi S, Robinson P (1997) Children of mothers with eating disorders: a preliminary study. European Eating Disorders Review 5: 11–24.

Hoek H (1991) The incidence and prevalence of anorexia nervosa and bulimia nervosa. Psychological Medicine 21: 455–60.

Hoffman L, Halmi K (1993) Psychopharmacology in the treatment of anorexia nervosa and bulimia nervosa. Psychiatric Clinics of North America 6: 767–78.

Holden N (1990) Is anorexia nervosa an obsessive-compulsive disorder? British Journal of Psychiatry 157: 1–5.

Holden N, Robinson P (1988) Anorexia nervosa and bulimia nervosa in British Blacks. British Journal of Psychiatry 152: 544–9.

Holland A, Sicotte N, Treasure J (1988) Anorexia nervosa: evidence for a genetic basis. Journal of Psychosomatic Research 32: 561–71.

Hooper M, Garner D (1986) Application of the eating disorders inventory to a sample of black, white and mixed race schoolgirls in Zimbabwe. International Journal of Eating Disorders 5: 161–8.

Hornyak L, Baker E (1989) Experiental Therapies for Eating Disorders. New York: Guildford Press.

Howard R (1990) Art therapy as an isomorphic intervention in the treatment of a client with post-traumatic stress disorder. American Journal of Art Therapy 28: 79–86.

Hsu G (1983) The aetiology of anorexia nervosa and bulimia nervosa. Psychological Medicine 13: 231–8.

Hsu G (1987) Outcome and treatment effects. In Beumont P, Burrows J, Casper R (Eds) (1987) Handbook of Eating Disorders. London: Eisevier Science Publishers.

Hsu G (1990) Eating Disorders. New York: Guildford.

Hsu G (1996) Outcome of early-onset anorexia nervosa – what do we know? Journal of Youth and Adolescence 25: 563–8.

Hsu G (1996) Epidemiology of the eating disorders. The Psychiatric Clinics of North America 19: 681–700.

Hsu G, Chesler B, Santhouse R (1990) Bulimia nervosa in eleven sets of twins: a clinical report. International Journal of Eating Disorders 9: 275–82.

Hudson J, Pope H, Jonas J (1983) Family history study of anorexia nervosa and bulimia. British Journal of Psychiatry 142: 133–8.

Hudson J, Pope H, Jonas J (1985) Treatment of anorexia nervosa with antidepressants. Journal of Clinical Psychopharmacology 5: 17–23.

Hudson J, Pope H, Jonas J, Yurgelum-Todd D (1987) A controlled family study of bulimia. Psychological Medicine 17: 883–90.

Hurst A (1936) British Encyclopaedia of Medical Practice. London: Butterworth.

Iannos M, Tiggemann M (1997) Personality of the excessive exerciser. Personality and Individual Differences 22: 775–8.

Irving L (1990) Mirror images – effects of the standard of beauty on women's self and body esteem. Journal of Social and Clinical Psychology 9: 230–42.

Jacobs B, Isaac S (1986) Pre-pubertal anorexia – a retrospective controlled study. Journal of Child Psychology and Psychiatry 27: 237–50.

Jacobson E (1938) Progressive Relaxation. Chicago: University Chicago Press.

Jacobson R, Robins C (1989) Social dependency and social support in bulimic and non-bulimic women. International Journal of Eating Disorders 8: 665–70.

James A (1990) The good, the bad and the delicious: the role of confectionery in British society. The Sociological Review 38: 667–88.

Jimerson J, Lesem M, Kaye W (1990) Eating disorders and depression: is there a serotonin connection. Biological Psychiatry 28: 443–54.

Johnson C (1984) The Initial Consultation for Patients with Anorexia Nervosa and Bulimia. In Garner D, Garfinkel P (eds) (1984) Handbook of Psychotherapy for Anorexia Nervosa and Bulimia. New York: Guildford Press.

Johnson C, Berndt D (1983) Preliminary investigations of bulimia and life adjustment. American Journal of Psychiatry 140: 774–7.

Johnson C, Larson R (1982) Bulimia: an analysis of moods and behaviour. Psychosomatic Medicine 44: 341–51.

Johnston C, Stuckey M, Lewis L (1982) Bulimia, a descriptive survey of 316 cases. International Journal of Eating Disorders 2: 3–18.

Johnson W, Tsoh J, Varnado P (1996) Eating disorders – efficacy of pharmacological and psychological interventions. Clinical Psychology Review 16: 457–78.

Kagan D, Squires R (1983) Dieting, compulsive eating and feelings of failure among adolescents. International Journal of Eating Disorders 3: 15–26.

Kalucy R, Crisp A, Harding B (1977) A study of 56 families with anorexia nervosa. British Journal of Medical Psychology 50: 381–95.

Kaplan A, Woodside D (1987) Biological aspects of anorexia nervosa and bulimia nervosa. Journal of Consulting and Clinical Psychology 55: 645–53.

Kassett J, Gershon E, Maxwell M, Guroff J (1989) Psychiatric disorders in the first degree relatives of probands with bulimia nervosa. American Journal of Psychiatry 146: 1468–71.

Katz J (1985) Some reflections on the nature of eating disorders on the need for humility. International Journal of Eating Disorders 4: 617–26.

Katzman M, Weiss L, Wolchik S (1986) Speak don't eat! Teaching women to express their feelings. Women and Therapy 5: 143–51.

Keel P, Mitchell J (1997) Outcome in bulimia nervosa. American Journal of Psychiatry 154: 313–21.

Keller M, Herzog D, Lavori P (1992) The naturalistic history of bulimia nervosa. Extraordinarily high rates of chronicity, relapse, recurrence and psychosocial morbidity. International Journal of Eating Disorders 12: 1–10.

Kelly Y, Lai M, Alfred H, Wong C (1995) Case study: early onset anorexia nervosa in a Chinese boy. Journal of the American Academy of Child Adolescent Psychiatry 34: 383–6.

Kendler K, Maclean C, Neale M, Kessler R, Heath A (1991) The genetic epidemiology of bulimic nervosa. American Journal of Psychiatry 148: 1627–37.

Kennedy S, Goldbloom D (1989) Current perspectives on drug therapies for anorexia nervosa and bulimia nervosa. Drugs 141: 367–77.

Khandelwal S, Saxena S (1990) Anorexia nervosa in people of Asian extraction. British Journal of Psychiatry 157: 784–7.

Khandelwal S, Sharan P, Saxena S (1995) Eating disorders: an Indian perspective. International Journal of Social Psychiatry 41: 132–46.

Kielhofner G (1985) A Model of Human Occupation: Theory and Application. Baltimore: Williams & Wilkins.

King M (1989) Eating Disorders in a General Practice Population: Prevalence, Characteristics and Follow-Up at 12 to 18 Months. Great Britain: Cambridge University Press.

King M (1991) Epidemiological study of eating disorders: time for a change of emphasis. Psychological Medicine 21: 287–91.

King M, Bhugra D (1989) Eating disorders: lessons from a cross-cultural study. Psychological Medicine 19: 955–8.

Kinzl J, Traweger C, Guenther V, Biehl W (1994) Family background and sexual abuse with eating disorders. American Journal of Psychiatry 151: 1127–31.

Kleifield E, Wagner S, Halmi K (1996) Cognitive-behavioural treatment of anorexia nervosa. Psychiatric Clinics of North America 19: 715–9.

Klerman G, Weissman M, Rounsaville B, Chevron E (1984) Interpersonal Psychotherapy of Depression. New York: Basic Books.

Kok L, Tian C (1994) Susceptibility of Singapore Chinese schoolgirls to anorexia nervosa – Part II (family factors). Singapore Medical Journal 35: 609–12.

Koran L, Agras W, Rossiter E, Arnow B, Schneider J (1995) Comparing the cost-effectiveness of psychiatric treatments – bulimia nervosa. Psychiatry Research 58: 13–21.

Kotler L, Katz L, Anyan W, Comite F (1994) Case study of the effects of prolonged and severe anorexia nervosa on bone mineral density. International Journal of Eating Disorders 15: 395–9.

Kron L, Katz J, Gorzynski G, Wuner H (1978) Hyperactivity in anorexia nervosa. A fundamental clinical feature. Comprehensive Psychiatry 19: 433–40.

Kuboki T, Nomura S, Ide M, Suematsu H, Araki S (1996) Epidemiological data on anorexia nervosa in Japan. Psychiatry Research 62: 11–6.

Lacey H (1983) Bulimia nervosa, binge eating and psychogenic vomiting: A controlled treatment study and long-term outcome. British Medical Journal 286: 1609–13.

Lacey H (1992) Homogamy: the relationships and sexual partners of normal weight bulimic women. British Journal of Psychiatry 161: 638–42.

Lacey H, Crisp A, Kalucy R, Hartman M (1976) Study of EEG sleep characteristics in patients with anorexia nervosa before and after restoration of weight. Postgraduate Medical Journal 52: 45–9.

Lacey H, Dolan B (1988) Bulimia in British Blacks and Asians: a catchment area study. British Journal of Psychiatry 152: 73–9.

Lacey H, Evans D (1986) The impulsivist: a multi-impulsive personality disorder. British Journal of Addiction 81: 641–9.

Lacey H, Gibson E (1985) Controlling weight by purgation and vomiting: a comprehensive study of bulimics. Journal of Psychiatric Research 19: 337–41.

Lacey H, Smith G (1987) Bulimia nervosa: the impact of pregnancy on mother and baby. British Journal of Psychiatry 150: 777–81.

Laessle R, Beumont P, Butow P, Lennerts W, O'Connor M (1991) A comparison of nutritional management with stress management in the treatment of bulimia nervosa. British Journal of Psychiatry 159: 250–61.

Lam R, Goldner E, Solyom L, Remick R (1994) A controlled study of light therapy for bulimia nervosa. American Journal of Psychiatry 151: 744–50.

Lam R, Solyom L, Tompkins A (1991) Seasonal mood symptoms in bulimia nervosa and seasonal affective disorder. Comprehensive Psychiatry 32: 552–8.

Langer L, Warheit G, Zimmerman R (1991) Epidemiological study of problem eating behaviours and related attitudes in the general population. Addictive Behaviours 16: 167–73.

La Porte D (1996) Influence of gender, amount of food and speed of eating on external raters' perceptions of binge-eating. Appetite 27: 119–27.

Laseque E (1873) Translated from 'De L'Anorexia Hysterique'. Archives of General Medicine 21: 388.

Lask B, Bryant-Waugh R (1992) Early onset anorexia nervosa and related eating disorders. Journal of Child Psychology and Psychiatry 33: 281–300.

Laube J (1990) Why group therapy for bulimia? International Journal of Group Psychotherapy 40: 169–87.

Lavic V, Clausen S, Pedersen W (1991) Eating behaviour, drug use, psychopathology and parental bonding in adolescents in Norway. Acta Psychiatrica Scandinavia 84: 387–90.

Lawrence M (1984) The Anorexia Experience. London: Women's Press.

Lawrence C, Thelen M (1995) Body image, dieting and self-concept. Their relation in African-American and Caucasian children. Journal of Clinical Child Psychology 24: 41–8.

Leach A (1995) The psychopharmacotherapy of eating disorders. Psychiatric Annals 25: 628–33.

Leavitt R, Pill C (1995) Composing a self through writing – the ego and the ink. Smith College Studies in Social Work 65: 137–49.

Lee S (1991) Anorexia nervosa in Hong Kong: A Chinese perspective. Psychological Medicine 21: 703–11.

Lee A, Lee S (1996) Disordered eating and its psycho-social correlates among Chinese adolescent females in Hong Kong. International Journal of Eating Disorders 20: 177–83.

Lee S, Rush A (1986) Cognitive-behavioural group therapy for bulimia. International Journal of Eating Disorders 5: 599–615.

Lee S, Hsu G. Wing Y (1992) Bulimia nervosa in Hong Kong Chinese patients. British Journal Psychiatry 161: 545–51.

Le Grange D, Eizler I, Dare C, Russell G (1992) Evaluation of family treatments in adolescent anorexia nervosa: a pilot study. International Journal of Eating Disorders 12: 347–57.

Le Grange D, Telch C, Agras W (1997) Eating and general psychopathology in a sample of Caucasian and ethnic minority subjects. International Journal of Eating Disorders 21: 285–93.

Le Grange D, Tibbs A, Noakes T (1994) Implications of a diagnosis of anorexia nervosa in a ballet school. International Journal of Eating Disorders 15: 369–76.

Leonard D (1980) Sex and Generation. London: Tavistock.

Lester R (1997) The (dis) embodied self in anorexia nervosa. Social Science and Medicine 44: 479–89.

Licavoli L, Orland R (1997) Psychotherapy pharmacotherapy and nutritional therapy in the treatment of eating disorders. In Session – Psychotherapy in Practice 3: 57–78.

Littlewood R (1995) Psychopathology and personal agency: Modernity, culture change and eating disorders in South Asian societies. British Journal Medical Psychology 68: 45–63.

Lucas A, Beard M, O'Fallon M, Kurland L (1991) Fifty year trends in the incidence of anorexia nervosa in Rochester Minnesota: A population-based study. American Journal of Psychiatry 148: 917–22.

Lupton D (1994) Food, memory and meaning. The symbolic and social nature of food events. Sociological Review 2: 665–85.

Mackensie M (1980) The Politics of Body Size: Fear of Fat. Los Angeles: Pacifica Tape Library.

Maclancy J (1992) Consuming Culture. London: Chapman.

Mahowald J (1992) To be or not to be a woman: anorexia nervosa, normative gender roles and feminism. Journal of Medicine and Philosophy 17: 233–51.

Mallinckrodt B, McCreary B, Robertson A (1995) Co-occurrence of eating disorders and incest: The role of attachment, family environment and social competencies. Journal of Counselling and Psychology 42: 178–86.

Maloney M, McGuire J, Daniels S (1988) Reliability testing of a children's version of the Eating Attitudes Test. Journal American Academy of Child and Adolescent Psychiatry 27: 541–3.

Maloney M, Mcguire J, Daniels S, Specke B (1989) Dieting behaviour and eating attitudes in children. Paediatrics 84: 482–9.

Mangweth B, Pope H, Hudson J (1995) Bulimia nervosa in two cultures: a comparison of Austrian and American college students. International Journal of Eating Disorders 17: 403–12.

Mann T, Nolenhoeksema S, Huang K, Burgand D, Wright A (1997) Are two interventions worse than none? Joint primary and secondary prevention of eating disorders in college females. Health Psychology 16: 215–25.

Maresh D, Willard C (1996) Anorexia nervosa in an African-American female of a lower socio-economic background. European Eating Disorders Review 4: 95–9.

Margittae K, Blouin A, Perez E (1986) A study of drop-out and psychopharmacological research with bulimics. International Journal of Psychiatric Medicine 16: 297–303.

Martin J (1985) Body Image: Anorexia nervosa patients and occupational therapy students. British Journal of Occupational Therapy 48: 96–8.

Martin J (1989) Bulimia – a literature review. British Journal of Occupational Therapy 52: 138–42.

Martin J (1990) Bulimia: a review of the medical, behavioural and psychodynamic models of treatment. British Journal of Occupational Therapy 53: 495–500.

Martin J (1991) Occupational therapy in bulimia. British Journal of Occupational Therapy 54: 48–52.

Mason N, Chaney J (1996) Bulimia nervosa in undergraduate women – factors associated with internalisation of the sociocultural standard of thinness. Applied and Preventive Psychology 5: 249–59.

Mavisskalian M (1982) Anorexia nervosa treated with response preventions and prolonged exposure. Behaviour Research and Therapy 20: 27–31.

McCourt J, Waller G (1996) Factors on the eating psychopathology of Asian women in British society. European Eating Disorders Review 4: 74–83.

McDonald D, Hodgdon J (1991) Psychological Effects of Aerobic Fitness Training. Research and Theory. New York: Springer Verlag.

McElroy S, Keck P, Phillips (1995) Kleptomania, compulsive buying and binge-eating disorder. Journal of Clinical Psychiatry 56: 14–27.

McKisack C, Waller G (1996) Why is attendance variable at groups for women with bulimia nervosa? The role of eating psychopathology and other characteristics. International Journal of Eating Disorders 20: 205–9.

McKisack C, Waller G (1997) Factors influencing the outcome of group psychotherapy for bulimia nervosa. International Journal of Eating Disorders 22: 1–13.

Merrill C, Mines R, Starkey R (1987) The premature drop-out in the group treatment of bulimia. International Journal of Eating Disorders 6: 293–300.

Meyer D (1997) Co-dependency as a mediator between stressful events and eating disorders. Journal of Clinical Psychology 53: 107–16.

Mickley D (1994) The Prozac hype. Journal of Treatment Prevention 2: 188–92.

Miller D, McCluskey-Fawcett K, Irving L (1993) Correlates of bulimia nervosa: early family mealtime experience. Adolescence 28: 621–35.

Minuchin S, Rosman B, Baker L (1978) Psychosomatic Families. Cambridge MA: Harvard University Press.

Mishkind M, Rodin A, Silberstein L, Striegel-Moore R (1986) The embodiment of masculinity: cultural, psychological and behavioural dimensiions. American Behavioural Scientist 29: 545–62.

Mitchell J, Boutacoff L, Hatsukami D, Pyle R (1986) Laxative abuse as a variant of bulimia. Journal of Nervous and Mental Disease 174: 174–6.

Mitchell J, Hatsukami D, Eckert E, Pyle R (1985) Characteristics of 275 patients with bulimia. American Journal of Psychiatry 142: 482–5.

Mitchell H, Pyle R, Eckert E (1981) Frequency and duration of binge-eating episodes in patients with bulimia. American Journal of Psychiatry 138: 835–6.

Mitchell J, Pyle R, Eckert E, Hatsuikami D (1990) A comparison study of anti-depressants and structured intensive group psychotherapy in the treatment of bulimia nervosa. Archives of General Psychiatry 47: 149–57.

Mitchell J, Pyle R, Hatsukami D, Eckert E (1988) Chewing and spitting out food as a clinical feature of bulimia. Psychosomatics 29: 81–4.

Moller-Madsen S, Nystrup J, Nielsen S (1996) Mortality in anorexia nervosa in Denmark during the period 1970-1987. Acta Psychiatrica Scandinavia 94: 454–9.

Mondina S, Favoro A, Santonastaso P (1996) Eating disorders and the ideal of feminine beauty in Italian newspapers and magazines. European Eating Disorders Review 4: 112–20.

Moreno J (1946) Psychodrama. Beacon NT: Beacon House.

Morgan W (1979) Negative addiction in runners. Physician Sports Medicine 7: 57–70.

Morgan H, Purgold J, Wellbourne J (1983) Management and outcome in anorexia nervosa: a standardised prognostic study. British Journal Psychiatry 144: 282–7.

Morgan H, Russell G (1975) Value of family background and clinical features as predictors of long-term outcome in anorexia nervosa, 4 year follow-up study. Psychological Medicine 5: 355–71.

Morris A, Cooper T, Cooper P (1989) The changing shape of female fashion models. International Journal of Eating Disorders 8: 593–6.

Morton R (1689) Phthisiologia, Seu exercitationes de phthisi. London: Smith & Walford.

Morton R (1694) Phthisiologia: Or a Treatise of Consumption. London: Smith & Walford.

Mukai T, Crago M, Shisslak M (1994) Eating attitudes and weight preoccupation among female high school students in Japan. Journal of Child Psychology and Psychiatry 35: 677–88.

Mumford D (1992) Eating disorders among Asian girls in Britain. British Journal of Psychiatry 160; 719–23.

Mumford D, Whitehouse A, Choudry I (1992) Survey of eating disorders in English-medium schools in Lahore Pakistan. International Journal of Eating Disorders 11: 173–84.

Mumford D, Whitehouse A, Platts M (1991) Sociocultural correlates of eating disorders among Asian schoolgirls in Bradford. British Journal of Psychiatry 158: 222–8.

Murcott A (1982) On the social significance of the 'cooked dinner' in South Wales. Social Science Information 21: 677–96.

Murcott A (1983) 'Its a Pleasure to Cook for Him'. Food, mealtimes and gender in some South Wales households. In Garmarnikow E, Morgan D, Puruis J (1983) The Public and the Private. London: Heinemann.

Murcott A (1985) The Sociology of Food and Eating. Aldershot: Gower.

Nasser M (1986) Comparative study of the prevalence of abnormal eating attitudes among Arab female students of both London and Cairo universities. Psychological Medicine 16: 621–5.

Nasser M (1997) Culture and Weight Consciousness. London: Routledge.

Nattiva A, Agostini R, Drinkwater B, Yeager K (1994) The female athlete triad: the interrelatedness of disordered eating, amenorrhea and osteoporosis. Clinical Sports Medicine 13: 405–18.

Nemeroff C, Stein R, Diehl N, Smilack C (1994) From the Cleavers to the Clintons: role choices and body orientation as reflected in magazine article content. International Journal of Eating Disorders 16: 167–76.

Neumark-Sztainer D (1996) School-based programs for preventing eating disturbances. Journal of School Health 66: 64–71.

Nichter M, Nichter M (1991) Hype and Weight. Medical Antrophology 13: 249–84.

Nielsen S (1990) The epidemiology of anorexia nervosa in Denmark from 1973–1987: A nationwide register study of psychiatric admission. Acta Psychiatrica Scandinavica 81: 507–14.

Norring C, Sohlberg S (1993) Outcome recovery, relapse and mortality across six years in patients with clinical eating disorders. Acta Psychiatrica Scandinavica 87: 43–4.

Nylander I (1971) The feeling of being fat and dieting in a school population. Acta Sociomedica Scandinavica 17–26.

Oakley A (1974) The Sociology of Housework. London: Martin Roberton.

Ogden J, Mundray K (1996) The effect of the media on body satisfaction: the role of gender and size. European Eating Disorders Review 4: 171–82.

Ogles B, Masters K, Richardson S (1995) Obligatory running and gender: an analysis of participative motives and training habits. International Journal of Sport Psychology 26: 249–61.

Okasha A, Kamel M, Sadek A, Lotaif F (1977) Psychiatric morbidity among university students in Egypt. British Journal of Psychiatry 131: 149–54.

Olivardia R, Pope H, Mangweth B, Hudson J (1995) Eating disorders in college men. American Journal of Psychiatry 152: 1279–85.

Olmsted M, Davis R, Rockert W, Irvine M (1991) Efficacy of a brief group psychoeducational intervention for bulimia nervosa. Behaviour Research and Therapy 27: 71–83.

Olmsted M, Kaplan A, Rockert W (1994) Rate and prediction of relapse in bulimia nervosa. American Journal of Psychiatry 151: 738–43.

Oncerdin P (1979) Compulsive eating in college women. Journal of College Student Personnel 20: 153–7.

Ono Y, Berger D, Saitos S, Takahanshi Y, Kuboki T (1996) Relationship of childhood abuse to psychiatric distress, social adjustment and eating disorder severity in Japanese bulimics. European Eating Disorders Review 4: 121–30.

Oppenheimer R, Howells K, Palmer R, Chaloner D (1985) Adverse sexual experiences in childhood and clinical eating disorders. Journal of Psychiatric Research 19: 357–61.

Orbach S (1984) Fat is a Feminist Issue: The Anti-Diet Guide to Permanent Weight Loss. London: Hamlyn.

Orbach S (1993) Hunger Strike: The Anorectic's Struggle as a Metaphor for Our Age. London: Penguin.

Osler N (1981) Principles and Practice of Medicine. New York: D Appleton & Co.

Oyebode F, Boodhoo J, Schapiro K (1988) Anorexia nervosa in males. International Journal of Eating Disorders 7: 121–4.

Palazzoli M (1974 and 1978) Self-Starvation from the Intrapsychic to the Transpersonal Approach to Anorexia Nervosa. London: Chancer.

Palazzoli M (1985) Anorexia nervosa. A syndrome of the affluent society. Transcultural Psychiatric Research Review 22: 199–205.

Palmer R (1979) The dietary chaos syndrome: a useful new term? British Journal Medical Psychology 52: 187–90.

Palmer R, Oppenheimer R, Dignon A, Chaloner D (1990) Childhood sexual experiences with adults reported by women with eating disorders. British Journal of Psychiatry 156: 699–703.

Parry-Jones B, Parry-Jones W (1993) Self-mutilation in four historical cases of bulimia. British Journal of Psychiatry 163: 394–402.

Peacock M (1991) A personal construct approach to art therapy in the treatment of post-sexual abuse trauma. Journal of Art Therapy 29: 100–9.

Peloquin S (1989) Sustaining the art of practice in occupational therapy. American Journal of Occupational Therapy 43: 219–26.

Petrie T (1996) Differences between male and female college lean sport athletes. Non-lean sport athletes and non-athletes on behavioural and psychological indices of eating disorders. Journal of Applied Sport Psychology 8: 218–30.

Pill R (1985) An apple a day . . . some reflections on working class mothers' views on food and health. In Murcott A (1985) The Sociology of Food and Eating. Gower.

Pitts C, Waller G (1993) Self-denigratory beliefs following sexual abuse: association with the symptomatology of bulimic disorders. International Journal of Eating Disorders 13: 407–10.

Pliner P, Chaiken S (1990) Eating social motives and self-presentation in women and men. Journal of Experimental Social Psychology 26: 240–54.

Pope H, Hudson J (1987) Anti-depressant medication in the treatment of bulimia nervosa. Psychopathology 20: 123–9.

Pope H, Hudson J (1992) Is childhood sexual abuse a risk factor for bulimia nervosa. American Journal of Psychiatry 149: 455–63.

Pope H, Hudson J, Jonas J, Yurgelum-Todd D (1983) Bulimia treated with imipramine: a placebo-controlled double-blind study. American Journal of Psychiatry 140: 554–8.

Pope H, Hudson J, Jonas J, Yurgelum-Todd D (1985) Anti-depressant treatment of bulimia: a two year follow-up study. Journal of Clinical Psychopharmacology 5: 320–7.

Pope H, Hudson J, Yurgelum-Todd D, Hudson M (1984) Prevalence of anorexia nervosa and bulimia in three student populations. International Journal of Eating Disorders 3: 45–52.

Powell A, Kahn A (1995) Racial differences in women's desires to be thin. International Journal of Eating Disorders 17: 191–5.

Pribor E, Dinwiddle S (1992) Psychiatric correlates of incest in childhood. American Journal of Psychiatry 149: 52–6.

Prince R (1985) The concept of culture-bound syndromes: anorexia nervosa and brain fag. Social Sciences and Medicine 22: 197–203.

Pruitt J, Kappius R, Gorman P (1992) Bulimia and fear of intimacy. Journal of Clinical Psychology 48: 472–6.

Pumariega A (1986) Acculturation and eating attitudes in adolescent girls. a comparative and cultural study. Journal of the American Academy of Child and Adolescent Psychiatry 25: 276–9.

Pumariega A, Edwards P, Mitchell C (1984) Anorexia nervosa in black adolescents. Journal of the American Academy of Child Psychiatry 23: 111–14.

Pumariega A, Gustavson C, Gustavson J, Motes P (1994) Eating attitudes in African-American women: The 'Essence' eating disorders survey. International Journal of Eating Disorders 2: 5–16.

Pyle R, Neuman P, Halvorson P, Mitchell J (1991) An ongoing cross-sectional study of the prevalence of eating disorders in freshman college students. International Journal of Eating Disorders 6: 667–77.

Rand C, Kuldau J (1990) The epidemiology of obesity and self-defined weight problems in the general population: gender, race, age and social class. International Journal of Eating Disorders 9: 329–43.

Ratnasuriya R, Eisler I, Szmukler G, Russell G (1991) Anorexia nervosa: outcome and prognostic factors after 20 years. British Journal of Psychiatry 158: 495–502.

Ratner G, Tury F, Szabo P, Geyer M, Rumpold G (1995) Prevalence of eating disorders and minor psychiatric morbidity in central Europe before the political changes in 1989: a cross-cultural study. Psychological Medicine 25: 1027–35.

Reeves M (1913) Round About a Pound a Week. London: Bell.

Riess H, Rutan T (1992) Group therapy for eating disorders: a step-wise approach. Group 16: 79–82.

Rigotti N, Neer R, Jameson L (1986) Osteopenia and bone fracture in a man with anorexia nervosa and hypogonadism. Journal of the American Medical Association 256: 385–88.

Robin A, Siegel M, Koepke T, Moye A, Tice S (1995) Family therapy versus individual therapy for adolescent females with anorexia nervosa. Journal of Developmental and Behavioural Pediatrics 15: 111–6.

Robinson P, Andersen A (1985) Anorexia nervosa in American Blacks. Journal of Psychiatric Research 19: 183–8.

Robinson P, Holden N (1986) Bulimia nervosa in the male: a report of nine cases. Psychological Medicine 16: 795–803.

Rolland K, Farnill D, Griffiths R (1997) Body figure perceptions and eating attitudes among Australian school children aged 8 to 12 years. International Journal of Eating Disorders 21: 273–8.

Rollins N, Piazza E (1978) Diagnosis of anorexia nervosa. American Academy of Child Psychiatry 17: 126–37.

Root M, Fallon P (1988) The incidence of victimization experiences in a bulimic sample. Journal of Interpersonal Violence 3: 161–73.

Root M, Fallon P (1989) Treating the victimized bulimic. Journal of Interpersonal Violence 4: 90–100.

Rorty M, Yager J, Rossotto E (1993) Why and how do women recover from bulimia nervosa? The subjective appraisals of 40 women recovered for a year or more. International Journal of Eating Disorders 14: 249–60.

Rorty M, Yager J, Rosotto E (1994) Childhood sexual, physical and psychological abuse in bulimia nervosa. American Journal of Psychiatry 151: 1122–6.

Rorty M, Yager J, Rossotto E (1995) Aspects of childhood physical punishment and family environment correlates in bulimia nervosa. Child Abuse and Neglect 19: 659–67.

Rosen J (1997) Cognitive-behavioural body image therapy for eating disorders. In Garner D, Garfinkel P (Eds) (1997) Handbook of treatment for eating disorders. New York: Guildford Press.

Rosen J, Leitenberg H (1982) Bulimia nervosa: treatment with exposure and response prevention. Behaviour Therapy 13: 117–24.

Rosen J, Tracey B, Howell D (1990) Life stress, psychological symptoms and weight reducing behaviour in adolescent girls. A prospective analysis. International Journal of Eating Disorders 9: 17–26.

Rosen L, McKeag D, Hough D (1986) Pathogenic weight-control behaviour in female athletes. Physician Sports Medicine 14: 79–86.

Ross T (1936) An Enquiry Into Prognosis In The Neuroses. Cambridge: Cambridge University Press.

Rothenberg A (1986) Eating disorder as a modern obsessive – compulsive syndrome. Psychiatry 49: 45–53.

Rowntree S (1901) Poverty: A Study of Town Life. London: Macmillan.

Royal College Of Psychiatrists (1992) UK. Report to the College Section of General Psychiatry by the Eating Disorders Working Group London: Royal College of Psychiatrists CR14.

Russell G (1970) Anorexia nervosa its identity as an illness and its treatment. Modern Trends in Psychological Medicine 2: 131–64.

Russell G (1979) Bulimia nervosa: an ominous variant of anorexia nervosa. Psychological Medicine 9: 429–38.

Russell G (1986) The Secret Trauma: Incest In The Lives Of Girls And Women. New York: Basic Books.

Russell G, Checkley S, Feldman J (1988) A controlled trial of D-fenfluramine in bulimia nervosa. Clinical Neuropharmacology 11: 146–9.

Russell G, Szmukler G, Dare C, Eisler I (1987) An evaluation of family therapy in anorexia nervosa and bulimia nervosa. Archives of General Psychiatry 44: 1047–56.

Sabine E, Yonace A, Farrington A, Barratt K (1983) Bulimia nervosa: a placebo controlled double-blind therapeutic trial of mianserin. British Journal Clinical Pharmacology 15: 195–202.

Santonastaso P, Zambenedetti M, Favaro A, Pavan T (1997) Family psychiatric morbidity in eating disorders. European Eating Disorders Review 5: 3–10.

Schmidt U, Tiller J, Treasure J (1993) Self-treatment of bulimia nervosa: a pilot study. International Journal of Eating Disorders 13: 273–7.

Schneider J, Agras W (1985) A cognitive-behavioural group treatment of bulimia. British Journal of Psychiatry 146: 66–9.

Schneider J, O'Leary A, Jenkins S (1995) Gender sexual orientation and disordered eating. Psychology and Health 10: 113–28.

Schork E, Eckert E, Halmi K (1994) The relationship between psychopathology eating disorder diagnosis and clinical outcome at 10 year follow-up in anorexia nervosa. Comprehensive Psychiatry 35: 113–23.

Schupak-Neuberg E, Nemeroff C (1993) Disturbances in identity and self-regulation in bulimia nervosa: Implications for a metaphorical perspective of 'body as self'. International Journal of Eating Disorders 13: 335–47.

Schwalberg M, Barlow D, Alger S, Howard L (1992) A comparison of bulimics, obese binge eaters, social phobics and individuals with panic disorder on co-morbidity across DSM-III-R anxiety disorders. Journal of Abnormal Psychology 101: 675–81.

Schwartz H (1986) Bulimia: psychoanalytical perspectives. Journal of the American Psychoanalytical Association 34: 439–62.

Schwartz R, Barratt M, Saba G (1985) Family therapy for bulimia. In Garner D, Garfinkel P (eds) (1985) A Handbook Psychotherapy For Anorexia and Bulimia. New York: Guildford.

Schwitzer J, Neudorfer C, Fleischhacker W (1993) Seasonal bulimia treated with fluoxetine and phototherapy. American Journal of Psychiatry 150: 1752–3.

Scourfield J (1995) Anorexia by Proxy: Are the children of anorexia mothers an at-risk group? International Journal of Eating Disorders 18: 371–4.

Scurlock H, Timimi S, Robinson P (1997) Case report: osteoporosis as a complication of chronic anorexia nervosa in a male. European Eating Disorders Review 5: 42–6.

Sharp C, Clark S, Dunan J, Blackwood D, Shapiro C (1994) Clinical presentation of anorexia nervosa in males: 24 new cases. International Journal of Eating Disorders 15: 125–34.

Shisslak C, Crago M, Schnaps L, Swain B (1986) Interactional group therapy for anorexic and bulimic women. Psychotherapy 23: 598–607.

Shisslak C, Gray N, Crago M (1989) Health care professionals' reaction to working with eating disorder patients. International Journal of Eating Disorders 8: 689–94.

Shugar G, Krueger S (1995) Aggressive family communication, weight-gain and improved eating attitudes during systemic family therapy for anorexia nervosa. International Journal of Eating Disorders 17: 23–31.

Siever M (1994) Sexual orientation and gender as factors in socioculturally acquired vulnerability to body dissatisfaction and eating disorders. Journal of Consulting and Clinical Psychology 62: 252–60.

Silber T (1986) Anorexia nervosa in blacks and Hispanics. International Journal of Eating Disorders 5: 121–8.

Silberstein L, Mishkind M, Striegel-Moore R, Tinko C (1989) Men and their bodies: A comparison of homosexual and heterosexual men. Psychomatic Medicine 51: 337–46.

Silverstein B, Perdue L (1988) The relationship between role concerns, preferences for slimness and symptoms of eating problems among college women. Sex Roles 18: 101–6.

Silverstein B, Perdue L, Peterson B, Kelly E (1986) The role of the mass media in promoting a thin standard of bodily attractiveness for women. Sex Roles 14: 519–32.

Slade P, Russell G (1973) Awareness of body dimensions in anorexia nervosa, cross-sectional and longitudinal studies. Psychological Medicine 3: 188–9.

Sloan G, Leichner P (1986) Is there a relationship between sexual abuse or incest and eating disorders? Canadian Journal of Psychiatry 3: 161–73.

Smith D, Marcus M, Eldredge K (1994) Binge-eating syndromes: A review of assessment and treatment with an emphasis on clinical application. Behaviour Therapy 25: 635–58.

Smith J, Waldorf V, Trembath D (1990) 'Single white male looking for this very attractive . . .' Sex Roles 23: 675–85.

Snow J, Harris M (1986) An analysis of weight and diet content in five women's interest magazines. Journal of Obesity and Weight Regulation 5: 194–214.

Sohlberg S, Norring C, Holmgren S, Rosmark B (1989) Impulsivity and long-term prognosis of psychiatric patients with anorexia nervosa/bulimia nervosa. Journal of Nervous and Mental Disease 177: 249–58.

Soomro G, Crisp A, Lynch D, Tran D, Joughin N (1995) Anorexia nervosa in 'non-white populations'. British Journal of Psychiatry 167: 385–9.

Soundy T, Lucas A, Suman V, Melton L (1995) Bulimia nervosa in Rochester Minesota from 1980-1990. Psychological Medicine 25: 1065–71.

Spivack G, Platt J, Shure M (1974) The Problem-Solving Approach To Adjustment. San Francisco: Jossey-Bass.

Sprechner S (1989) The importance to males and females of physical attractiveness, earning potential and expressiveness in initial attraction. Sex Roles 21: 591–607.

Srinivasagam N, Kaye W, Plotnicov K, Greeno C (1995) Persistent perfectionism, symmetry and exactness after long-term recovery from anorexia nervosa. American Journal of Psychiatry 152: 1630–4.

Steiger H (1989) Anorexia – nervosa and bulimia in males: lesson from a low risk population. Canadian Journal of Psychiatry 34: 419–24.

Steiger H, Zanko M (1990) Sexual traumata among eating - disordered, psychiatric and normal female groups. Journal of Interpersonal Violence 5: 74–86.

Steiner-Adair C (1986) The body politic: normal female adolescent development and the development of eating disorders. Journal of the American Academy of Psychoanalysis 14: 95–114.

Steinhausen H, Rauss-Mason C, Seidel R (1991) Follow-up studies of anorexia nervosa: A review of four decades of outcome research. Psychological Medicine 21: 447–57.

Stern S, Dixon K, Nemzer E (1984) Affective disorder in the families of women with normal weight bulimia. American Journal of Psychiatry 141: 1224–7.

Stice E, Schupak-Neuberg E, Shaw H, Stein R (1994) Relation of media exposure to eating disorder symptomatology: an examination of mediating mechanisms. Journal of Abnormal Psychology 103: 836–40.

Stoner S, Fedoroff I, Andersen A, Rolls B (1996) Food preferences and desire to eat in anorexia and bulimia nervosa. International Journal of Eating Disorders 19: 13–22.

Story M (1986) Nutrition management and dietary treatment of bulimia. Journal of American Dietetic Association 86: 517–19.

Story M, French S, Resnick M, Blum R (1995) Ethnic/racial and socio-economic differences in dieting behaviour and body image perceptions in adolescents. International Journal of Eating Disorders 18: 173–9.

Story M, Hauck F, Bronssard B, White L (1994) Weight perceptions and weight control practices in American Indian and Alaska native adolescents. Archives of Paediatrics and Adolescent Medicine 148: 567–71.

Stoutjesdyk D, Jevne R (1993) Eating disorders among high performance athletes. Journal of Youth and Adolescence 22: 271–6.

Striegel-Moore R (1995) Psychological factors in the aetiology of binge eating Addictive Behaviours 20: 713–23.

Striegel-Moore R, Kearney-Cooke A (1994) Exploring parents' attitudes and behaviours about their children's physical appearance. International Journal of Eating Disorders 15: 377–85.

Striegel-Moore R, Schreiber G, Pike K, Wifley D, Rodin J (1995) Drive for thinness in black and white preadolescent girls. International Journal of Eating Disorders 18: 59–69.

Striegel-Moore R, Tucker N, Hsu G (1990). Body image dissatisfaction and disordered eating in lesbian college students. International Journal of Eating Disorders 9: 493–500.

Strober M (1980) Personality and symptomatological features in young, non-chronic anorexia nervosa patients. Journal of Psychosomatic Research 24: 353–9.

Strober M, Humphrey L (1987) Familial contributions to the aetiology and course of anorexia and bulimia. Journal of Consulting and Clinical Psychology 55: 654–9.

Strober M, Yager J (1985) A developmental perspective on the treatment of anorexia nervosa in adolescents. In Garner D,Garfinkel P (eds) (1985) Handbook of Psychotherapy for Anorexia and Bulimia. New York: Guildford Press.

Stunkard A (1959) Eating patterns and obesity. Psychiatric Quarterly 33: 284–95.

Suematsu H, Ishitawa H, Kuboki T, Ito T (1985) Statistical studies on anorexia nervosa in Japan: detailed clinical data on 1,011 patients. Psychotherapy and Psychosomatics 43: 96–101.

Sullivan P (1995) Mortality in anorexia nervosa. American Journal Psychiatry 152: 1073–6.

Sunday S, Reeman I, Eckert E, Halmi K (1996) Ten-year outcome in adolescent onset anorexia nervosa. Journal of Youth and Adolescence 25: 533–44.

Susuki K, Takeda A, Matsushita S (1995) Coprevalence of bulimia with alcohol abuse and smoking among Japanese male and female high school students. Addiction 90: 971–5.

Swift W, Ritholzm M, Kalin N (1987) A follow-up study of thirty hospitalised bulimics. Psychosomatic Medicine 49: 45–55.

Sykes D, Currie K, Gross M (1987) The use of group therapy in the treatment of bulimia. International Journal of Psychosomatics 34: 7–10.

Sykes D, Gross M, Subishin S (1986) Preliminary findings of demographic variables in patients suffering from anorexia nervosa and bulimia. International Journal of Psychosomatics 33: 27–30.

Szabo P, Tury F (1991) The prevalence of bulimia nervosa in a Hungarian college and secondary school population. Psychotherapy and Psychosomatics 56: 43–7.

Szmukler G, Eisler I, Gillies C, Hayward M (1985) The implications of anorexia nervosa in a ballet school. Journal of Psychiatric Research 19: 177–81.

Szyrynski V (1973) Anorexia nervosa and psychotherapy. American Journal of Psychotherapy 27: 492–505.

Taipale V, Larkio-Miettinen K, Valanne E, Moren R (1972) Anorexia nervosa in boys. Psychosomatics 16: 23–7.

Talerico C (1995) The expressive arts as a form of therapeutic experience in the field of mental health. Journal of Creative Behaviour 65: 137–49.

Taub D, Blinde E (1994) Disordered eating and weight control among adolescent female athletes and performance squad members. Journal of Adolescent Research 9: 483–97.

Thackwray D, Smith M, Bodfish J, Meyers A (1993) A comparison of behavioural and cognitive - behavioural interventions for bulimia nervosa. Journal of Consulting and Clinical Psychology 61: 639–45.

Theander S (1970) Anorexia nervosa: A psychiatric investigation of 94 female patients. Acta Psychiatrica Scandinavia (Supp) 214: 1–194.

Theander S (1985) Outcome and prognosis in anorexia nervosa and bulimia. Journal of Psychiatric Research 19: 493–508.

Thelen M, Farmer J, McLaughlin M, Pruitt J (1990) Bulimia and interpersonal relationships. A longitudinal study. Journal of Counselling Psychology 37: 85–90.

Thomas J, Szmukler G (1985) Anorexia nervosa in patients of Afro-Caribbean extraction. British Journal of Psychiatry 146: 653–6.

Thompson B (1992) 'A way out a no way'. Eating problems among African, American, Latina and white women. Gender and Society 6: 546–61.

Thorton B, Leo R, Alberg K (1991) Gender role typing, the superwoman ideal and the potential for eating disorders. Sex Roles 25: 469–84.

Timini S (1995) Adolescence in immigrant Arab families. Psychotherapy 32: 141–9.

Timini S, Robinson P (1996) Disturbances in eating of patients with eating disorders. European Eating Disorders Review 4: 183–8.

Tobin D, Griffing A (1996) Coping, sexual abuse and compensatory behaviour. International Journal of Eating Disorders 20: 143–8.

Tordjman S, Zittoun C, Anderson G, Flament M, Jeammet P (1994) Preliminary study of eating disorders among French female adolescents and young adults. International Journal of Eating Disorders 16: 301–5.

Toriola A, Dolan B, Evans C, Adetimole O (1996) Weight satisfaction of Nigerian women in Nigeria and Britain: Inter-generational and cross-cultural influences. European Eating Disorders Review 4: 84–94.

Toro J, Nicolau R, Gervera M, Castro J, Blecua M (1995) A clinical and phenomenological study of 185 Spanish adolescents with anorexia nervosa. European Child and Adolescent Psychiatry 4: 165–74.

Totler I, Stryer B, Micheli L, Herman L (1996) Physical and emotional problems of elite female gymnasts. The New England Journal of Medicine 335: 281–3.

Touyz S, Kopec-Schrader E, Beumont P (1993) Anorexia nervosa in males: A report of 12 cases. Australian and New Zealand Journal of Psychiatry 27: 512–7.

Treasure J, Schmidt U (1993) Getting Better Bit (E) By Bit (E): A Survival Kit for Sufferers of Bulimia Nervosa and Binge Eating. Hove U.K: Lawrence Erlbaum Associates.

Treasure J, Schmidt U, Troop N, Tiller J, Todd G (1994) First step in managing bulimia nervosa – controlled trial of therapeutic manual. British Medical Journal 308: 686–9.

Treasure J. Todd G, Brolly M, Tiller J, Nehmed A (1995) A pilot-study of a randomised trial of cognitive analytical therapy Vs educational behavioural-therapy for adult anorexia nervosa. Behaviour Research and Therapy 33: 363–7.

Treasure J, Ward A (1997) Cognitive analytical therapy in the treatment of anorexia nervosa. Clinical Psychology and Psychotherapy 4: 62–71.

Tseng M, Lee M, Lee Y (1989) A clinical study of Chinese patients with eating disorders. Chinese Psychiatry 3: 17–21.

Turnbull S, Schmidt Y, Troop N, Tiller J, Todd G (1997) Predictors of outcome for two treatments for bulimia nervosa - short and long term. International Journal of Eating Disorders 21: 17–22.

Vandereycken W (1987) The constructive family approach to eating disorders: Critical remarks on the use of family therapy in anorexia nervosa and bulimia. International Journal of Eating Disorders 6: 455–67.

Vandereycken W, Vanhoudenhove V (1996) Stealing behaviour in eating disorders – characteristics and associated psychopathology. Comprehensive Psychiatry 37: 316–21.

Varela P, Marcos A, Navarro M (1992) Zinc status in anorexia nervosa. Ann Nutr Metab (Switzerland) 36: 197–202.

Varney W (1996) The Briar around the strawberry patch. Women's Studies International Forum 19: 267–76.

Wade T, Tiggemann M, Heath A, Abraham S, Treloar S (1996) Structure of disordered eating in a twin's community sample. International Journal of Eating Disorders 19: 63–71.

Walford G, McCune N (1991) Long-term outcome in early-onset anorexia nervosa. British Journal of Psychiatry 159: 383–9.

Waller G (1992) Sexual abuse and the severity of bulimic symptoms. British Journal of Psychiatry 161: 90–3.

Waller G (1993) Sexual abuse and eating disorders – borderline personality disorder as a mediating factor? British Journal of Psychiatry 162: 771–5.

Waller G, Hamilton K, Rose N, Sumra J, Baldwin G (1993) Sexual abuse and body-image distortion in the eating disorders. British Journal of Clinical Psychology 32: 350–2.

Wallin U, Roijen S, Hansson K (1996) Too close or too separate: family function in families with an anorexia nervosa patient in two Nordic countries. Journal of Family Therapy 18: 397–414.

Walsh B, Stewart J, Roose S, Gladis M (1984) Treatment of bulimia with phenelzine. Archives of General Psychiatry 41: 1105–9.

Walsh T, Gladis M, Roose S, Stewart J (1988) Phenelzine Vs Placebo in fifty patients with bulimia. Archives in General Psychiatry 45: 471–6.

Walsh B, Kissileff H, Cassidy S, Dantzic S (1989) Eating behaviour in women with bulimia. Archives in General Psychiatry 46: 54–60.

Walsh B, Wilson G, Loeb K, Devlin M, Pike K, Roose S (1997) Medication and psychotherapy in the treatment of bulimia nervosa. American Journal of Psychiatry 154: 523–53.

Warde A, Hetherington K (1994) English household and routine food practices: a research note. Sociology Review 2: 759–71.

Warheit G, Langer L, Zimmermann R, Biafora F (1993) Prevalence of bulimic behaviours and bulimia among a sample of the general population. American Journal of Epidemiology 137: 569–76.

Welch S, Fairburn C (1996) Childhood sexual and physical abuse as risk factors for the development of bulimia nervosa: a community–based case control study. Child Abuse and Neglect 20: 633–42.

Weltzin T, Bulik C, McConaha C, Kaye (1995) Laxative withdrawal and anxiety in bulimia nervosa. International Journal of Eating Disorders 17: 141–6.

Weltzin T, Fernstrom M, Hansen D, McConaha C (1991) Abnormal caloric requirements for weight maintenance in patients with anorexia and bulimia nervosa. American Journal of Psychiatry 148: 1675–82.

Weltzin T, Hsu G, Pollice C, Kaye W (1991) Feeding patterns in bulimia nervosa. Biological Psychiatry (USA) 30: 1093–110.

Wenlock R (1986) The Diets of British School-Children: A Preliminary Report of a Nutritional Analysis of a Nationwide Dietary Survey of British School-Children. London: HMSO.

Whitaker A, Davis C, Shaffer D (1989) The struggle to be thin: a survey of anorexic and bulimic symptoms in a non-referred adolescent population. Psychological Medicine 19: 143–63.

Wichman S, Martin D (1992) Exercise excess: Treating patients addicted to fitness. The Physican and Sports Medicine 20 193–200.

Wiederman M, Pryor T (1996) Substance use among women with eating disorders. International Journal of Eating Disorders 20: 163–8.

Wiener J (1976) Identical male twins discordant for anorexia nervosa. Journal of the American Academy of Child Psychiatry 15: 523–34.

Wilfley D, Schreiber G, Pike K, Striegel-Moore R, Wright D (1996) Eating disturbance and body image: A comparison of a community sample of adult black and white women. International Journal of Eating Disorders 20: 377–87.

Willi J, Glacometti G, Limacher B (1990) Update on the epidemiology of anorexia nervosa in a defined region of Switzerland. American Journal of Psychiatry 147: 1514–17.

Williamson D, Netemeyer R, Jackman L, Andersen D (1995) Structural equation modelling of risk factors for the development of eating disorder symptoms in female athletes. International Journal of Eating Disorders 17: 387–93.

Wilson G (1996) Treatment of bulimia nervosa – when CBT fails. Behaviour Research and Therapy 34: 197–212.

Wilson T, Eldredge K, Smith D, Niles B (1991) Cognitive-behavioural treatment with and without response prevention for bulimia. Behaviour Research Therapy 29: 575–83.

Wilson G, Fairburn C, Agras W (1997) Cognitive-behavioural therapy for bulimia nervosa. In Garner D, Garfinkel P (eds) (1997) Handbook of Treatment for Eating Disorders. New York: Guildford Press.

Windauer U, Lennerts W, Talbot P, Touyz S, Beumont P (1993) How well are 'cured' anorexia nervosa patients? An investigation of 16 weight-recovered anorexia patients. British Journal of Psychiatry 163: 195–200.

Wiseman M, Gray J, Mosimann J, Ahrens A (1992) Cultural expectations of thinness in women. An update. International Journal of Eating Disorders 11: 85–9.

Wlodarczyk-Bisaga K, Dolan B (1996) A two-stage epidemiological study of abnormal eating attitudes and their prospective risk factors in Polish schoolgirls. Psychological Medicine 26: 1021–32.

Wolf J, Willmuth M, Watkins A (1986) Art therapy's role in the treatment of anorexia nervosa. The American Journal of Art Therapy 25: 39–46.

Wonderlich S, Donaldson M, Carson D, Staton D, Gertz L (1996) Eating disturbance and incest. Journal of Interpersonal Violence 2: 195–207.

Wonderlich S, Ukestad L, Perzacki R (1994) Perceptions of nonshared childhood environment in bulimia nervosa. Journal of American Child and Adolescent Psychiatry 33: 741–7.

Woodside B (1995) A review of anorexia nervosa and bulimia nervosa. Current Problems in Paediatrics 25: 67–89.

Woodside D, Lackstrom J, Shekter-Wolfson L, Heinmaa M (1996) Long-term follow up of patient reported family functioning in eating disorders after intensive day hospital treatment. Journal of Psychosomatic Research 41: 269–77.

Woodside D, Shekter-Wolfson L (1990) Parenting by patients with anorexia nervosa and bulimia nervosa. International Journal of Eating Disorders 9: 303–9.

Wooley S, Wooley O (1979) Obesity and women. A closer look at the facts. Women's Studies International Quarterly 2: 69–79.

Wooley S, Wooley O (1985) Intensive outpatient and residential treatment for bulimia. In Garner D, Garfinkel P (Eds) (1985) Handbook of Psychotherapy for Anorexia Nervosa. New York: Guildford Press.

Wurman V (1989) A feminist interpretation of college student bulimia. Journal of College Student Psychotherapy 3: 167–80.

Yager J (1994) Psychosocial treatments for eating disorders. Psychiatry – Interpersonal and Biological Processes 57: 153–64.

Yates A (1991) Compulsive Exercise and the Eating Disorders. Toward An Integrative Theory. New York: Brunner/Mazel Inc.

Zerbe K (1996) Feminist psychodynamic psychotherapy of eating disorders. The Psychiatric Clinics of North American 19: 811–22.

Zlotnick C, Holstein L. Shea M, Pearlstein T, Recupero P (1996) The relationship between sexual abuse and eating behaviour. International Journal of Eating Disorders 20: 129–34.

Zunino N, Agoos E, Davis W (1991) The impact of therapist gender on the treatment of bulimic women. International Journal of Eating Disorders 10: 253–63.

Index

X